TISTICAL AREAS
ET TO APRIL 8, 1966

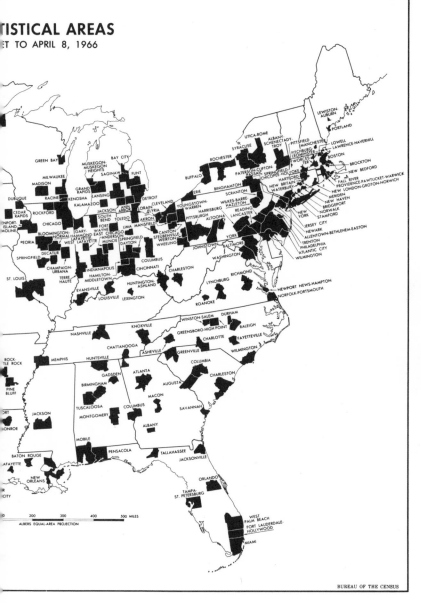

BUREAU OF THE CENSUS

0   200   300   400   500 MILES

ALBERS EQUAL-AREA PROJECTION

Metropolitan America

Metropolitan America

Fiscal Patterns
and Governmental Systems

ALAN K. CAMPBELL and
SEYMOUR SACKS

The Free Press, New York
Collier-Macmillan Limited, London

Copyright © 1967 by The Free Press

A DIVISION OF THE MACMILLAN COMPANY

Printed in the United States of America

Collier-Macmillan Canada, Ltd., Toronto, Ontario

Library of Congress Catalog Card Number: 67-14373

First Printing

PREFACE

Since the end of World War II, probably no domestic phenomenon has received more attention than the metropolitanization of America. In the early stages of this redistribution of population and economic activity, attention and concern was concentrated on the rapidly expanding suburbs. As the sorting-out process continued, interest shifted to the problems of the central city. It was the deterioration of the central business district and the concentration of disadvantaged population in the city's ghettoes which attracted most attention.

There are almost as many ways to analyze the process of metropolitanization as there are analysts. This study is an attempt to examine that process through its fiscal dimensions and consequences. It is hoped that this approach provides a useful contribution to understanding the entire phenomenon, as well as contributing to a classification of the public policy alternatives available for solving or ameliorating some of the problems caused by this major reorganization of American society.

The study concentrates on explaining the differences in local fiscal outputs from city to city and between cities and their own suburbs. In addition to analyzing the determinants of the differences, the patterns of the differences themselves are presented. Standing alone, these patterns explain much about the problems of a metropolitan society.

Since one of the primary characteristics of metropolitan America is the fragmentation of its governmental system, special attention is given to describing this system. Variations in the interrelationships between state governments and their local subdivisions is subject to careful analysis to determine their relevance to differences in fiscal performance.

A study of this kind is completely dependent on the quality of data provided by the various reporting agencies in the country. The authors must, therefore, give thanks first, to the Governments Division of the Bureau of the Census for its first-rate reporting of state and local fiscal data. Although such a task presents a momentous challenge to any data-collecting agency, the Bureau of the Census has responded by continually improving the form and content of its state and local fiscal reporting. Every student of American governmental institutions is indebted to this division of the Census Bureau and its Director, Mr. Allen Manvel.

The authors also express their appreciation to The Brookings Institution for the financial assistance they provided for the research on which the findings reported in this volume are based. Several graduate students worked directly on the project. Most notably Yong Hyo Cho and Woo Sik Kee completed Ph.D. dissertations in the process—Mr. Cho in political science and Mr. Kee in economics. Their contribution was vital to the entire study and their diligent attention to the undertaking is greatly appreciated.

Many of the findings as they emerged in this study were used by both authors in their seminars in the Metropolitan Studies Program at Syracuse University. The students made significant contributions through their questions and suggestions. Particularly helpful were the following past and present graduate students: David Plavin, Philip Meranto, David Ranney, Donna Shalala and Judith Launer Palkovitz.

Many colleagues read the manuscript in various stages and their assistance is appreciated. Professor Jesse Burkhead was particularly helpful, as were Norman Beckman, Selma Mushkin, Harold Pellish, Robert Harris and Eugene P.

McLoone. The Syracuse University Computing Center as a whole, and in particular Professor Otway O'M. Pardee, was most generous in extending time and facilities for the processing of the data on which this study so heavily relies.

Finally, the excecutive secretary of the Metropolitan Studies Program, Mrs. Jane Rood, was unfailingly patient as she was asked to type, retype, and then type again the various drafts which this report has gone through. In addition, she aided the authors immeasurably by assuming competently and willingly many of the administrative duties connected with the study.

ALAN K. CAMPBELL and
SEYMOUR SACKS

Metropolitan Studies Program
Maxwell Graduate School
Syracuse University

CONTENTS

ix

LIST OF TABLES

xiii

CHAPTER 1

The Metropolitan Context for Fiscal Decision-Making

America becomes Metropolitan

Although no single word, phrase, or sentence can summarize the domestic changes occurring in the United States, it is clear that underlying many of them is the metropolitanization of the country. The dual movement of people, jobs, and economic activity from countryside to city and from city to suburb has changed drastically the nature of American society: it has become a metropolitan society. A change of this magnitude did not occur overnight; its origins, in fact, can be traced into the last half of the nineteenth century, but its full flowering is a post-World War II phenomenon with the result that, "now, when the last rural threads of American society are being woven into the national urban fabric the idea of cities is becoming indistinguishable from the idea of society."[1]

Many value judgments have been made about the character of the new society, particularly about the significance of the redistribution of population, which, in many ways, defines the change. Philosophers, statesmen, social critics, journalists, and scholars all debate the merits of this revolution with a colorful, although imprecise, language. Of the names the new environment is called, a few are flattering but most are damning and hardly any are value free; urban sprawl, scatteration, crazy quilt, cancerous growth, and slurbs are but a few of the critical phrases that are being used. A few commentators, however, view the phenomenon in a more positive way. They argue that the new society provides for urban man or, perhaps better said, metropolitan man, a range of choices in living conditions and life styles that never before existed. They find "in the dissolution of the urban settlement a liberation of human energies and a proliferation of opportunities for human interaction."[2]

Although all do not agree about the quality of the new society, all do agree that it is different from the past and that it requires a reorientation of public thinking about domestic affairs. Old policies and timeworn slogans applicable to an earlier age are simply not relevant to the new society. One student of public affairs, in discussing the metropolitanization of the country, argues that "this inexorable trend poses the question of whether men will become further dehumanized and corrupted in megalopolis, or whether a national government sensitive to urban needs can take the leadership, through policy on education, cultural subsidies, television and other mass media, city planning and redevelopment, recreation, transportation, expansion of civil rights, in making megalopolis not only habitable but hospitable to man."[3] Whether the responsibility for public policy leadership in metropolitan areas is entirely that of the national government, as this quote implies, is not self-evident. In contrast, the position taken in this study is that the country's total governmental system—national-state-local—must respond and is in fact responding to the metropolitanization of the nation.

Measuring the Public Policy Consequences

While the quality of the change is debated and its supposed consequences for public policy are discussed, the real consequences and the actual public policy responses are occurring daily. This study is an attempt to measure the fiscal dimension of these public policy responses and to relate the responses to the characteristics of metropolitanism.

These responses, of course, are many and varied, ranging from changes in land-use control techniques to the reapportionment of state legislatures. Of all the types of responses, however, the one that serves best as a proxy for most of the others is the fiscal response. In addition to its inclusive quality it has the further advantage, for analytical purposes, of its quantitative dimension.

Because fiscal decisions are the products of governmental systems, these decisions provide a means of analyzing the nature of the governmental systems and in turn the impact of the systems themselves on fiscal behavior. It is the governmental systems that allocate resources to the public sector and that divide these resources among the services provided by these systems. Fiscal behavior, therefore, is related to both the policy consequences of metropolitanism and to the governmental systems that formulate and execute these policies.

In the course of the present study it is demonstrated that within metropolitan areas[4] the mix of local public services is different from that of nonmetropolitan areas. Even among metropolitan areas the basket of services provided differs from one place to another. Further, the combinations of services required or demanded in different parts of any one metropolitan area may be quite different.

What is the relevance of metropolitanism to variations in fiscal behavior in the United States? Does metropolitanism provide any help in understanding these variations? Further, are differences in fiscal behavior between metropolitan and nonmetropolitan areas, and, within metropolitan areas, between central cities and outside central cities,[5] caused by the same factors or different ones?

The Role of Governmental Systems

The fiscal responses to metropolitanism work themselves out through the governmental decision-making system that exists in each metropolitan area. No aspect of metropolitanism has received more attention than the local governmental units that serve these population concentrations. In fact, the existence of many jurisdictions operating in the same area has resulted in some students defining *the* metropolitan problem as governmental fragmentation: "The basis of the problem is the absence of general local government organizations broad enough to cope with metropolitan matters."[6]

Important as fragmentation may be, the interaction of the levels of government operative in metropolitan areas is equally important. These areas are governed not only by local institutions, but by state and federal governments as well. All of these levels interact, and the possibility that variations in governmental systems from area to area have important consequences for the nature of the fiscal response must be taken into account. To measure the impact of these differences it is necessary to design an index of governmental systems. The measure used in this study is the difference in assignment of expenditure and revenue responsibilities by states among the governmental units within the state-local system. The question to be answered is: What is the impact of these variations of assignment on fiscal behavior within state-local governmental systems?

The chapters to follow, then, comprise a study of fiscal responses to measurable aspects of metropolitanism and to the local governmental systems operative within metropolitan areas. From this analysis there emerges a fairly clear picture of the differences in fiscal behavior between metropolitan and nonmetropolitan areas and between central cities and their outlying areas within metropolitan areas.

To understand the differences in response of the component parts of a metropolitan society, a great variety of governmental, socioeconomic, and fiscal variables are correlated with the fiscal responses in the different areas examined. However, throughout the analysis great stress is placed on using common variables for all levels of analysis in order that differences in their impact may be clearly seen.

These common variables—the measures of personal income, governmental systems, and selected fiscal and social variables—are examined in great detail. The variables selected for intensive analysis were those that showed greatest explanatory power when used in combination with many others. By consistently employing common variables throughout the study, it is possible to compare the results and clarify the fiscal responses of local governments in different parts of metropolitan areas (primarily central cities and outside central cities), among metropolitan areas, and between metropolitan and nonmetropolitan areas.

Before proceeding with the analysis of the fiscal responses to metropolitanism, it is important to define the context within which these responses are occurring. Of particular importance is the fiscal changes that have taken place over the past decade.

A Decade of Fiscal Growth[7]

The most dynamic part of the American economy today is the state-local public sector. Although public discussion and debate about the appropriate role of government centers on the national government, that level of the system is relatively stagnant when compared to the state-local level. In fact, the rate of growth in expenditures, revenues, and employment at the state and local levels of government outstrips the growth rate of all other parts of the economy, public or private.

One measure of the comparative growth of the state and local sector is its relation to the federal sector. During the past decade federal general expenditures increased 24 per cent, whereas state-local expenditures grew by 126 per cent.[8]

This greater growth of state and local expenditures has caused its proportion of all general expenditures (federal, state, and local) to approach the pre-World War II relationship of federal and state-local expenditures. State and local expenditures in 1963/64 constituted 41.7 per cent of total general expenditures, the highest proportion it has reached since the early 1940s.

If defense and foreign policy expenditures are excluded and only domestic expenditures compared (Table 1-1), the growth of the state and local sector, relative to the national sector, is even more pronounced. Measured in this way, state and local expenditures in 1963/64 constituted 64 per cent of all general expenditures; the similar figure for 1946 was 44 per cent. The 1963/64 proportion is comparable to the pattern of the 1920s.

These comparisons demonstrate the growing role of state

TABLE 1-1: *Proportion of General Domestic Expenditures* by Level of Government, 1922–1963/64*

	Federal	State	Local	State and local
1922	34.6%	12.9%	52.5%	65.4%
1936	48.7	14.9	36.4	51.3
1946	56.1	12.6	31.3	43.9
1952	39.5	20.1	40.5	60.6
1954	39.8	19.8	40.3	60.1
1962	37.2	21.2	41.5	62.7
1963/64	36.3	22.3	41.4	63.7

(Totals do not add to 100 per cent because of rounding)
* Excludes defense and foreign policy expenditures.

SOURCE: U. S. Bureau of the Census, *Census of Governments: 1962*, Vol. VI, No. 4 (*Historical Statistics on Governmental Finances and Employment*).

U. S. Bureau of the Census, *Governmental Finances in 1963–64*. Series G-GF64-No. 1.

Fiscal Decision-Making

and local government in the total governmental system of the country, but of even greater interest is the role of the state and local sector in the total economy. In 1964 total government purchases of goods and services constituted 19.16 per cent of Gross National Product (based on 1965 revision in GNP), a figure that shows a small decline from 1954, when it was 21.84 per cent. In other words, the total public sector as measured by purchases of goods and services has not increased its proportion of the total economy during the past decade.

This overall stability, however, hides important internal shifts. For this same ten-year period federal government purchases, as a proportion of the Gross National Product, declined from 13.96 per cent to 10.01 per cent, whereas the state and local sector grew from 7.89 per cent to 9.14 per cent (Table 1-2). In relative terms, therefore, the proportion of Gross National Product represented by the state and local expenditures for goods and services increased 16 per cent, whereas similar federal expenditures declined 28 per cent during the last decade.

This overall growth in expenditure levels has been accompanied by different rates of growth for the functions performed

TABLE 1-2: *Government Purchases of Goods and Services as a Per Cent of GNP 1929–1965 (in 1958 Constant Dollars)*

	GNP Billion	ALL GOVERNMENT Billion	Per cent of GNP	FEDERAL GOVERNMENT Billion	Per cent of GNP	STATE AND LOCAL Billion	Per cent of GNP
1929	$203.6	$ 22.0	10.81%	$ 3.5	1.72%	$18.5	9.09%
1940	227.2	36.4	16.02	15.0	6.60	21.4	9.42
1946	312.6	48.4	15.48	30.1	9.63	18.4	5.89
1950	355.3	52.8	14.86	25.3	7.12	27.5	7.74
1952	395.1	92.1	23.31	63.8	16.15	28.4	7.19
1954	407.0	88.9	21.84	56.8	13.96	32.1	7.89
1962	530.0	107.5	20.28	60.0	12.00	47.5	8.62
1964	577.6	110.7	19.16	57.8	10.01	52.8	9.14
1965	609.0	112.8	18.52	57.2	9.39	55.6	9.13

SOURCE: U. S. Department of Commerce, Office of Business Economics, *Survey of Current Business*, XLV (August 1965), Table 2.

by state and local governments (Table 1-3). Although total state and local general expenditures have increased by 126 per cent during the past decade, education has increased by 151 per cent. The large growth in expenditures for education added to the large proportion of the total expenditures represented by this function, results in most other functions increasing less than the average increase for all functions. One exception is local parks and recreation, which has grown 141 per cent since 1954, but the absolute amount in this category is so small that the proportion of total expenditures had increased to only 1.5 per cent of the total by 1963–64. Interest on debt, too, has increased more than the overall increase, 224 per cent. The other large increase was in the census category called "other and unallocable expenditures."

TABLE 1-3: *State and Local General Expenditures With and Without Education: Growth and Proportion, by Function, 1954–1963/64*

| | | PROPORTION OF TOTAL EXPENDITURES 1954, 1963/64 | | | |
| | Growth 1954–63/64 | With Education | | Without Education | |
		1954	1963/64	1954	1963/64
Total	125.7%	100.0%	100.0%		
Education	151.3	34.4	38.3		
Local schools	127.9	29.1	29.4		
Insts. of higher ed.	289.6	4.6	7.9		
Noneducation	112.3	65.6	61.7	100.0%	100.0%
Highways	111.0	18.0	16.8	27.4	27.3
Public welfare	88.4	10.0	8.3	15.2	13.5
Hospitals and health	103.8	7.8	7.1	12.0	11.5
Police	109.4	3.7	3.6	5.6	5.5
Local fire protection	87.1	2.1	1.8	3.2	2.9
Sanitation	114.3	3.5	3.3	5.2	5.3
Natural resources	140.8	2.4	2.6	3.8	4.3
Parks and recreation	141.0	1.4	1.5	2.1	2.4
Hous. and comm. redev.	86.9	2.0	1.6	3.0	2.7
General control	86.7	4.5	3.7	6.8	6.0
Interest on debt	223.6	2.3	3.4	3.6	5.5
Non-hwy. transportation	110.3	1.0	0.9	1.5	1.5
Others and unallocable	137.2	6.9	7.2	10.5	11.7

SOURCE: U. S. Bureau of the Census, *Census of Governments: 1962*, Vol. VI, No. 4 (*Historical Statistics on Governmental Finances and Employment*).

U. S. Bureau of the Census, *Governmental Finances in 1963–64*.

The education expenditure increase reveals an interesting contrast when it is divided between local schools and higher education. Local school expenditures have increased at just about the average national increase—a growth of 127.9 per cent. The higher growth rate for education is accounted for by the increase of 289.6 per cent for institutions of higher education, the greatest increase for any major function.

Because educational expenditures dominate the total figures, it is revealing to analyze separately noneducation expenditures, which had an overall increase of 112 per cent. Looked at this way, the greatest growth for a large function was highways, which increased its expenditures by 111.0 per cent, whereas welfare, with an increase of 88.4 per cent, is growing less rapidly than the average of all noneducation functions.

Despite the different rates of growth for individual functions, the proportionate allocation of the total resources used in the state and local sector has not changed drastically over the last ten years. The biggest gainer has been education, which has climbed from 34 per cent of the total to 38. Welfare has declined; highways just about held its own.

This growth experience of the past decade raises the question of what will happen in the future—will the present pattern continue, will there be a leveling off, or will rates of change increase or decline? The easy and correct answer is that nobody knows. Nevertheless, informed guesses are possible, and in recent years several have been made that are based on an analysis of need and resource availability as measured by such factors as potential increase in school population and economic growth.[9]

Contrasting three of these predictions with mechanical straight-line projections indicates that in the opinion of the soothsayers, future growth will proceed at a somewhat slower pace than that of the past decade. For one of the projections[10] it is possible to check its current accuracy because it was made in 1958 and estimates annual increases over the next decade (Table 1-4).

When current expenditures are translated into the definitions used in the one prediction made for annual changes, the actual growth has been greater than the prediction. Such direct comparison is not possible for the other projections because

TABLE 1-4: *A Comparison of Analytical Projections of State and Local Expenditures to Straight Line Projections*[1] *(Billions in 1958 Constant Dollars)*

PROJECTIONS: ECKSTEIN DEFINITIONS

	Substantive	Straight Line
1962	$ 43.3	$ 44.8 (actual)
1963	45.2	49.2
1964	47.4	53.4
1968	53.7	68.8
1970		75.7
1972		82.1

PROJECTIONS: NETZER DEFINITIONS

	Substantive	Straight Line
1962		60.2 (actual)
1963		66.4
1964		72.4
1968		93.9
1970	65.8–78.4	103.6
1972		112.6

PROJECTIONS: COLM-HELZNER DEFINITIONS

	Substantive	Straight Line[2]
1962		61.9 (actual)
1963		70.2
1964	64.6	78.2
1968		107.3
1970	90.0	120.3
1972		132.4

SOURCE: See footnote 9.

[1] A straight line projection is provided for each of the other projections. In each case the straight line projection follows the definitions and constant dollar assumptions used by the authors of the other projections.

[2] The 1962 figures of the straight line projections are actual figures adjusted for appropriate definitions and constant dollars. The straight line projections are based on the experience of the 1952–1962 period.

they were not made on an annual basis. Nevertheless, when these projections are compared to straight-line projections based on the actual experience of 1952–1962, the indications of both the substantive and mechanical projections is for continued growth. It seems fair to assume, therefore, that a larger and larger portion of the total national product will be allocated to the state and local sector of the economy.

The overall general revenue increases that support these expenditure increases have had to be equally large. Therefore, the significant revenue questions relate to changes in sources of revenue and shifts in the intensiveness of their use. As with general expenditures, federal tax revenues have increased less rapidly in the past decade than similar state and local revenues (Table 1-5). As a proportion of national income, state and local taxes have increased from 7.3 per cent in 1954 to 9.2 per cent in 1963. Federal tax revenue in 1954 equalled 20.6 per cent of national income and declined by 1964 to 18.0 per cent.

Despite the large increase in total tax revenue, the sources of state and local tax revenue have not shifted markedly during the past decade. Perhaps most remarkable, particularly in view of many dire predictions about its productivity, has been

TABLE 1-5: *Tax Revenues as a Per Cent of National Income, 1940–1963/64*

	All govts.	Federal	State	Local	State and local	National income (Billion)
1940	15.64%	6.01%	4.09%	5.55%	9.63%	$ 81.1
1946	25.51	19.96	2.72	2.84	5.55	181.8
1950	21.19	14.60	3.29	3.31	6.60	241.1
1952	27.14	20.49	3.40	3.26	6.62	291.4
1954	27.86	20.59	3.66	3.62	7.28	303.1
1962	27.05	17.98	4.50	4.59	9.09	457.7
1963/64	27.25	18.04	4.60	4.60	9.20	481.1

SOURCE: U. S. Bureau of the Census, *Census of Governments; 1962,* Vol. VI, No. 4 (*Historical Statistics on Governmental Finances and Employment*).

U. S. Bureau of the Census, *Governmental Finances in 1963–64,* Series G-GF64-No. 1.

The U. S. Department of Commerce, Office of Business Economics, *Survey of Current Business,* XLV (August 1965), Table 4.

the performance of the property tax. In 1954 the property tax contributed 45.2 per cent of state and local *tax* revenues; in 1963/64, 44.6 per cent. At the local level its proportion was 87.2 per cent in 1954 and an almost identical 87.5 per cent in 1963/64.

Over a longer time span the significant change in the property tax has been its abandonment by most state governments, causing it to become almost exclusively a local source of revenue. For example, 37 per cent of state tax revenues in 1922 were provided by the property tax. This percentage had declined by 1940 to 8 per cent, to 4 per cent in 1952, and to 3 per cent in 1962. This change in the jurisdiction that uses the property tax, however, has not reduced its total contribution to state and local finance. In other words, its abandonment by the state has simply resulted in its being more intensively used by local governments.

The abandonment by the state governments of the property tax as a major source of revenue has resulted during the last quarter of a century in their adopting nonproperty taxes and

TABLE 1-6: *Per Cent of State Government Revenues Contributed by Revenue Source, 1940–1963/64*

	1940	1946	1950	1952	1954	1962	1963/64
Total gen. rev.*	100.0%	100.0%	100.0%	100.0%	100.0%	100.0%	100.0%
Taxes	75.5	78.6	70.4	73.5	72.5	66.1	64.4
Indiv. income	4.7	6.2	6.4	6.8	6.6	8.8	9.1
Corp. income	3.5	7.0	5.2	6.2	5.0	4.2	4.5
Sales	42.3	44.6	41.5	42.7	43.0	38.6	37.1
Property	5.9	4.0	2.7	2.8	2.6	2.6	1.9
Licenses	8.8	7.0	6.7	6.9	7.2	5.4	5.1
Other	10.3	9.8	7.9	8.1	8.2	7.0	6.7
Charges	7.9	7.7	8.1	8.1	8.7	10.0	10.5
Intergov'tal rev.	16.5	13.8	21.5	18.5	18.8	24.0	25.1
From federal	15.2	12.8	20.2	17.3	17.4	22.8	24.0
From local	1.3	1.0	1.3	1.2	1.4	1.2	1.1

SOURCE: U. S. Bureau of The Census, *Census of Governments; 1962*, Vol. VI, No. 4 (*Historical Statistics on Governmental Finances and Employment*).

U. S. Bureau of the Census, *Governmental Finances in 1963–64*. Series G-GF64-No. 1.

* Due to rounding, the totals do not add to exactly 100.0 per cent.

nontax sources of revenue. By 1952 a new pattern of revenue
sources had been established. All states, with the exception of
Nebraska, had adopted by 1966 one or two broad-based
taxes—the individual income tax and/or the sales tax. New
Hampshire's income tax is a limited one and the state has
responded to its fiscal pressure with a state-sponsored lottery.
The revenue results of the New Hampshire experiment have
been disappointing.

Although the overall pattern of state general revenue
sources had been established by 1952, the contribution made
by the various sources of revenue has shifted somewhat in the
past decade (Table 1-6). Gains have been made in the proportion of general revenue contributed by the individual income
tax, fees and charges, and federal aid. The individual income
tax had increased its proportion of total state general revenues
from 6.6 to 9.1 per cent; fees and charges increased from 8.7
per cent to 10.5 per cent; and most significantly, federal aid
had grown from 17.4 per cent to 24.0 per cent.

The pattern of local general revenue sources has not shifted
as much during this same period as has the state pattern
(Table 1-7). Over a longer period, about the last four
decades, the significant change in local revenue has been the

TABLE 1-7: *Per Cent of Local Government General Revenues Contributed by Revenue Source, 1940–1963/64*

	1940	1946	1950	1952	1954	1962	1963/64
Total gen. rev.	100.0%	100.0%	100.0%	100.0%	100.0%	100.0%	100.0%
Taxes	64.9	62.6	57.0	55.8	56.1	54.7	53.4
Indiv. income	0.3	0.4	0.5	0.5	0.6	0.8	0.9
Sales	1.9	2.2	3.5	3.7	3.6	3.8	4.1
Property	60.1	57.6	50.2	48.9	49.0	48.0	46.5
Others	2.6	2.4	2.8	2.7	2.9	2.1	1.9
Charges and misc. rev.	7.3	11.2	11.4	13.0	13.6	14.9	15.2
Intergov'tal rev.	27.8	26.0	31.6	31.2	30.3	30.4	31.4
From federal	4.0	0.6	1.5	1.4	1.5	1.5	2.2
From state	23.8	25.4	30.1	29.8	28.8	28.4	29.2

SOURCE: U. S. Bureau of the Census. *Census of Governments; 1962*, Vol. VI,
No. 4 (*Historical Statistics on Governmental Finances and Employment*).

U. S. Bureau of the Census, *Governmental Finances in 1963–64*. Series
G-GF64-No. 1.

increasing proportion of local general revenues provided by state aid. During the last ten years, however, the various sources have remained relatively constant in their contribution to general revenues. The only source, that shows a major proportionate increase is charges and miscellaneous revenues, which has increased from 13.6 per cent to 15.2 per cent of total revenues.

Overall, the most remarkable aspect of state and local revenue sources during the past decade has been the stability of their proportional contribution. There have not been any dramatic developments in traditional revenue sources nor have there been any major new sources found.

It seems likely, therefore, that the additional revenue needed to finance the increasing expenditures of both state and local governments will simply come from the same sources, unless more massive changes are made in federal aid. The property tax has been found to be remarkably responsive to new needs, and recent studies indicate that at least in suburban areas it is a fairly adequate surrogate for a local income tax because a high relationship has been found between residential property values and income levels.[11] It is possible that many of those states, that have adopted only one of the two broad-based taxes, may well adopt the other, as New York State did in 1965 when it added a general sales tax.

Because these changes and growth in the levels of state and local finance occurred simultaneously with the metropolitanization of the country, it is likely that there are interrelationships between the two phenomena. The nature of these interrelationships can be uncovered by the examination of differences in the fiscal responses in metropolitan and nonmetropolitan areas and in the different parts of metropolitan areas and the differences, if any, in the forces operative in these different types of areas.

Although the specific variables used in the analysis are

lescribed when employed statistically, it is useful to examine
beforehand the general characteristics of metropolitan
America, for it is from these general characteristics that the
specific variables used in this study are drawn. Basically
metropolitanism is defined by a redistribution of population.
This redistribution involves not only the move from countryside to urban areas, but from city to suburb as well. The
resulting patterns of settlement and the interactions that result
are metropolitanism.

Population Characteristics of Metropolitanism

In 1960 there were in the United States 212 standard metropolitan statistical areas (SMSAs). These areas possessed 63
per cent of the country's total population, which was about
evenly divided between central cities and outside central city
areas (Table 1-8). This distribution of population between
metropolitan and nonmetropolitan areas and within the
metropolitan areas is the product of many years of population
growth and movement. As Table 1-9 shows, those areas
classified as metropolitan in 1960 have grown consistently
more rapidly than nonmetropolitan portions of the conterminous United States.[12] The difference in population growth
in metropolitan and nonmetropolitan areas is illustrated by
the relationship of their separate growth rates to the rate of
growth of the total population by decade from 1900 to 1960.

TABLE 1-8: *Population Distribution Between and Within Metropolitan
and Nonmetropolitan Areas, 1960*

	SMSAs	Per cent of SMSA Population	Non-SMSAs	Per cent of Non-SMSA Population
Total	112,883,757	100.0%	66,441,914	100.0%
Central cities	58,010,482	51.4	—	
Outside central city area	54,873,275	48.6	—	
Other urban	41,560,998	36.8	25,712,303	38.7
Rural nonfarm	11,675,448	10.3	28,921,542	43.5
Rural farm	1,636,829	1.5	11,808,069	17.8

SOURCE: U. S. Bureau of the Census, *U. S. Census of Population: 1960. General
Social and Economic Characteristics, U. S. Summary.* Final Report PC(1)-1C.

The least difference between these two growth rates occurred
in the depression decade, when the population growth in the
nonmetropolitan areas of the country equaled 75 per cent of
the United States average growth rate and the metropolitan
rate was 122 per cent of that rate. The greatest difference in
the growth rate occurred in the decades of 1920–1930 and
1940–50..The areas outside metropolitan areas grew only 34
per cent of the average rate for the whole population from
1920 to 1930 and 31 per cent 1940–1950, whereas the SMSA
growth was 168 per cent and 156 per cent of this growth for
these two periods (Table 1-10).

While the metropolitan areas of the country were increasing
their share of total population, the internal shifts in population
were altering the distribution of population within SMSAs.

TABLE 1-9: *Population Growth in the United States, in Metropolitan and
Nonmetropolitan Areas and the Proportion of Population in Metropolitan
Areas, 1900–1965 (Conterminous U. S. only)*

	UNITED STATES		SMSA		NON-SMSA		SMSA population as
	Popula-tion U. S. (000)	Per cent increase by decade	Popula-tion (000)	Per cent increase by decade	Popula-tion (000)	Per cent increase by decade	per cent of total population
1900	75,995	—	31,836	—	44,159	—	41.9%
		21.0%		32.0%		13.1%	
1910	91,972		42,012		49,960		45.7
		14.9		25.0		6.5	
1920	105,711		52,508		53,203		49.7
		16.1		27.1		5.4	
1930	122,775		66,712		56,063		54.3
		7.2		8.8		5.4	
1940	131,669		72,576		59,093		55.1
		14.5		22.6		4.5	
1950	150,697		88,964		61,733		59.0
		18.4		26.3		7.0	
1960	178,464		112,385		66,079		63.0
		7.5*		10.2*		3.4*	
1965	192,185		123,813		68,372		64.4

SOURCE: U. S. Bureau of the Census, *U. S. Census of Population: 1960, Selected Area
Reports: Standard Metropolitan Statistical Areas.* Final Report PC(3)-1D, p. 1.

* Five-year growth.

At the turn of the century about 62 per cent of total SMSA
population resided within central cities, with the remainder
outside (Table 1-11). By 1965 the proportion within central
cities had declined to 48 per cent of total metropolitan
population.

Up to 1920, the central city proportion of total SMSA
population had been increasing and then began to decline,
with the largest decline occurring in the most recent decade.
To some extent these figures understate central city decline since
they include that part of the growth caused by continuing
annexations of new areas to these cities.

TABLE 1-10: *The Relation of Metropolitan Area and Nonmetropolitan
Area Growth to Total Population Growth, 1900–1960 (U. S. Average
= 100)*

	Per cent growth of total population	Ratio of SMSA growth to average U. S. Growth	Ratio of non-SMSA growth to average U. S. Growth
1900–1910	21.0%	152	62
1910–1920	14.9	168	44
1920–1930	16.1	168	34
1930–1940	7.2	122	75
1940–1950	14.5	156	31
1950–1960	18.4	143	38

SOURCE: U. S. Bureau of the Census, *U. S. Census of Population: 1960. Selected
Area Reports: Standard Metropolitan Statistical Areas.* Final Report PC(3)-1D.

TABLE 1-11: *The Distribution of SMSA Population Between Central
Cities and Outside Central Cities, 1900–1965 (Conterminous U. S.)*

	Total SMSA population (000)	Per cent of SMSA population within central cities	Per cent of SMSA population outside central cities
1900	31,895	62.2%	37.8%
1910	42,094	64.6	35.4
1920	52,631	66.0	34.0
1930	66,915	64.6	35.4
1940	72,834	62.7	37.3
1950	89,317	58.7	41.3
1960	112,895	51.4	48.6
1965	123,813	48.1	51.9

SOURCE: U. S. Bureau of the Census, *U. S. Census of Population: 1960. Selected
Area Reports: Standard Metropolitan Statistical Areas.* Final Report PC(3)-1D.

Table 1-12 shows the growth inside and outside central cities with and without annexations for all metropolitan areas and by size category for the 1950 to 1960 decade. Overall, central cities grew by about 11 per cent in this ten-year period, but if annexations are excluded the growth is only 1.5 per cent. In fact, when growth caused by annexation is eliminated, the central cities in metropolitan areas with a population between one and three million show a decline in population. Only in the West did central cities show a sizeable increase within their 1950 boundaries, and that reflected the growth of

TABLE 1-12: *Population Growth in Metropolitan Areas With and Without Central City Annexations, 1950–1960*

	Total change (per cent)	Change without annexations (per cent)
All SMAs		
Central cities	+10.8%	+ 1.5%
Outside central cities	+48.5	+61.7
Total	+26.4	+26.4
SMSAs, population of:		
3,000,000 or more		
Central cities	+ 1.0	+ 0.6
Outside central cities	+71.3	+72.2
Total	+23.2	+23.2
1,000,000 to 3,000,000		
Central cities	+ 5.6	− 2.2
Outside central cities	+44.8	+52.7
Total	+25.0	+25.0
500,000 to 1,000,000		
Central cities	+21.4	+ 4.8
Outside central cities	+57.4	+81.1
Total	+36.0	+36.0
250,000 to 500,000		
Central cities	+16.2	+ 2.2
Outside central cities	+36.2	+51.9
Total	+25.6	+25.6
100,000 to 250,000		
Central cities	+24.4	+ 4.6
Outside central cities	+27.6	+54.5
Total	+25.8	+25.8
Under 100,000		
Central cities	+29.2	+ 8.6
Outside central cities	+10.9	+69.9
Total	+24.4	+24.4

SOURCE: U. S. Bureau of the Census, *U. S. Census of Population: 1960*, Vol. (*Characteristics of the Population*), Part A: Number of Inhabitants.

only Los Angeles and San Diego, which had considerable undeveloped land within their corporate boundaries.

These national population figures hide significant regional differences (Table 1-13). The North and West have a considerably larger proportion of their population in metropolitan areas than the South does, although the rates of metropolitanization, current and long term, are much greater in the South. Since 1910 the proportion of southern population that is metropolitan has increased by 90.1 per cent,

TABLE 1-13: *SMSA Population as Proportion of Total Population by Region, 1910–1960*

	U. S.	North	South	West
1910	45.7%	55.8%	25.3%	49.2%
1920	49.6	60.2	28.2	52.2
1930	54.3	64.6	32.3	59.3
1940	55.1	65.1	34.5	60.2
1950	59.0	67.1	41.2	65.3
1960	63.0	68.9	48.1	70.0

SOURCE: U. S. Bureau of the Census, *U. S. Census of Population: 1960. Selected Area Reports: Standard Metropolitan Statistical Areas.* Final Report PC(3)-1D.

TABLE 1-14: *Population Growth in Central Cities and Outside Central Cities by Regions, 1900–1960*

	North	South	West
1900–1910			
Central cities	32.4%	41.2%	89.0%
Outside central cities	21.7	18.3	64.7
1910–1920			
Central cities	24.6	37.8	37.7
Outside central cities	20.8	10.3	39.2
1920–1930			
Central cities	18.8	38.3	45.1
Outside central cities	31.7	19.6	63.8
1930–1940			
Central cities	2.4	14.4	11.9
Outside central cities	9.7	23.7	29.3
1940–1950			
Central cities	7.4	29.9	33.0
Outside central cities	24.9	43.5	79.3
1950–1960			
Central cities	0.3	28.5	31.9
Outside central cities	43.7	47.7	65.9

SOURCE: U. S. Bureau of the Census, *U. S. Census of Population: 1960. Selected Area Reports: Standard Metropolitan Statistical Areas.* Final Report PC(3)-1D.

whereas the comparable figures for the North and West are 23.4 and 42.3 per cent.

The distribution of population within metropolitan areas and the relative growth rates of central city and outside central city areas are marked by regional variations, too (Table 1-14). Central city growth, for example, remains fairly strong in the South and West for the 1950–1960 decade, but it is practically zero in the North. In contrast, all sections of the country show strong outside-central-city growth.

One final aspect of the central city-outside central city population comparisons is worth noting. The numerical stability of central city population has obscured a tremendous amount of population movement as measured by the proportion of persons living in the same house in 1960 as in 1955. By this measure of movement there is only a minor difference between central city and outside central city areas: 52.3 compared to 47.7 per cent.

Income Characteristics

These population shifts have resulted in measurable differences in the social and economic characteristics between metropolitan and nonmetropolitan areas and between central cities and outside central cities. Most revealing, perhaps, are the differences in income levels (Table 1-15).

TABLE 1-15: *Per Capita Income in Metropolitan and Nonmetropolitan Areas by Region, 1959*

	Regional per capita income	Per capita income in SMSAs	Per capita income in non-SMSAs	Amount SMSA income is higher than non-SMSA income	SMSA income as proportion of non-SMSA
United States	$1,850	$2,113	$1,388	$725	152.2%
Northeast	2,086	2,182	1,675	507	130.3
North Central	1,405	2,176	1,480	696	147.0
South	1,420	1,771	1,130	641	156.7
West	2,121	2,282	1,700	582	134.2

SOURCE: Computed from census aggregate income data as provided in U. S. Bureau of the Census, *County and City Data Book, 1962* (A Statistical Supplement).

For the United States in 1959, median family income in metropolitan areas was $6,324, compared to $4,485 for non-metropolitan areas. On a per capita basis for the same year, the comparable figures are $2,113 and $1,388. The higher level of income in metropolitan areas exists in all regions of the country. The differences between metropolitan and non-metropolitan areas are greatest in relative terms in the South, the least metropolitan region; these differences are least, both relatively and absolutely, in the Northeast, the most metropolitan region.

Although the average income level in the South is lower than for the rest of the country, its metropolitan level is proportionately higher than its nonmetropolitan income. It seems clear that metropolitanism has had less impact beyond metropolitan area borders in this region than in other sections of the country. As metropolitanization advances in the South it seems likely that the gap between metropolitan and nonmetropolitan income will decline there, too.

Just as there are distinctions between metropolitan and non-metropolitan areas, there are similar distinctions within these areas. The highest income areas are the urban portions of the outside central city areas (urban fringe and other urban); in nonmetropolitan areas it is the urban places that have the highest incomes. Table 1-16 presents the median family income breakdown for both metropolitan and nonmetropolitan areas. Although these figures are for 1959, the relationships have remained approximately the same since that date but the levels have increased for all area types.

TABLE 1-16: *Median Family Income in Metropolitan and Nonmetropolitan Areas, 1959*

	SMSA	Non-SMSA
United States	$6,324	$4,485
Central city	5,940	—
Urban fringe	7,114	—
Other urban	7,002	5,296
Rural nonfarm	5,830	4,303
Rural farm	4,543	3,061

SOURCE: U. S. Bureau of the Census, *U. S. Census of Population: 1960. General Social and Economic Characteristics, U. S. Summary.* Final Report PC(1)-1C.

These median family income figures for different parts of metropolitan areas hide important contrasts in the income distribution within these areas. The usual picture of high income suburbs and low income cities needs considerable qualification, particularly when size categories of SMSAs are used in the analysis. Measuring low income by the proportion of families under $3,000 per year and high income by the proportion over $10,000, the picture of low income cities and high income suburbs holds for nationwide averages but not for every size category. Central cities of metropolitan areas have 17.6 per cent of their families under $3,000, whereas the comparable figure for outside central city areas is 12.5 per cent. On the high income side central cities have 16.5 per cent over $10,000; 21.2 per cent outside central cities are in this category.

Examining income differences for entire metropolitan areas it is found that only in the large areas, those possessing over a million in population, is the proportion over $10,000 greater than the proportion under $3,000. In the case of the largest size category, population over three million, the proportion over $10,000 is almost double that of the proportion under $3,000: 23.0 compared to 12.6 per cent. It is in this category, too, that the central cities have a higher proportion over $10,000 than under $3,000: 19.5 per cent compared to 15.4 per cent.

TABLE 1-17: *Per Cent of Families with Incomes Under $3,000 and Over $10,000 by Size of Standard Metropolitan Statistical Area, 1959*

| | | PER CENT OF FAMILIES WITH INCOMES | | | | | |
| | | UNDER $3,000 | | | OVER $10,000 | | |
Population of SMSA	Number of SMSAs	Entire SMSA	Central city	Outside central city	Entire SMSA	Central city	Outside central city
United States average	212	15.1%	17.6%	12.5%	18.8%	16.5%	21.2%
Over 3,000,000	5	12.6	15.4	8.9	23.0	19.5	27.6
1,000,000 to 3,000,000	19	13.0	17.1	10.0	20.8	16.6	23.9
500,000 to 1,000,000	29	17.2	19.8	14.2	16.4	14.6	18.4
250,000 to 500,000	48	17.6	18.7	16.6	14.6	14.7	14.5
100,000 to 250,000	89	19.5	19.6	19.3	13.7	14.3	12.9
Less than 100,000	22	20.7	18.8	27.2	13.8	14.4	12.0

SOURCE: U. S. Bureau of the Census, *U. S. Census of Population, 1960. Selected Area Reports: Standard Metropolitan Statistical Areas.*

Another important distinction by size is the decreasing proportion over $10,000 outside central cities, as size declines. For the largest metropolitan areas the proportion over $10,000 outside central cities is 27.6 per cent; for the smallest size category, less than 100,000 population, the comparable percentage is 12.0. As the proportion over $10,000 for areas outside central cities declines, the proportion under $3,000 increases: from 8.9 per cent for the largest category to 27.2 per cent for the smallest.

The larger metropolitan areas, it is clear, have less poverty proportionately than the smaller areas. On the other hand, if the measurement is of comparative affluence inside and outside central cities, this contrast is greatest for the largest areas. In the over three million population category, for every 100 families in central cities under $3,000 there are 127 over $10,000, whereas outside central cities the comparable number over $10,000 is 312 for every 100 under $3,000. Stated another way, the difference in the number of families with incomes of $10,000 and over per 100 families under $3,000 for outside central city areas to the comparable number for central cities is 184.8. The size of this difference between central city and outside central city declines as size decreases and, in fact, reverses itself for the two size categories below 250,000 population, as shown in Table 1-18.

TABLE 1-18: *The Ratio of Number of Families with Incomes Over $10,000 to Those Families Under $3,000 per 100 Families, by SMSA Size, 1959*

Population of SMSA	Entire SMSA	Central city (CC)	Outside central city (OCC)	Difference in ratio: (OCC-CC)
United States	124.2%	93.9%	169.4%	75.5
Over 3,000,000	183.0	126.7	311.5	184.8
1,000,000 to 3,000,000	160.5	97.3	238.9	141.6
500,000 to 1,000,000	95.6	73.8	129.3	55.5
250,000 to 500,000	82.8	78.6	87.4	8.8
100,000 to 250,000	70.3	73.1	66.6	− 6.5
Less than 100,000	67.0	76.3	44.0	−32.3

SOURCE: U. S. Bureau of the Census, *U. S. Census of Population, 1960. Selected Area Reports: Standard Metropolitan Statistical Areas.* Fund Report PC(3)-1D.

Within metropolitan areas, therefore, the central cities of the largest metropolitan areas show both greater absolute affluence and relative poverty than the smaller areas, but these smaller areas have considerably less difference between central cities and outside central cities than the larger areas. And in the areas with population of less than 250,000 the central cities possess relative opulence compared to their surrounding areas.

In summary, metropolitan areas have considerably higher incomes than nonmetropolitan areas whether viewed by region or, as will be shown in the next chapter, by state. This difference is greatest in the South, even though that region's average income level, combining metropolitan and nonmetropolitan areas, is the lowest in the nation.

By size categories the largest metropolitan areas are the most affluent, but the internal income distribution shows that the central city portions of the largest metropolitan areas are worse off relative to their outlying areas than is true of the smaller areas. For the smallest areas there is more affluence within than outside central cities. It is clear that in these smaller areas the suburban portion does not have the income characteristics normally associated with suburbia. Of importance in these smaller population metropolitan areas are the rural portions incorporated into metropolitan areas by census definition.

The significance of these income differences for fiscal behavior is tested throughout this study, and the influence of the proportion of the population that is rural is particularly important in the fiscal analysis of outside central city areas.

Education Characteristics

The residents of metropolitan areas are, on the whole, better educated than those living in nonmetropolitan areas. The median number of school years completed for residents of metropolitan areas over 25 years of age in 1960 was 11.1; the comparable national figure for outside metropolitan areas was 9.5. (Table 1-19). This difference in median school years completed is reflected in the proportions of those 25 years of age and over who have completed less than five years of schooling, and the proportion of those who completed high school, and those who have four years of college or more.

Within metropolitan areas there are also differences, with these being closely related to the income characteristics already explained. The outside central city residents have completed on the average more education than those in central cities (Table 1-20). Median school years completed in central cities was 10.7, compared to 12.0 for the urban areas outside central cities, although for the rural nonfarm and for the rural farm areas within metropolitan areas these figures were lower at 10.6 and 9.2, respectively.

TABLE 1-19: *School Years Completed for Persons 25 Years and Older in SMSAs and Non-SMSAs, 1960*

Completing:	SMSA	Non-SMSA
Less than five years of school	7.0%	10.7%
More than five years but less than four years of high school	40.0	48.3
Four years of high school or more	44.2	35.4
Four years of college or more	8.8	5.6
Exhibit:		
Median school years completed	11.1	9.5

SOURCE: U. S. Bureau of the Census, *U. S. Census of Population: 1960. General Social and Economic Characteristics, U. S. Summary.* Final Report PC(1)-1C.

TABLE 1-20: *Proportion Over 25 Years of Age Who Have Completed Four or More Years of College in SMSAs, by Region, 1960 (Conterminous U. S.)*

Region	SMSA	Central city	Outside central city
United States	8.8%	8.0%	9.8%
North	8.3	6.9	9.8
South	9.1	9.0	9.3
West	10.4	10.5	10.2

SOURCE: U. S. Bureau of the Census, *U. S. Census of Population: 1960. Selected Area Reports: Standard Metropolitan Statistical Areas.* Final Report PC(3)-1D.

TABLE 1-21: *Proportion Over 25 Years of Age Who Have Had No High School or Have Completed Four or More Years of College in SMSAs, by Size Classification, 1960*

Size	SMSA			CENTRAL CITY			OUTSIDE CENTRAL CITY		
	Four or more years of college	No high school	Ratio of those completing college to those with no high school	Four or more years of college	No high school	Ratio of those completing college to those with no high school	Four or more years of college	No high school	Ratio of those completing college to those with no high school
3,000,000 and over	8.9%	35.5%	25.1	7.5%	40.6%	18.4	10.8%	28.2%	38.3
1,000,000 to 3,000,000	9.9	34.0	29.1	8.2	39.0	21.0	11.3	30.0	37.6
500,000 to 1,000,000	8.5	35.4	24.0	7.8	38.3	20.2	9.4	22.1	29.3
250,000 to 500,000	7.8	37.1	21.0	8.1	36.8	22.0	7.4	37.5	19.7
100,000 to 250,000	8.1	38.0	21.3	9.1	37.1	24.6	6.7	39.4	17.0
Less than 100,000	7.8	38.2	20.4	8.1	37.1	21.8	6.6	41.9	15.6

SOURCE: U. S. Bureau of the Census, *U. S. Census of Population: 1960. Selected-Area Reports: Standard Metropolitan Statistical Areas.* Final Report PC(3)-1D.

There are, with education and with other characteristics, regional patterns that can be shown by contrasting the proportions of those who have completed four or more years of college by region.

Overall, the West has a considerably higher proportion completing four years or more of college than the rest of the country. Further, in the South and West there is not the sharp contrast between central cities and suburbs that there is in the East. These differences reflect the contrasting population growth patterns already described for these regions.

Differences in size are also important in understanding differences in education level. It is only in the size categories over 500,000 that the proportion completing four years of college is higher in the suburbs than in the central city.

The ratio of those completing college to those without any high school shows the educational contrasts between these two type areas. For metropolitan areas as a whole it is the largest areas that have the highest ratio—i.e., the higher the proportion who have completed college relative to the proportion with no high school. Yet it is in these large areas that the contrast is greatest between central cities and their outlying parts. Just as with income, the outside central city areas show the highest ratios and the greatest difference from the central city ratios. For the smaller areas the pattern reverses itself and the highest ratios are found in the central cities.

Again, only the larger metropolitan areas reflect the popular view of the suburbs as the place of residence of the well-to-do and highly educated. In the smaller metropolitan areas, many of the well educated remain in the central city, and the average educational level is reduced for the outside central city areas by the high proportion of the population that is rural (Table 1-21).

Of importance for fiscal analysis is not only the level of education already acquired by adults, but the proportion of school-age children in public schools. For the country as a whole the proportion in public schools is considerably higher in nonmetropolitan than in metropolitan areas, reflecting the concentration of parochial schools in the latter. In these areas 84.7 per cent of young people of high school age are in public schools, whereas the comparable figure for nonmetropolitan areas is 97.2 per cent (Table 1-22).

Within metropolitan areas the greatest contrasts are between the rural portions of metropolitan areas and the rest of the area, although non-public schools do play a larger role in central cities than they do in the urban fringe. The difference is greatest at the high school level, where 81.2 per cent of central city young people are in public schools; the comparable figure for suburban areas is 86.3 (Table 1-23).

These education characteristics can obviously affect fiscal behavior in several ways. The educational level of a community and the relation of educational aspirations to income, plus the availability of resources to devote to education, will all help determine the quantity of resources devoted to this function, as will the proportion of school-age children in public schools.

TABLE 1-22: *Proportion of School-Age Children in Public Schools in SMSA and Non-SMSA Areas, 1960 (Conterminous U. S.)*

	SMSA per cent	Non-SMSA per cent
Kindergarten	85.1%	87.7%
Elementary	81.1	92.5
High School	84.7	97.2

SOURCE: U. S. Bureau of the Census, *U. S. Census of Population: 1960. General Social and Economic Characteristics, U. S. Summary.* Final Report PC(1)-1C.

TABLE 1-23: *Proportion of School-Age Children in Public Schools Within SMSAs, 1960 (Conterminous U. S.)*

	SMSA	Central city	Other urban	Rural Non-farm	Rural Farm
Kindergarten	85.1%	83.4%	86.1%	88.7%	91.8%
Elementary	81.1	78.3	80.9	91.3	90.1
High School	84.7	81.2	86.3	92.4	94.1

SOURCE: U. S. Bureau of the Census, *U. S. Census of Population: 1960. General Social and Economic Characteristics, U. S. Summary.* Final Report PC(1)-1C.

[28]

Distribution of the Foreign-Born and Those of Foreign-Born and Mixed Parentage

The tendency of immigrants to reside in urban rather than rural areas is verified by the distribution of the foreign-born and of those with foreign-born or mixed parentage. The foreign-born and those who have one or both parents foreign-born constitute 23.8 per cent of the population of metropolitan areas compared to 10.7 per cent of nonmetropolitan areas. (Table 1-24). Somewhat surprising, perhaps, is that those with foreign or mixed parentage are of almost equal proportion in the population of both the central cities and the urban portion of the outside central city areas.

White—Nonwhite Distribution

Although the children of the foreign-born tend to move to the suburbs in the same proportion as their counterparts with native-born parents, such is not true of the nonwhite population. Whereas the proportion of nonwhites in the central cities has been increasing, their proportion in the suburban areas has been declining. Table 1-25 shows that the proportion of nonwhite population in the central cities has increased since 1900 from 6.8 per cent to 20.8 per cent in 1965, whereas

TABLE 1-24: *Proportion of Foreign-Born and Those with Foreign or Mixed Parentage of Total Population in SMSA and Non-SMSA Areas, 1960 (Conterminous U. S.)*

	SMSA		NON-SMSA	
	Foreign born	*Of foreign or mixed parentage*	*Foreign born*	*Of foreign or mixed parentage*
Total (United States)	7.2%	16.6%	2.4%	8.3%
Central city	8.8	17.2	—	—
Other urban	6.2	17.8	3.1	10.1
Rural nonfarm	3.4	10.6	2.1	7.1
Rural farm	3.6	11.2	1.4	7.4

SOURCE: U. S. Bureau of the Census, *U. S. Census of Population: 1960. General Social and Economic Characteristics, U. S. Summary.* Final Report PC(1)-1C.

in the areas outside central cities the nonwhite proportion has declined from 9.4 per cent to 5.0 per cent.

As the nonwhite population in metropolitan areas has become more and more concentrated in the central city portions of those areas, the proportion of nonwhites in metropolitan areas has been simultaneously growing (Table 1-26). In other words, the nonwhite population is distributing itself more like the white population between metropolitan and nonmetropolitan areas, but not between central cities and outside central city areas.

This movement of nonwhites to metropolitan areas, combined with the decreasing proportion of nonwhite population

TABLE 1-25: *Proportion of Population in SMSAs that is Nonwhite, 1900–1965 (Conterminous U. S.)*

Year	Per cent nonwhite in SMAs	Per cent nonwhite in central city	Per cent nonwhite outside central city
1900	7.8%	6.8%	9.4%
1910	7.3	6.9	8.1
1920	7.2	7.3	7.0
1930	8.1	9.0	6.4
1940	8.6	10.1	6.0
1950	10.0	13.1	5.7
1960	11.7	17.8	5.2
1965	12.6	20.8	5.0

SOURCE: U. S. Bureau of the Census, *U. S. Census of Population: 1960. Selected Area Reports: Standard Metropolitan Statistical Areas.* Final Report PC(3)-1D.

TABLE 1-26: *Nonwhite Proportion of Total U. S. Population and SMSA Population, 1900–1965 (Conterminous U. S.)*

Year	Nonwhite proportion of total U. S. population	Nonwhite proportion of SMSA population
1900	12.1%	7.8%
1910	11.1	7.3
1920	10.3	7.2
1930	10.2	8.1
1940	10.2	8.6
1950	10.7	10.0
1960	11.4	11.7
1965	11.9	12.6

SOURCE: U. S. Bureau of the Census, *U. S. Census of Population: 1960. Selected Area Reports: Standard Metropolitan Statistical Areas.* Final Report PC(3)-1D.

in the areas outside central cities, results in a growing concentration of nonwhites in central cities. In the North this population shift is reinforced by the decline in total central city population.

The regional exception to this large increase in the nonwhite proportion of central city population is the South, where the proportion increased only from 24.9 per cent to 26.1 from 1940 to 1960 (Table 1-27). In contrast, the proportion of nonwhites in the suburbs in the South has decreased for this same time period from 18.4 per cent to 11.8. More important, however, is the mobility pattern of the southern Negro who apparently moves first from rural areas to a nearby city and then moves from that city to a northern city. As a result, the proportion of Negroes in southern central cities is relatively stable, whereas the proportion in northern cities is growing.

This high proportion of the nonwhite population in central cities, in contrast to outside central cities, accounts, in part, for the differences between these areas already found for income, occupation, and education.

TABLE 1-27: *Nonwhite Proportion of Population in SMSAs by Region, 1940–1960 (Conterminous U. S.)*

	Nonwhite proportion of SMSA population	Nonwhite proportion of central city population	Nonwhite proportion of outside central city population
North			
1940	5.1%	6.5%	2.6%
1950	7.1	9.9	2.9
1960	9.4	15.5	3.0
South			
1940	22.5	24.9	13.4
1950	21.5	24.4	14.6
1960	19.9	26.1	11.8
West			
1940	3.9	4.3	3.2
1950	5.7	7.5	3.8
1960	7.2	11.1	4.0

SOURCE: U. S. Bureau of the Census, *U. S. Census of Population: 1960. Selected Area Reports: Standard Metropolitan Statistical Areas.* Final Report PC(3)-1D.

Metropolitan Characteristics: A Synthesis

The United States, over the past half century, has become a metropolitan nation. This transition involves more than is usually conveyed in the concept of urbanization because people have moved not only from countryside to urban areas, but from city to suburbs as well. The nature of urbanism has changed. "Our very concept of the city has been exploded by the massive expansion of modern urbanization."[13]

This new areal distribution of people within urban and metropolitan areas has followed a kind of "sorting out" pattern. Metropolitan areas are distinguishable from one another by size and regional location. The socioeconomic characteristics of different parts of metropolitan areas make them distinguishable from each other, and these differences are also influenced by both size and region.

Metropolitan areas are growing faster in population than nonmetropolitan areas; this is particularly true in the South and the West. Income is higher in metropolitan than in non-metropolitan areas. In the South the general level of income is lower than for the rest of the country, but in this region metropolitan income is proportionately higher than non-metropolitan income.

Within metropolitan areas income levels are higher on the average in outside central city areas than in central cities, but these differences hide important differences based on the size of areas. In the largest metropolitan areas the number of families over $10,000 per year substantially exceeds the number below $3,000, but the ratio of those over $10,000 to those under $3,000 is much greater in the suburbs than in the central cities of these areas. As a result of this pattern, in these same large areas the position of the central cities in relation to their own outlying parts is one of relative poverty.

In the smaller metropolitan areas the income position of central city and outlying areas is reversed. The income distribution is more heavily weighted in the below $3,000 category than in the over $10,000, and the proportion below $3,000 is greater in the outside central city areas than in the central cities.

The better educated in the larger metropolitan areas live in the outside central city areas, as do larger proportions of the holders of professional and managerial positions. It is noteworthy, however, that despite the slightly larger proportions of these professional groups living outside central cities, substantial numbers of these continue to live in central cities.

Although the foreign-born are more heavily concentrated in central cities than outside them, such is not true for their children. Nonwhites are moving in larger and larger numbers into metropolitan areas and within these areas tend to live in central cities. In all parts of the country, except in the South, the proportion of nonwhites is increasing substantially in central cities.

Although these characteristics do not add up to the usual picture of the differences between central cities and suburbs, they do make clear that patterns are sufficiently different to justify an examination of the implications of the differences for fiscal behavior. The modifications that must be made in the traditional view of the contrasts between these areas appear to be primarily a result of the size, regional, and rural characteristics of these areas. The smaller an area, the less likely it will

TABLE 1-28: *Proportion of Population, White and Nonwhite, Residing in Central Cities and in the Urban Fringe, by Economic Status, 1960*

	(Highest status)	High	Low	(Lowest status)	
Total population					
Central cities	13.7%	42.4%	35.2%	8.6%	100%
Urban fringe	22.8	50.1	23.4	3.7	100%
White population					
Central cities	16.0	46.8	31.1	6.1	100%
Urban fringe	23.7	51.3	22.0	3.0	100%
Nonwhite population					
Central cities	3.0	21.9	54.5	20.6	100%
Urban fringe	3.6	25.2	52.7	18.4	100%

SOURCE: U. S. Bureau of the Census, *Current Population Reports, Technical Studies*, Series P 23, No. 12, July 31, 1964.

fit the model, and regionally the North fits better than the South or West.

Despite these qualifications, the differences between cities and suburbs are substantial. The Census Bureau recently attempted to measure these differences through the use of a socioeconomic status scale. Combining measures of occupation, income, and education, the scale developed was applied to the population residing in central cities and in the urban fringe portion of the outside central city areas. The results are given in Table 1-28.

The suburbs have more of their residents in the highest status category than do the central cities; at the other end of the scale central cities have over twice as high a proportion of their population in the lowest category. On the average, therefore, the impressionistic image of the differences between suburbs and central cities holds true.[14]

Governmental Systems, Metropolitanism, and Fiscal Behavior

Although the socioeconomic characteristics of metropolitanism can be described for such sociogeographic divisions as metropolitan/nonmetropolitan and central/outside central cities, fiscal decisions are not made by such units. Instead, fiscal decisions are made by all levels of government—federal-state-local—and at the local level by many different kinds of local jurisdictions. Put another way, the assignment of responsibility for different functions and taxing powers is made to federal, state, and the various kinds of local governments in a wide variety of different combinations.

It is this variety of governmental jurisdictions that complicates any analysis that attempts to measure fiscal behavior in metropolitan terms. For this reason nearly all analyses of subnational fiscal behavior have used either state variations in state-local totals as the dependent variables to be explained or they have dealt with the finances of specific cities. This lumping together of fiscal behavior by states or the concentration of attention on only a single city, hides the possible significance that variations in governmental systems may have for fiscal behavior, as well as the relevance of metropolitanism to such behavior.

Despite the addition of the metropolitan dimension, the stream of literature into which this study most clearly fits is that devoted to state and local public finances. Although most of the publications in this field are cited, with respect to their specific findings, where relevant, a brief summary of the historical background of these earlier analyses will help to fit this study into that body of literature.

Early studies of state and local finances focused on the large cities whose tills had been pilfered during the last decades of the 19th century. Muckraker and academic alike analyzed the "shame of the cities." Drives for municipal reform concentrated their energies on individual cities. Bureaus of municipal research were established and more adequate state reporting of local finances was begun in Wisconsin and New York; however, except in special cases, the analysis was restricted to the areas covered.

While the political scientist clamored for reform of local government, at first demanding economy but afterwards modifying his demands in terms of efficiency, students of public finance and members of the aroused citizenry were attacking the general property tax as an inequitable means of raising the revenues to meet increasing local government costs. The demand for greater efficiency necessitated reorganizing local governments. Such reorganization required state-enabling legislation; curtailing the general property tax meant an increase in direct state responsibility and greater state aid.

Evidence of the trends of the twenties were contained in Lent Upson's annual comparison of tax rates in cities with populations over 30,000 and the National Industrial Conference Board's "Studies in Taxation and Public Finance."[15]

The increases in costs demonstrated by these studies had already created new demands that local government services be improved. Grading cities became an important occupation in its own right. "Measuring the Results of Government," "Municipal Batting Averages," "Score Cards To Be Used in the Selection of School Building Sites," and "A Statistical Study of American Cities by Students of Reed College," all joined Clarence E. Ridley in *Measuring Municipal Government*.[16] Mabel L. Walker's 1930 volume on *Municipal Expenditures*[17] summarized the interest in a more scientific approach to the individual city, which now included the smaller community. Comparisons were made of like communities, but not of interrelated metropolitan areas.

The development, however, of a framework for the analysis of metropolitan area finances was a slow process. The initial work of Haig[18] and the concomitant work within the Census Bureau provided the beginning of a framework. But the restrictions to a small number of large cities and the slow development of governmental services outside these cities reduced the pressure for a detailed analysis beyond cities. Paul Studenski's 1930 study, *The Government of Metropolitan Areas in the United States*,[19] opened the way to consideration of metropolitan fiscal characteristics, as did Victor Jones's pioneering study, *Metropolitan Government*.[20]

The developments of the 1930s created a new era of fiscal interdependence as the various levels of government became increasingly dependent on each other for the raising and spending of money. The first steps had been taken in the form of state aid to local governments for education, then the welfare crisis brought in both federal and state governments to an unprecedented extent.

This crisis, plus the development of more refined statistical tools, led to the development of studies of the determinants of variations in levels of expenditures. The first major study of these determinants used interstate differences in operating expenses of state and local government for the year 1942 as its data for analysis.[21] This study chose the three factors that have since formed the basis for the analysis of per capita expenditures by function: per capita income, population density, and per cent urban. These variables, plus others, are used in this study in order to enhance the cumulative quality of work in this field.

Others[22] followed the path laid down in the original study, applying the same variables to new data or with the introduction of intergovernmental aids, federal and state, as a new independent variable.[23]

Increasingly sophisticated studies led gradually to an analysis of metropolitan fiscal behavior. Early emphasis in this field was on differences in tax burden in different parts of the same metropolitan area.[24]

The analysis of specific areas was more limited than was generally understood even though they were formulated in a metropolitan context. The changing framework of federal-state-local relations were further modified by changes in the local level itself, producing important variations within and among metropolitan areas. Even in the case of the studies of central cities, the magnitude of the differences was simply not appreciated.

Another step forward was made by Harvey Brazer in his study of city expenditures.[25] Unlike previous studies, Brazer raised most of the conceptual problems of local finances. The use of ingenious proxies for fundamental differences gave this study a far more solid base than its predecessors, but it failed to provide the generalized framework for the analysis of local (or state) finances. The emphasis on comparable common functions, statewide data, and the recognition of interstate differences, all pointed to the necessity of a broader framework. These were followed by analyses of individual metropolitan areas.[26]

Integration of the state and local systems was made a

realistic possibility by the 1957 Census of Governments and its successor analyses. By breaking down local finances into county area units with subcounty detail on the central city and its overlying units, the governments division provided data consistent with a general framework for analyzing the metropolitan areas. Further, by the analysis of the assignment of revenue and expenditure responsibilities of the state and local governments within each state, interstate comparisons became a possibility. In spite of many limitations associated primarily with the geographic pattern of direct state expenditures, the generalized conceptual pattern appropriate to the analysis of metropolitan finances has become operational.

The first step to analyze metropolitan finance nationally was taken by Ross Stephens and Henry Schmandt in their "Revenue Patterns of Local Governments."[27] Their pioneering work was limited because of its failure to incorporate variations in the state and local assignment systems. In addition, the use of equally weighted county data to draw metropolitan and regional inferences contained some basically unresolved conceptual problems. In a successor article on "Local Government Expenditures,"[28] no attempt was made to segregate metropolitan and nonmetropolitan areas. Implicit "metropolitan" results exist in this article if account is taken of size categories, but these have to be inferred from the results rather than from the presentation.

Harvey Shapiro, in his analysis of "Economics of Scale and Local Government Finance,"[29] recapitulated the results of the 1957 Census of Governments and threw his emphasis on an analysis of states by county area population-size groups. However, like the Stephens and Schmandt studies, the failure to use an assignment of tax and expenditures responsibility reduces the comparability of the findings of local governments as between states.

The analysis of metropolitan local government finances must take place within the framework of state-local finances.

Since Solomon Fabricant made his important contribution, the necessity of viewing the total picture has been generally appreciated. Building on these earlier studies of state-local fiscal behavior and adding to them governmental variables, this study will provide the most general findings to date about the determinants of local finances in metropolitan areas. It is believed, too, that use of governmental variables will help to make the policy implications clear.

References

1. Melvin M. Webber, "Order in Diversity: Community Without Propinquity" in *Cities and Space: The Future Use of Urban Land*, ed. Lowdon Wingo Jr. (Baltimore: Johns Hopkins Press, 1963), 23.
2. Webber, 18.
3. James McGregor Burns, *The Deadlock of Democracy: Four-Party Politics in America* (Englewood Cliffs, N.J.: Prentice-Hall, Inc., 1963), 5.
4. The Census Bureau definition of metropolitan areas and of its component parts is followed throughout this study. That definition is as follows: "Except in New England, a standard metropolitan statistical area (an SMSA) is a county or group of contiguous counties which contain at least one city of 50,000 inhabitants or more or 'twin cities' with a combined population of at least 50,000. In addition to the county, or counties, containing such a city or cities, contiguous counties are included in an SMSA if, according to certain criteria, they are essentially metropolitan in character and are socially and economically integrated with the central city." In New England, towns are used instead of counties.
5. The phrase *outside central cities* is generally used throughout this study instead of suburbia; the latter term is not sufficiently inclusive of the range of types of areas included in the Census Bureau definition of the non-central city portions of metropolitan areas.

6. Council of State Governments (John C. Bollens, Director of Study), *The States and the Metropolitan Problem* (1956), 17.

7. This section is based on an earlier article that grew out of this overall study: Alan K. Campbell, "Most Dynamic Sector," *National Civic Review*, LIII (February 1964).

8. Unless otherwise stated, comparisons are of general expenditures as that term is defined by the Census Bureau, comprising "all expenditures other than (*a*) benefit and refund payments of public-employee retirement and other social insurance systems and (*b*) spending for state and local liquor stores and for local water, electric, transit, and gas utilities."

9. Otto Eckstein, *Trends in Public Expenditures in the Next Decade*, Committee for Economic Development, 1959. Gerhard Colm and Manuel Helzner, "Financial Needs and Resources Over the Next Decade: At All Levels of Government," and Dick Netzer, "Financial Needs and Resources over the Next Decade: State and Local Governments," in *Public Finances: Needs, Sources and Utilization, A Report of the National Bureau of Economic Research, New York* (Princeton: University Press, 1961).

10. Eckstein, *op. cit.*

11. Robert Fairbanks, *Property Tax Behavior in New York State, 1949-1961* (D. S. Sc. Dissertation, Syracuse University, 1963); and Jesse Burkhead, *State and Local Taxes for Public Education* (Syracuse, N.Y.: Syracuse University Press, 1963).

12. Wherever historical data of metropolitan areas are used, the Census Bureau's practice of tracing the areas defined as metropolitan in 1960 back to the turn of the century is followed. In explaining this practice the Bureau states: "The delineation of SMSAs in terms of counties or other administratively defined areas facilitates tracing the population of the areas as defined in 1960 back through the censuses to the beginning of the century. (No determination has been made of the actual metropolitan character or integration of particular counties at earlier dates, however.) The population of central cities cannot be traced for constant areas, since the data pertain to areas as incorporated at the time of enumeration. Hence, the historical data on the population of SMSAs pertain to constant areas for the total SMSA and to changing incorporated areas for the central city. An SMSA is not included until the census

at which the population of its central city attained 2,500. Very few areas were affected by this restriction, however."

13. Jean Gottman, "Mankind is Reshaping its Habitat," in *Metropolis: Values in Conflict*, ed. C. E. Elias, Jr., James Gillies, and Svend Riemer (Belmont, Ind.: Wadsworth Publishing Company, 1964), 5.

14. For a thorough analysis of central city—outside central city differences, see Advisory Commission on Intergovernmental Relations, *Metropolitan Social and Economic Disparities: Implications for Intergovernmental Relations in Central Cities and Suburbs* (Washington, D.C., September 1964).

15. The Upson tax rate compilations appeared annually in the *National Municipal Review* in the 1930s and 1940s. The National Industry Conference Board Studies contained volumes on individual states and on interstate comparisons.

16. Clarence E. Ridley, *Measuring Municipal Government: Suggested Standards for Measuring the Results of Fire, Health, Police and Public Works Departments* (New York: Municipal Administration Service, Publication No. 4), 1927.

17. Baltimore: The Johns Hopkins Press, 1930.

18. Robert M. Haig and Roswell C. McCrae, *Regional Survey of New York and its Environs*. Vol. I: *Major Economic Factors in Metropolitan Growth and Arrangement: A Study of Trends and Tendencies in the Economic Activities within the Region of New York and its Environs* (Regional Plan Association of New York, 1927).

19. National Municipal League, Committee on Metropolitan Government. New York, 1930.

20. (Chicago: University of Chicago Press, 1942).

21. Solomon Fabricant, *Trend of Government Activity in the United States Since 1900* (New York: National Bureau of Economic Research, 1952), 122–131; and Josef Berolzheimer, "Influences Shaping Expenditure for Operations of State and Local Governments," *Bulletin of the National Tax Association*, XXXII (March 1947), 237–244.

22. Glenn W. Fisher, "Determinants of State and Local Government Expenditures: A Preliminary Analysis," *National Tax Journal*, XIV (December 1961), 349–355, and "Interstate Variation

in State and Local Government Expenditures," *National Tax Journal*, XVII (March 1964), 57–74.

23. Seymour Sacks, Robert Harris, and John J. Carroll, *The State and the Local Government . . . The Role of State Aid*, Comptroller's Studies in Local Finance No. 3 (New York State Department of Audit and Control, 1963).

24. For a survey of these studies of specific metropolitan areas see Ruth L. Mace, *Municipal Cost-Revenue Research in the United States* (Chapel Hill, N.C.: Institute of Government, The University of North Carolina, 1961), 151–168; and Alan K. Campbell, "Taxes and Industrial Location in the New York Metropolitan Region," *National Tax Journal* (September 1958), 195–218.

25. Harvey E. Brazer, *City Expenditures in the United States*, Occasional Paper 66 (New York: National Bureau of Economic Research, Inc., 1959).

26. St. Louis—Werner Z. Hirsch, "Measuring Factors Affecting Expenditure Levels for Local Government Services," *Metropolitan St. Louis Survey*, (St. Louis, 1957); Dayton—John C. Bollens, with G. Ross Stephens, *Metropolitan Challenge* (Dayton: Metropolitan Community Studies, November 1959); Cleveland—Seymour Sacks and William F. Hellmuth, Jr., *Financing Government in a Metropolitan Area* (New York: The Free Press, 1961); New York City—Robert C. Wood and Vladimir V. Almendinger, *1400 Governments* (Cambridge, Mass.: Harvard University Press, 1961); and Hartford—Seymour Sacks, *Municipal Taxation and Regional Development* (East Hartford, Conn.: Capitol Regional Planning Agency, March 1963).

27. *National Tax Journal*, (December 1962), 432–437. The findings of this study are given detailed consideration in Chapter 2.

28. Henry J. Schmandt and G. Ross Stephens, *Land Economics*, XXXIX (November 1963), 397–406.

29. *Land Economics*, XXXIX (May 1963), 175–186.

State-Local and Local Systems of Finance: The Context of Metropolitan Fiscal Behavior

The general description of metropolitanism and of the state-local fiscal behavior provided in the previous chapter indicates the overall environment in which metropolitan fiscal behavior occurs. In the present chapter the analysis is of the determinants of variations in local and state-local fiscal levels. This analysis is to some extent a diversion from the central concern of this study—metropolitan fiscal behavior. The local and state-local analysis, however, is vital to understanding metropolitan fiscal behavior, because the local and state-local governmental systems are, in fact, the context of metropolitan fiscal behavior.

There is a rather extensive body of literature about the determinants of expenditure variations by state of total *state-local* fiscal levels. There is considerably less information and fewer findings concerning state-local tax variations and even less about local fiscal behavior. This latter gap is of great importance for any study of metropolitan fiscal behavior, which is basically local, although influenced by intergovernmental flows of funds.

The independent variables used for analyzing state-local and local fiscal performance are those that have been used by other students in their analysis of expenditure variations with the addition in this study of the expenditure and tax assignment variables. The "traditional" variables used in this expenditure literature are per capita income, urbanization, density, and state and federal aid. The relationship of these variables to taxes as well as to expenditures are examined in the pages that follow and, additionally, the assignment variables are included in the analysis. Because these assignment variables have not been used before, they need further explanation.

There are 50 state-local governmental systems (51 if the District of Columbia system is included) in the United States, each with its own unique characteristics. Some method for classifying them had to be developed, therefore, if their relevance to fiscal activity was to be measured. The classification system developed for this study uses as its primary measure the differences in state-to-state assignments of local governmental responsibilities for expenditures and taxes. These differences in assignment are measured by the proportion of expenditures and taxes, that are a local responsibility.

The assignment of expenditure responsibility to local government varies greatly from state to state although there are regional patterns. In 1962 direct local government expenditures ranged from 39.4 per cent of total state-local expenditures in Vermont and 42.3 per cent and 44.9 per cent in Kentucky and West Virginia, respectively, to highs of 77.8 per cent in New York, 74.8 per cent in Wisconsin, and 74.4 per cent in New Jersey.

The general differences in local expenditure assignment

reflect patterns of state and federal aid and the degree of urbanization. The most important single component of interstate differences in assignment of responsibility is the division of public welfare expenditures between state and local governments.[1] There are 33 states in which state governments take primary responsibility for this function and 17 in which local government is given such responsibility. Because of the large role that welfare plays in determining the nature of the assignment system, its division between state and local government is substituted for the assignment variable when analysis of the fiscal behavior of less than a whole state is undertaken (i.e., metropolitan areas and their parts). This substitution is necessary because it is impossible to compute a general assignment variable for a part of a state.

Related to local expenditure assignment is the role of state aid, which, other things being equal, tends to increase the local assignment proportion. In 1962 this source of local revenue varied from $10.54 per capita in New Hampshire to $96.81 per capita in California, or as a proportion of local expenditure it varied from 6.6 per cent in New Hampshire to 52 per cent in New Mexico, with California's high per capita figure being equivalent to only 31.4 per cent of its local expenditures.

It is a combination of local expenditure assignment and the amount of state aid that determines, in part, the other assignment variable—tax assignment. As would be expected, local tax variations are greater than those for local expenditures. Per capita local taxes varied from $35.97 in South Carolina to $175.85 in New York, a substantially greater proportional variation than the differences in local expenditures, which varied from a low of $103 to a high of $310 per capita. The variation in local tax assignment is from 22.2 per cent in Delaware to 71.1 per cent in neighboring New Jersey.

State-Local Systems

If it is assumed that the differences in proportional assignment to local subdivisions makes no differences in state-local fiscal levels, it is possible to compare state-local totals without regard to differences in these assignments. All studies of determinants of state-local fiscal levels to date have made this assumption, without ever testing whether, in fact, assignment does or does not make a difference.

Even if the assumption is true for overall state-local fiscal totals, the omission of the assignment variables raises other serious problems. It is quite possible, for example, that the significance and importance of other variables is distorted by this omission. The significance of such determinants of fiscal levels as income, urbanization and state aid may be drastically altered by including the assignment variable, because of a possible functional relationship between these variables and assignment. This could be true even if assignment had no independent power in explaining state-local fiscal levels.

Further, comparisons of local fiscal levels are impossible unless account is taken of the assignment variables. Comparisons of local fiscal levels across state lines often assume a common assignment system where none, in fact, exists. Comparison, for example, of fiscal levels between New York and Chicago city governments can be completely misleading unless differences in the state-local assignment system are taken into account. The census reports that in 1963 per capita expenditures in New York City were $332.34, whereas those in Chicago were only $122.92. This difference is in large part accounted for by differences in assignment between the two states. Welfare is a city function in New York, and in Illinois it is a combined state-county function. Education is provided in Chicago by an independent school district, in New York by a dependent school district.

Even if all overlying local expenditures are totaled for

Chicago, there remain significant differences between Chicago and New York in the expenditure of all overlying local governments because of differences in local assignment in the two states. Welfare expenditures, as already noted, are in part a state function in Illinois, but are almost entirely local in New York State. If the expenditures made in the two cities are put on a comparable basis, the result is per capita expenditures of $369.93 for New York City and $344.46 for Chicago.

Unless these differences in state-local assignment among the states are taken into account, local comparisons across state lines cannot be made. One method used to overcome the problems caused by differences in assignment without taking them directly into account is to compare only functions that are entirely local in all systems. The difficulty with this approach is that it leaves very few functions to be compared. Further, it omits the possibility of finding that the assignment system itself might have an impact beyond the one of simply reflecting which level of government performs the function. It may have an independent influence on fiscal levels, both local and state-local levels. This significance of the assignment variable can only be determined when it is related to other determinants of fiscal behavior.

The Dependent Variables

As already noted, the existing literature has focused on the determinants of state-local expenditures, both totals and various categories of functions. State-local expenditure totals have been analyzed for a variety of years but have concentrated on the years in which there has been a Census of Governments. Because the results for 1957 and 1962 are basically similar, the data used here are for the latter year.

Particular emphasis in this analysis will be an examination of the extent to which the two basic aggregates, per capita total general expenditures and per capita taxes, respond to given forces (independent variables) on the state-local and local levels by state.

In the examination of metropolitan fiscal behavior a number of other dependent variables will also be analyzed. These are as follows: per capita education expenditures, per capita non-education expenditures, per capita education tax proxy (education expenditures less state aid), and per capita non-education tax proxy (noneducation expenditure less state aid).

The Independent Variables

Following the work of Fabricant, Fisher, and Sacks-Harris-Carroll[2] five basic independent variables are utilized to explain the observed variations in local and state-local fiscal behavior. These variables, as shown in Table 2-1, are: density as measured by the 1962 population per square mile; per cent urban as reported in the 1960 population census; 1962 per capita income; 1962 state aid per capita; and 1962 federal aid per capita. All these variables have been tested for earlier years to determine their impact on state-local expenditure behavior. They have not, however, been tested in association with taxes or with the assignment variables already discussed. Nor have they been used to explain local fiscal behavior.

Per capita personal income is assumed to be positively and significantly associated with variations in local and state-local expenditures. On the state-local level it is assumed that density will be associated negatively with state-local expenditures but not with taxes. Because the principal reason for this expectation involves highway costs, where federal aid plays an important role, it is assumed that, if anything, density would be associated positively with taxes. On the local level it has been presumed that urbanization is associated positively with a higher level of both per capita expenditures and taxes.

It is assumed that the appropriate assignment variables would have no influence on state-local behavior, but would be associated positively with local expenditures and taxes. The noninfluence assumption about state-local totals is based on the proposition that the division of responsibility between a state and its local governments will not influence the overall total state-local fiscal levels.

The "expected" patterns are summarized in Table 2-1 for the density, urbanization, income, the state and federal aid variables, and the two assignment variables.

The results of the statistical analysis are presented in terms of: *a.* the estimating equations, and *b.* the elasticities of each of the independent variables with respect to the dependent variable. The purpose is to see the extent to which each is significant when the other independent variables are included in the equation. Further, it is assumed that the combination of all the variables will not only be significant but will in fact account for a major portion of the total variation in the dependent variables.

The results are presented in a modified stepwise manner, first for local expenditures and then for state-local expenditures. A similar stepwise analysis of local taxes and state-local taxes is provided. The stepwise approach permits an analysis of the effect of the addition of a given variable, not only on the dependent variable, but on the other independent variables as well. On the local level it is assumed that the addition of the assignment variables, after the other five variables have been taken into account, will lead to a basic increase in the total explanatory power of the estimating equation, whereas in the

TABLE 2-1: *Hypotheses Concerning the Relationships Between Selected Independent and Dependent Variables*

| | DEPENDENT VARIABLES | | | |
| | STATE-LOCAL | | LOCAL | |
Independent variables	Expenditures	Taxes	Expenditures	Taxes
Density	−	0	−	+
Urbanization	+	+	+	+
Per capita income	+	+	+	+
State aid	0	0	+	−
Federal aid	+	−	+	−
Expenditure assignment	0		+	
Tax assignment		0		+

case of the state-local totals, assignment is not expected to make any contribution to the total explanatory power. Even at the state-local level, however, assignment may affect some of the other independent variables.

The Determinants of Local Expenditures

The results of the regression analysis using the five variables enumerated above are clearly significant with an adjusted coefficient of multiple correlation, $\bar{R} = .872$. The regression equation, including the standard errors for per capita local expenditures (P. C. Exp.$_L$) in 1962, is shown below. Given 41 degrees of freedom, a regression coefficient is accepted as significant when it is more than 2.02 times its standard error at the .05 level of probability, which is designated by a single asterisk (*). When it is more than 2.71 times its standard error, it is asterisked twice (**), indicating significance at the .01 level of probability.

$$\text{P. C. Exp.}_L = -.049^*$$
$$(.023)$$
$$+.987^* \text{ Per Cent Urban}$$
$$(.428)$$
$$+.065^{**} \text{ P. C. Income}$$
$$(.013)$$
$$+.737^{**} \text{ P. C. State Aid}$$
$$(.199)$$
$$+.252 \text{ P. C. Federal Aid} - \$61.04$$
$$(.186)$$
$$\bar{R} = .872 \qquad \bar{R}^2 = .760$$

The combined power of all the variables ($\bar{R}^2$ at .760) is somewhat higher than that achieved by the simple coefficient of determination (r^2) for per capita income.

Adding the assignment variable, it is hypothesized that in addition to improving the level of explanation, this variable should contribute substantially to understanding the roles played by each of the other variables. Specifically, it is to be expected that the result will be a much higher coefficient of multiple determination, and basic changes may be shown in the relationships between the other independent variables.

These expectations are borne out as indicated by the new estimating equation:

$$
\begin{aligned}
\text{P. C. Exp.}_L = &-.023 \text{ Density} \\
&(.014) \\
&+ .107 \text{ Per Cent Urban} \\
&(.280) \\
&+ .052^{**} \text{ P. C. Income} \\
&(.007) \\
&+ .467^{**} \text{ P. C. State Aid} \\
&(.125) \\
&+ .849^{**} \text{ P. C. Federal Aid} \\
&(.133) \\
&+ 3.359^{**} \text{ Local Exp. Assignment} \\
&(.395) \\
&- \$195.35
\end{aligned}
$$

$$\bar{R} = .956 \qquad \bar{R}^2 = .914$$

The importance of the income, state, and federal aid variables are all enhanced by the introduction of the local expenditure assignment variable. It appears that the coefficients for density and urbanization actually are a reflection of other variables, because their significance is considerably reduced by the addition of the assignment variable; this is especially true in the case of urbanization. When the local expenditures assignment variable is included, the overall estimating equation explains 91.4 per cent of the observed variation in per capita local general expenditures by state. This figure, of course, contrasts with the 76.1 per cent explanation obtained when the assignment variable was excluded. The signs and the significance of the independent variables are in accord with the hypotheses cited earlier.

Using the elasticity concept, it is possible to determine the impact of a one per cent change in the independent variable on the dependent variable being tested. Again, as in the case of the estimating equation, certain hypotheses have been formulated. It is assumed from prior work[3] that the elasticities of income and state and federal aid will be positive— that is, the proportionate increase in local expenditure will be greater than the proportionate increase in aid or income. Further, it is hypothesized that on the local level the assignment variable will have a unitary elasticity—that is, a one per cent increase in assignment should lead to a one per cent increase in expenditures. The observed elasticities of each of the independent variables on local expenditures at the mean are as follows:

Density	− .018
Per Cent Urban	.035
Per Capita Income	.606
Per Capita State Aid	.131
Per Capita Federal Aid	.229
Local Expenditure Assignment	1.045

The findings are slightly higher for income than those of the earlier, more limited studies of local expenditures by Brazer and others.[4] Income is positive but not of unitary elasticity; a one per cent increase in this variable being associated with a 0.606 per cent increase in per capita local expenditures, whereas a one per cent increase in state aid is associated with 0.131 per cent increase in local expenditures. The comparable figure for federal aid is 0.229 per cent.

The crucial variable is clearly the assignment variable, which has an elasticity of close to unity, indicating that differences in assignment are of major importance in accounting for interstate differences in local expenditures. At this stage it should be noted that although this new variable tremendously increases the explanatory power of the estimating equation, it does not have any effect beyond the obvious one.

The Determinants of Local Taxes

There has been practically no previous comprehensive analysis of the determinants of interstate variations of local taxes, and therefore there is little literature to which the findings in this section can be compared. If, however, the same variables are used in explaining differences in the level of taxation as were used in explaining expenditure variation (with the exception that tax assignment is used instead of expenditure assignment), the results are even more interesting than they were in the case of expenditures.

The expected findings for local taxes are assumed to vary slightly from those hypothesized for expenditures. It is anticipated that density will be unrelated to tax levels, but that income and urbanization will be positively correlated with these levels. On the other hand, it is assumed that state aid will hold down local tax levels and therefore will be negatively associated with tax levels. The same assumption is made for federal aid.

With the same stepwise methods as used for local expenditures, the multiple correlation for the five basic variables (that is, with the tax assignment variable omitted) is .766. These five basic variables therefore explain only 58.7 per cent of the interstate variation in per capita local taxes. This figure is not much better than that found for the per capita income variable with an r equal to $+ .722$ and an r^2 of .521. The estimating equation for local taxes per capita (P. C. Taxes$_L$) is as follows:

$$P.\ C.\ Taxes_L = -\ .015\ Density$$
$$(.022)$$
$$+\ .620\ Per\ Cent\ Urban$$
$$(.426)$$
$$+\ .057^{**}\ P.\ C.\ Income$$
$$(.012)$$
$$-\ .491^{*}\ P.\ C.\ State\ Aid$$
$$(.198)$$
$$+\ .166\ P.\ C.\ Federal\ Aid$$
$$(.185)$$
$$-\ \$46.60$$

$$\bar{R} = .766 \quad \bar{R}^2 = .587$$

The addition of the local tax assignment variable changes the overall picture drastically. The addition of this variable to the estimating equation increases the multiple correlation from .766 to .974. Stated another way, the proportion explained is increased from 58.7 per cent for the five basic variables, whereas the introduction of the tax assignment variable increases the total explanatory power to 94.8 per cent.

When the assignment variable is included, the estimating equation is as follows:

$$P.\ C.\ Taxes_L = +\ .009\ Density$$
$$(.008)$$
$$-\ .042\ Per\ Cent\ Urban$$
$$(.1569)$$
$$+\ .020^{**}\ P.\ C.\ Income$$
$$(.005)$$
$$+\ .425^{**}\ P.\ C.\ State\ Aid$$
$$(.089)$$
$$+\ .155^{*}\ P.\ C.\ Federal\ Aid$$
$$(.066)$$

+ 2.807** Local Tax Assignment
(.165)

−$103.06

$$\bar{R} = .975 \qquad \bar{R}^2 = .948$$

The introduction of the tax assignment variable thus has an impact on the significance of the other variables, as well as on the overall significance. The significance of the income variable is reduced and the role of both state and federal aid is enhanced, with state aid becoming positive. The dominance of the assignment variable in explaining interstate differences in local taxes is clearly evident.

Examining the observed elasticities of each of the independent variables on per capita local taxes at the mean, the results are as follows:

Density	.013
Per Cent Urban	− .027
Per Capita Income	.444
Per Capita State Aid	.228
Per Capita Federal Aid	.080
Local Tax Assignment	1.301

The low income elasticity is assumed to be the result of the fact that local taxes are more closely related to their property tax base rather than to their income base. Local taxes respond positively to state and federal aid, rather than having the expected negative relationship. This analysis of local taxes indicates that aid is not negatively elastic as hypothesized; instead increases in aid lead to increases in local taxes when the tax assignment variable is explicitly included.

At the mean, local tax assignment has an elasticity of 1.301 with respect to local taxes. In other words, a one per cent increase in local tax assignment results in a 1.301 per cent increase in local taxes. Because the relationship is not unitary it demonstrates that high local tax assignment reflects more than simply a transfer of tax responsibility to the local level.

It is apparent that when tax assignment to the local level is high, the result is higher local taxes than would be anticipated if assignment were a matter of indifference. If that were the case, the elasticity would be approximately unitary.

If this stimulative effect of changes in the level of local tax assignment on local tax levels is genuine, it should show itself at the combined state-local level as well as at the local level. In other words, high local tax assignment should result in a higher state-local tax level than would a low tax assignment. In contrast, since the elasticity found for expenditure assignment was unitary, it follows that the expenditure assignment variable should have no impact on state-local expenditure totals. To test this proposition the analysis now turns to an examination of the determinants of variations in state-local expenditure and tax levels.

State-Local Fiscal Behavior

Unlike the study of interstate variations in local fiscal behavior, state-local expenditure behavior has been, as was noted earlier, the subject of detailed analyses. On the other hand, such state-local analysis has not been expanded to encompass the tax side of the picture. Finally, no attempt has been made to determine the relationships of local to state-local fiscal behavior.

Table 2-2 shows the cross-sectional long-term relationships of state-local per capita general expenditures to selected variables. Of particular interest is the association between per capita state-local expenditures and per capita income, with the simple correlation of .920 in 1900 falling to .645 in 1962. This decline is undoubtedly the result of the gradual departure of state-local total expenditures from their own resources and their growing dependence on other sources. In other words, it is a measure of the evolving importance of the intergovernmental flow of funds and of the use of tax bases without income counterparts.

The stability of the relationship of taxes to income, however, is quite great.[5] The simple correlation between state-local per capita taxes and income has actually increased since 1932, from .782 to .843. This greater stability and higher correlation does indicate that taxes more than expenditures do respond to income, which is further confirmation of the significance of intergovernmental aid on the expenditure side. Thus for taxes, in contrast to expenditures, income is a fairly good measure of ability to support public services.

Because it will be necessary in some parts of this study to use 1957 data, it is worth noting the great stability in all of the relationships from 1957 to 1962. As will be shown in more detail later, there is no reason to suspect that the use of 1957 data will distort the current relationships that this study is attempting to show.

The same variables and the same stepwise regression and elasticity analysis as that used in the examination of local

TABLE 2-2: *Simple Correlations Between Per Capita Total State and Local Expenditures and Taxes and Selected Variables for Selected Years, 1903–1964–65 (48 Conterminous States)*

	Density	Per cent urban	Per capita income
Per capita expenditures			
1903	.086	.605**	.920**
1932	n.a.	n.a.	.839**
1942	.233	.595**	.821**
1957	−.079	.499**	.658**
1962	−.032	.342*	.645**
1964–65	−.075	n.a.	.558
Per capita taxes			
1932	n.a.	n.a.	.782**
1942	.161	.371*	.795**
1957	.203	.580**	.720**
1962	.236	.613**	.843**
1964–65	.240	n.a.	.787

* Significant at .05 level of confidence
** Significant at .01 level of confidence

SOURCES: All data, U. S. Bureau of the Census except personal income for 1900, which comes from Richard A. Easterlin, "State Income Estimates," in *Population Redistribution and Economic Growth, United States, 1870–1950*, Vol. I, *Methodological Considerations and Reference Tables*, ed. Simon Kuznets and Dorothy S. Thomas (American Philosophical Society, 1957).

fiscal behavior is applied to state-local behavior. However, the basic underlying hypotheses, especially those involving state aid and the assignment variables, will have to be changed and the importance of federal aid is expected to be considerably greater. The density and urbanization variables will be kept, not because of their expected significance, but to assure continuity with earlier analyses. Income is assumed to be a significant determinant of state-local fiscal behavior, perhaps even more important than in the case of local fiscal behavior.

As noted earlier, the hypothesis about state aid's impact on state-local fiscal behavior is nil on the assumption that such aid acts as a substitute for local expenditures and taxes and, therefore, does not raise overall totals. If aid, on the other hand, stimulates or reduces overall state-local fiscal levels then the aid variable will show a positive or negative relationship. This same logic for state aid can be used for the assignment variables. Unless differences in assignment stimulate or reduce overall state-local fiscal levels, the relationships will have values close to zero. The assumption of the indifference of the assignment variable impact is based on the common sense proposition that overall state-local levels will not be influenced by the placement of responsibility. The division of responsibility simply indicates which level of government does the financing of public services.

Previous analyses have shown that federal aid should play a far more important role in explaining interstate variations in state-local fiscal behavior than in the case of the more restricted local fiscal behavior, because most federal aid goes directly to state governments for state purposes. There is, of course, some federal aid that is paid directly to local government, but most federal aid received by local governments is funneled through the state to them. It is assumed that the "pure" effects of federal aid and state aid may be more easily measured on the tax side than on the expenditure side.[6]

When all variables except local expenditure assignment are

used, the five basic ones explain more of the observed variations in state-local expenditures than they do in the case of
local expenditures, with coefficients of multiple determination
of .859 and .761, respectively. Income, state aid, and federal
aid are all important. Further, it should be noted that the
coefficient of multiple determination for 1962 is virtually
identical with that for 1957.[7]

The estimating equation for state-local per capita expenditure (P. C. Exp.$_{SL}$) (48 conterminous states, 1962) is as
follows:

$$
\begin{aligned}
\text{P. C. Exp.}_{SL} = & - .041 \text{ Density} \\
& (.022) \\
& + .248 \text{ Per Cent Urban} \\
& (.401) \\
& + .092^{**} \text{ P. C. Income} \\
& (.011) \\
& + .690^{**} \text{ P. C. State Aid} \\
& (.187) \\
& + 1.557^{**} \text{ P. C. Federal Aid} \\
& (.174) \\
& - \$10.44
\end{aligned}
$$

$$\bar{R} = .927 \qquad \bar{R}^2 = .859$$

The inclusion of the local expenditure assignment as an
explicit variable does not alter the coefficient of multiple
determination nor does it alter the regression coefficients to
any extent.

The estimating equation for the same state-local per capita
expenditures (48 conterminous states, 1962) is as follows:

$$
\begin{aligned}
\text{P. C. Exp.}_{SL} = & - .038 \text{ Density} \\
& (.022) \\
& + .150 \text{ Per Cent Urban} \\
& (.436)
\end{aligned}
$$

$$+ .091^{**} \text{ P. C. Income}$$
$$(.012)$$

$$+ .660^{**} \text{ P. C. State Aid}$$
$$(.194)$$

$$1.624^{**} \text{ P. C. Federal Aid}$$
$$(.207)$$

$$+ .374 \text{ Local Exp. Assignment}$$
$$(.614)$$

$$- \$25.41$$

$$\bar{R} = .929 \qquad \bar{R}^2 = .859$$

Variations in income, state aid, and federal aid variables clearly have important effects on the level of state-local expenditures. The local expenditure assignment does not improve the overall explanatory power nor does it change much the role of each component.

TABLE 2-3: *Coefficients of Multiple (R^2) for Regressions of Per Capita General Expenditure Categories on The Three "Fabricant" Factors and with State Aid and Federal Aid Added, 1960*

Expenditure category	Three fabricant factors #	Appropriate state aid added	Appropriate federal aid added	Appropriate federal and state aid added
Total direct general	.532	.667	.813	.869
Highways	.370	.374	.834	.856
Public welfare	.114	.181	.830	.858
Local schools*	.604	.721	n.c.	n.c.
Health and hospitals	.435	.547	.472	.557
Not specifically aided and All other**	.577	.602	.627	.645

Three "Fabricant" factors are density, per cent urban, and per capita income.
n.c.—not computed
* All other education expenditures are included in the "Not Specifically Aided and All Other" category.
** The "Not Specifically Aided and All Other" category must be interpreted in relation to the functional grouping of this Table. Thus, this category includes fire, police, and general control.

SOURCE: Sacks and Harris, *National Tax Journal*, March 1964.

Of particular interest is the impact of federal and state aid on state-local expenditures. The variables, with or without assignment, have a coefficient of multiple determination of .859 with per capita total state-local expenditures.

It is of interest to note the differential impact of aid on individual functions (Table 2-3). Federal aid, for example, is of critical importance in accounting for the observed variations in highway and public welfare expenditures; state aid plays a role in accounting for variations in local schools and health and hospital expenditures.

The problems raised by Fisher[8] concerning the relationship between federal aid and expenditures cannot be directly answered on the expenditure side. The question can be more forthrightly faced on the tax side. Specifically, do federal aid and the other variables have a positive and significant effect on the level of state and local taxes? The political presumption is that although expenditures might go up as a result of federal aid, state-local taxes should go down. This will now be tested, as will be the hypothesis concerning the assignment of tax responsibility.

The Determinants of State-Local Taxes

The measurement of the determinants of per capita state-local taxes has the advantage over similar measurements for expenditures of getting at the underlying relationships between the raising of revenue from local sources and "community" characteristics. With expenditures there is always the problem of funds that flow into the system from outside, whereas the measurement of taxes deals exclusively with funds raised from within the system. It is possible, of course, that the external funds flowing into the system affect the amounts raised locally, but the advantage of using taxes as the dependent variable is that it makes possible a direct measurement of the influence of these external funds.

Using the five basic variables (excluding tax assignment), the estimating equation in state and local per capita taxes (P. C. Taxes$_{SL}$) (48 conterminous states, 1962) is:

P. C. Taxes$_{SL}$ = − .012 Density
     (.018)
     + .358 Per Cent Urban
     (.341)
     + .075** P. C. Income
     (.009)
     + .325* P. C. State Aid
     (.158)
     + .415* P. C. Federal Aid
     (.148)
     − $15.45

$$\bar{R} = .891 \qquad \bar{R}^2 = .794$$

With local tax assignment added, the equation is (48 conterminous states, 1962):

P. C. Taxes$_{SL}$ = − .001 Density
     (.015)
     + .030 Per Cent Urban
     (.289)
     + .057** P. C. Income
     (.008)
     + .779** P. C. State Aid
     (.164)
     + .405** P. C. Federal Aid
     (.122)
     + 1.392** Local Tax Assignment
     (.305)
     − $43.45

$$\bar{R} = .927 \qquad \bar{R}^2 = .859$$

The five basic variables account for 79.4 per cent of the variations in per capita state-local taxes as compared to 58.7 per cent for local taxes only. However, unlike the case of state-local expenditures, the introduction of the local tax assignment variable does make it possible to account for an increased proportion of the observed variation on state-local taxes; 79.4 per cent compared to 85.9 per cent. The coefficients of a multiple determination for state-local expenditure and state-local taxes are identical at 85.9.

Further, the introduction of local tax assignment not only increases the overall explanatory power to the level observed in the case of state-local expenditures, but the significance (and importance) of the state aid variable is substantially enhanced.

As already noted, the analysis of taxes makes possible a measurement of the direct effects of the aid and assignment variables. Thus, as shown in the estimating equation, per capita income is clearly significant, and state aid, federal aid, and tax assignment variables are also positive and clearly significant.

The initial hypothesis about the neutrality of state aid and local tax assignment on state-local taxes is clearly not confirmed. Neither of the variables are irrelevant to overall state-local fiscal totals. The additive effects of state and federal aid found on the expenditure side, and the similar finding for local tax assignment on the local tax side, are confirmed by the analysis of their "pure effects" on variations in per capita state-local tax patterns.

These findings about aid and assignment can be made even clearer by an examination of their elasticities. The elasticities for state-local and local expenditures and taxes at the mean are shown in Table 2-4.

The striking findings are the positive elasticities of state aid, federal aid, and local tax assignment with respect to per capita state-local taxes. The positive but less than unitary elasticity of income confirms the findings on the expenditure side. On a cross-sectional basis state-local taxes, like other aspects of aggregate fiscal behavior, are not income elastic, but reflect the existence of other factors.

These findings for aid (state and federal) and local assignment require further comment. One apparent reason for the stimulative effect of aid on local taxes is the matching requirement that most aid formulas possess. Secondly, it is evident that local and state-local taxes (unlike the expenditure variable) do not include state aid. Put another way, state aid is not a component of the number used to measure taxes. Thus, in this mechanical sense taxes do not reflect the level of aid directly but are free to respond to the tax resources that exist in a given community. The combination of these two influences, one the result of policy and the other the mechanical result of the measure of taxes, results in aid being stimulative of local effort rather than replacive of such effort.

The reasons for the stimulative effect of local tax assignment on the state-local tax totals are more complex. Part of this complexity lies in the fact that in the case of the expenditure assignment variable (the proportion of state-local expenditures made by local governments), variations from place to place in this proportion may be due to allocations of different functional responsibilities. The assignment value in one community, for example, may be due almost entirely to welfare, but in a second community with an identical assignment value,

TABLE 2-4: *Elasticity Coefficients: State-Local and Local Per Capita Expenditures and Taxes in Relation to Selected Variables, 1962*

	State-local expenditures	State-local taxes	Local expenditures	Local taxes
Density	−.174	.001	−.018	.013
Per cent urban	.003	.001	.035	−.027
Per capita income	.629	.598	.606	.444
Per capita state aid	.110	.197	.131	.228
Per capita federal aid	.260	.099	.229	.080
Local expenditure assignment	.069	n.c.	1.045	n.c.
Local tax assignment	n.c.	.392	n.c.	1.301
Exhibit: R²	.859	.859	.914	.948

n.c.—not computed

this value may reflect responsibility for, say, health and hospitals. It may be the case that the assignment of each different kind of functional responsibility does not interact with expenditures in the same manner, and in aggregate terms the components of expenditure assignment may cancel each other, resulting in no stimulative effect on expenditures whatsoever. Further, the dependent variable—expenditures— is complicated itself. As noted above, this variable is partly a reflection of the level of state aid. Thus the complex inter- relationship between expenditures, expenditure assignment, and state aid may hide the impact of expenditure assignment on the level of expenditures. The finding, however, that assignment has more of an impact on fiscal levels than the obvious and trivial one is borne out on the tax side.

Thus, while the results show an elasticity close to unity (1.045) between local expenditures and expenditure assign- ment, the coefficient on the tax side (between local taxes and tax assignment) is 1.301, indicating that, in fact, local tax assignment is stimulative of local taxes. There are similar results on the state-local level. The reason for this finding is difficult to interpret. A partial explanation for differences between the tax and expenditure findings is that the complexi- ties that plague the expenditure side are not present on the tax side. The dependent variable does not mechanically include state aid, nor does the tax assignment variable involve different functional assignments. The most logical explanation for the finding on the tax side would seem to rest with the impact on local government, which grows out of the high assignment of tax responsibility to the local parts of the governmental system. Such assignment apparently produces vigorous local governmental units and in this way increases their appetite for high quality performance. In other words, the very existence of a local governmental system with heavy respon- sibility creates a demand for services beyond that imposed by the legal assignment of responsibilities. The bureaucracies and public officials for these local units respond by providing more and better services than would be the case if the state provided the services. A kind of Parkinson's law (without any of the unfavorable normative qualities associated with that doctrine) seems to be at work.

Summary of Findings for Local and State-Local Fiscal Behavior

Variations in local fiscal behavior, whether measured on the expenditure or tax side, can be accounted for in large measure by a limited number of variables. The critical necessity for placing local fiscal behavior in its state-local contexts is also made clearly evident.

The analysis demonstrates, too, that the inclusion of the assignment variables both clarifies the operation of the remaining variables and shows an independent influence as well. Further, it is clear that intergovernmental flows of funds, as measured by state and federal aid, have a stimulative effect on local and state-local fiscal behavior. This relationship is shown best by the analysis of variations in per capita state-local taxes. Most interesting, perhaps, is the significant positive effect that the assignment of tax responsibility has on local tax levels.

Using the elasticity measure, it is found that a one per cent increase in income is related to a less than one per cent increase in expenditures and taxes at all levels, whereas the flow of funds from state governments to local governments, and the federal government to state and local governments, has a stimulative effect on local and state-local taxes. Finally, expenditures financed from a jurisdiction's own tax sources are stimulated by the assignment of tax responsibilities to that jurisdiction.

These results must be kept in mind in dealing with the various local governmental subsystems that form the basis of the remainder of this study. These subsystems, which were considered in very general terms and as totals in this chapter, will now be considered in detail. The detail will pertain to a division between metropolitan and nonmetropolitan areas and within metropolitan areas between central cities and their outlying areas. As has been clearly shown by the findings in this chapter, the state aid and assignment variables must be incorporated into the analysis if the results are to be meaningful. Failure to include them would diminish substantially the significance of any results found.

To measure the influence of these variables on metropolitan and nonmetropolitan fiscal behavior, it is first necessary to indicate the nature of the fiscal behavior of these divisions of the country. The next chapter, therefore, is devoted to an analysis of these fiscal patterns of metropolitan and non-metropolitan America.

References

1. Selma J. Mushkin, "Intergovernmental Aspects of Local Expenditure Decisions," in *Public Expenditure Decisions in the Urban Community*, ed. Howard G. Schaller, The Johns Hopkins Press, 1963).

2. Solomon Fabricant, *The Trend of Government Activity in the United States Since 1900* (New York: National Bureau of Economic Research, Inc., 1952); Glenn W. Fisher, "Determinants of State and Local Government Expenditure: A Preliminary Analysis," *National Tax Journal*, XIV (December 1961), 349–355; Glenn W. Fisher, "Interstate Variation in State and Local Government Expenditure," *National Tax Journal*, XVII (March 1964), 57–74; Seymour Sacks, Robert Harris and John J. Carroll, *The Role of State Aid*, New York State Comptroller's Studies in Local Finance, No. 3 (Albany: New York State Department of Audit and Control, 1963).

3. Brazer, Harvey E., *City Expenditures in the United States*—Occasional Paper 66 (New York: National Bureau of Economic Research, Inc., 1959); and Woo Sik Kee, *City Expenditures and Metropolitan Areas: Analysis of Intergovernmental Fiscal Systems* (Ph.D. Dissertation, Syracuse University, 1964).

4. Brazer, *op. cit.*, 27, found an income elasticity of 0.367 for common functions of 462 cities in 1951. Using a 304-city sample for 1961, Woo Sik Kee (*op. cit.*) found an income elasticity of 0.522 for general municipal functions.

5. Clara Penniman, "The Politics of Taxation," in *Politics in the American States: A Comparative Analysis*, ed. (Herbert Jacob and Kenneth N. Vines.) (Boston: Little, Brown and Company, 1965).

6. Seymour Sacks and Robert Harris, "The Determinants of State and Local Government Expenditures and Intergovernmental Flow of Funds," *National Tax Journal*, XVII (March 1964), 75–85.

7. *Ibid.*, 83.

8. Glenn W. Fisher, "Interstate Variations in State and Local Government Expenditures," *National Tax Journal*, XVII (March 1964), 71–73.

CHAPTER 3

Metropolitan Fiscal Behavior: National, Regional, and State Patterns

Examination of the determinants of variations in state-local and local fiscal behavior has established the context for analyzing metropolitan fiscal behavior. The first step in the metropolitan analysis is to demonstrate that metropolitanism makes a difference, that the division between metropolitan and nonmetropolitan behavior is a useful division for fiscal analysis.

Specifically, what are the effects on local government fiscal behavior of the concentration of almost two-thirds of the population and an even greater proportion of income and economic activity on less than one-tenth the land area of the country? Are the fiscal patterns of this concentration in metropolitan areas different from the fiscal patterns in the less concentrated nonmetropolitan areas? Finally, how do the local fiscal patterns of the metropolitan portion of the nation differ from those of the nonmetropolitan portion?

If there are differences between metropolitan and non-metropolitan portions of the nation, are these the result of differences in the response of the two "nations" or is it because the underlying conditions are different? Further, how do the differences between metropolitan areas compare with differences within metropolitan areas?

The discussion of national, regional, and state fiscal patterns that follows clearly shows that the unit of analysis (metropolitan or nonmetropolitan) has a determinate effect on observed fiscal behavior. ˙Preoccupation with national totals has obscured the fact that there are important differences when fiscal, and indeed all other characteristics, are examined within a metropolitan framework.

The local fiscal units, however, are not metropolitan and nonmetropolitan, but rather are the local jurisdictions (counties, cities, villages, and special districts), which provide government services in both metropolitan and nonmetropolitan areas. The analysis, therefore, of metropolitan fiscal behavior must take into account the governmental units being analyzed, as well as the more broadly defined social-economic classification of metropolitan/nonmetropolitan.

Whereas the last chapter dealt with fiscal behavior on a statewide basis, both local and state-local totals, the emphasis of this and the succeeding chapters is concentrated on various aspects of local governmental finances and metropolitanism. Particular emphasis is placed on contrasting, in an analytical manner, metropolitan and nonmetropolitan fiscal behavior on a national, regional, and state basis. In Chapter 4, emphasis will be placed on the component parts of the metropolitan areas— central cities and outside central cities—as well as the individual metropolitan areas taken as units.

National Patterns of Metropolitan and Nonmetropolitan Fiscal Behavior

In its report, *Local Government in Metropolitan Areas*,[1] the Governments Division of the Census Bureau has provided the first official statement of *aggregate local fiscal behavior* in the metropolitan and nonmetropolitan portions of the United States. On the basis of raw data contained in an earlier Census report, metropolitan and nonmetropolitan totals were computed for the year 1957.[2] Owing to the basic similarity of the two patterns, as shown in Table 3-2, and because of the contemporaneity and comparability with the statewide 1962 data, the national behavior patterns will be analyzed for the later year. When differences within metropolitan areas and among such areas are analyzed, 1957 will have to be used.

With an estimated 63.6 per cent of the population in metropolitan areas in 1962, 70.0 per cent of direct general expenditures, 74.0 per cent of taxes, but only 60.7 per cent of state aid was received by local governments in these areas. The picture is one in which local governments in metropolitan areas clearly have higher expenditures and taxes relative to their population than do nonmetropolitan areas, but at the same time receive proportionately less state aid.

These fiscal differences are explained, in part, by differences in fiscal resources. The population of metropolitan areas received 71.9 per cent of total personal income in 1959. Further, in 1961 metropolitan areas contained 69.1 per cent of the state and locally assessed property value subject to the local general property tax.[3] Except for acreage and farms and personal property, the proportions of locally assessed property, all other types of property (nonfarm residential, commercial, and industrial) showed even greater metropolitan concentration ratios. Thus, local government in metropolitan areas clearly had the basis for a higher level of local fiscal activity as measured by both their resources (income and property) and the service demands generated by their urban characteristics.

Information on aggregate fiscal activity and the resources available in metropolitan areas in earlier periods is very scanty and indirect. Clearly the aggregate level in metropolitan areas has gone up; the more crucial question involves the relative level. The period 1957 to 1962 is too brief for drawing any long-term inferences. The only long-term approach must be indirect. If one looks at the ten largest cities from 1913 to the present, they appear to show a relative secular decline in their per capita expenditures when compared to those of noncity local governments in their own states and in the nation as a whole.

This impression of a declining difference between metropolitan and nonmetropolitan fiscal levels is further strengthened by the reduced importance over time of income as a determinant of state-local expenditures and the increasing importance of state aid and direct state fiscal activities. It is presumed that such aid and direct state action tends to level out the differences in fiscal levels between metropolitan and nonmetropolitan areas.

Because of the size of metropolitan areas, the aggregate fiscal importance of these areas is enormously important. Indeed, from both a political and economic point of view it is quite useful to break the overall state-local fiscal problem down into three categories: *a*. direct expenditures and taxes of state governments relative to state-local totals, *b*. direct expenditures and taxes of local governments in metropolitan areas relative to state-local totals, and *c*. the direct expenditures and taxes of local governments in nonmetropolitan areas relative to the same state-local totals.

On the expenditure side state governments make 33.8 per cent of all state-local direct general expenditures. Local governments in metropolitan areas expend 46.3 per cent of state-local total direct general expenditures; in nonmetropolitan areas they spend only 19.8 per cent of the state-local total. The importance of local governments in metropolitan areas relative to the other two components of this tripartite breakdown holds on the tax side, too. State taxes as a proportion of total state-local taxes in 1962 were 50.5 per cent.

Local governments in metropolitan areas collected 37.4 per cent of total state-local taxes, but in nonmetropolitan areas the percentage was only 13.1.

The aggregate expenditure preeminence of local governments in metropolitan areas hides substantial variations from function to function. As shown in Table 3-1, per capita direct general expenditures of $235.92 in the metropolitan portion of the nation in 1962 were 136.1 per cent of the $176.65 in the nonmetropolitan portions of the nation. Despite this large difference there is a fundamental similarity between metropolitan and nonmetropolitan portions of the nation in the single most important expenditure category—education (local schools plus minor amounts for higher education). The per capita amounts expended were very close—$98.24 in metropolitan areas and $93.64 in nonmetropolitan areas. If capital outlay devoted to education is excluded, then there is an almost exact equality between per capita expenditures for the two areas, $80.68 in the metropolitan portion of the nation and $79.66 in the nonmetropolitan portion of the nation.

This similarity in educational expenditures is the result of very diverse forces, some of which can be easily quantified and others which cannot be. The public school enrollment ratio, the ratio of local school enrollment to the estimated population, is considerably higher in nonmetropolitan areas than in metropolitan areas (22.6 per cent as compared to 18.6 per cent). This difference in enrollment ratio explains, in fact, why per capita expenditures are more alike than per student expenditures are. In this latter case, expenditures in metropolitan areas are $513.85 per student compared to $409.58 in nonmetropolitan areas.

The near equality in per capita expenditures is also due to the fact that local schools receive the bulk of state aid, and aid is more important absolutely and relatively to nonmetropolitan finances than to metropolitan ones. Educational expenditures, as a result, are pushed upward in nonmetropolitan areas by these intergovernmental flows of funds that act as a substitute for the higher tax resources—income and property possessed by the metropolitan areas.

TABLE 3-1: *Local Direct General Expenditures by Function for Metropolitan and Nonmetropolitan Areas, 1962**

Expenditure category	U. S. per capita	SMSA per capita	Non- SMSA per capita	SMSA as a per cent of non-SMSA
Total expenditures	$243.67	$269.72	$198.13	136.1%
Direct general expenditures	214.35	235.92	176.65	133.6
Capital outlay	43.57	51.37	29.92	171.7
Other than capital outlay	170.78	184.55	146.73	125.8
Education	96.57	98.24	93.64	104.9
Capital outlay	16.26	17.56	13.98	125.6
Other than capital outlay	80.31	80.68	79.66	101.3
Noneducation	117.78	137.68	83.01	165.9
Capital outlay	27.31	33.81	15.94	212.1
Other than capital outlay	90.47	103.87	67.07	154.8
Noneducation nonhighway	97.75	119.04	60.56	196.6
Highways	20.03	18.64	22.45	83.0
Capital outlay	8.48	9.49	6.71	141.5
Other than capital outlay	11.55	9.17	15.71	58.4
Public welfare	13.86	16.30	9.59	169.9
Hospitals	9.66	10.60	8.01	132.3
Health	2.08	2.45	1.42	172.6
Police protection	9.98	12.72	5.18	245.6
Fire protection	6.05	7.87	2.86	275.5
Sewerage	6.85	8.53	3.91	217.9
Sanitation other than sewerage	3.69	4.96	1.47	337.5
Parks and recreation	4.77	6.50	1.74	373.0
Natural resources	2.14	1.99	2.40	82.7
Housing–urban renewal	6.16	8.77	1.59	551.7
Correction	1.54	2.05	.66	312.2
Libraries	1.72	2.07	1.11	186.3
Financial administration	2.98	3.19	2.62	121.6
Exhibit:				
Local school per student	471.84	513.85	409.58	125.5
Capital outlay	78.61	91.83	60.58	151.6
Other than capital outlay	392.48	422.72	348.99	121.1

* Population allocated on the basis of 1963 metropolitan/nonmetropolitan residence; 63.6% in metropolitan areas and 36.4% in nonmetropolitan areas. (U. S. Bureau of the Census, *Current Population Reports*, Series P-20, No. 131, September 4, 1964.)

SOURCE: U. S. Bureau of the Census, *Census of Governments: 1962*. Vol. V: *Local Government in Metropolitan Areas*. U. S. Government Printing Office, Washington, D.C.

As indicated, the similarity in per capita expenditures on education reflect basic differences in expenditures per enrolled student in local schools. Even if capital outlays—which are measurably higher in metropolitan areas—are excluded, expenditures per enrolled student in metropolitan areas are 21.1 per cent higher than their nonmetropolitan counterparts: $422.72 as compared to $348.99.

Because the per capita similarity in local school expenditures is combined with large differences in total per capita expenditures, the dissimilarity of the remainder of the fiscal packages for metropolitan and nonmetropolitan areas is necessarily large. The dissimilarity is enhanced when account is taken of expenditures for the highway and natural resource functions. These two functions alone show higher per capita expenditures in nonmetropolitan than in metropolitan areas.

When education and highway expenditures are excluded, the remainder of the services show expenditures about twice as great on a per capita basis in metropolitan areas than outside of SMSAs: $119.04 compared to $60.56 per capita. Of this portion of the package of services the general government component (financial administration, general control, and general public buildings) is only slightly higher in metropolitan areas than in nonmetropolitan areas: $11.87 as compared to $9.52. Somewhat surprising is the resemblance between the hospital expenditures within and outside SMSAs. Large differences, but still less than the average, occur in the case of public welfare, health, and library expenditures—the first two of which are highly aided functions.

In the case of those functions not highly aided, the differences in per capita expenditure between the metropolitan and nonmetropolitan areas are more clear-cut: metropolitan police, fire, and sewerage expenditures are more than twice as great; sanitation, parks, and recreation, and correction are more than three times as great; and housing and urban renewal, airports, and water transportation are more than five times as great as the levels in nonmetropolitan areas.

On the financing side, the picture is quite clear on an aggregate basis. Reflecting a combination of the political process and the availability of economic resources, metropolitan per capita taxes were 62.9 per cent higher than their nonmetropolitan counterparts, whereas state aid, reflecting the same set of circumstances, was higher in nonmetropolitan areas: $55.87 in metropolitan as compared to $63.20 in non-metropolitan areas. State aid was equal to 35.7 per cent of direct local general expenditures outside of metropolitan areas and only 23.7 per cent of such expenditures in metropolitan areas.

These major fiscal differences between metropolitan and non-metropolitan areas not only reflect income and property tax base differences, but differences in needs and responses per unit of population in the two areas as modified by the assignment of functional responsibility and state aid. It should be noted that total expenditures in metropolitan areas were 136 per cent of those in nonmetropolitan areas, but the like percentage for income was 152.

Because education and highway expenditures have much higher levels in nonmetropolitan areas relative to their income than other functions—owing to a combination of state aid and needs—most of the other functions have higher expenditures in metropolitan areas than is explainable by the higher income levels in these areas. This conclusion is reinforced by analyses of taxes that show the tax ratio between metropolitan and nonmetropolitan areas to be slightly higher than the comparable metropolitan/nonmetropolitan ratio of income. For 1957 (using the 1959 personal income data from the 1960 Census of Population) taxes in metropolitan areas were 172.9 per cent of those in nonmetropolitan areas as compared to the income ratio of 152 per cent. Therefore, metropolitan taxes as measured against income are higher than nonmetropolitan taxes: 4.68 per cent of income as compared to 4.12 per cent of income.

The differences found between nationwide metropolitan and nonmetropolitan fiscal levels herein presented are for the year 1962. It is useful, therefore, to make a comparison of the important categories with the 1957 data, because 1957 is the year that serves as the basis for the detailed analysis of the remainder of this study. The selection of that year was necessitated by the availability of data.

The comparison of total fiscal measures reveals a remarkable similarity in the relationships between metropolitan and nonmetropolitan fiscal levels for the two years. As Table 3-2 shows, the greatest change in percentage relationships between metropolitan and nonmetropolitan areas is for taxes: from 172.9 per cent in 1957 to 162.9 per cent in 1962. For state aid and general expenditures the percentage relationships show slightly less change.

Thus, in a period of unprecedented fiscal growth, the relative levels of local expenditures, taxes, and state aid have shown great stability, with a slight movement toward greater uniformity in the relationship of the fiscal behavior of the metropolitan and the nonmetropolitan portions of the nation. This movement, however small, toward greater uniformity adds some confirmation to the long term secular trend of

TABLE 3-2: *Nationwide Metropolitan and Nonmetropolitan Fiscal Levels, 1957 and 1962*

Per capita measure	Metropolitan	Non-metropolitan	Metropolitan less Non-metropolitan	Metropolitan as per cent of Non-metropolitan
General expenditure 1957	$175.49	$126.88	$48.46	138.0%
(1962)	(235.92)	(176.65)	(59.27)	(133.6)
Taxes 1957	98.88	57.18	41.70	172.9
(1962)	(131.44)	(80.68)	(50.76)	(162.9)
State Aid 1957	39.90	46.92	−7.02	85.0
(1962)	(55.87)	(63.20)	(−7.47)	(88.4)

SOURCE: U. S. Bureau of the Census, *Local Government Finances* (1957). U. S. Bureau of the Census, *Census of Governments: 1962.* Vol. V: *Local Government Finances.*

declining fiscal differences between metropolitan and non-metropolitan areas. Apparently as the nation-becomes more and more metropolitan, the influence of metropolitanism spreads beyond the boundaries of the metropolitan areas to encompass the whole society.

Regional Patterns of Metropolitan and Nonmetropolitan Fiscal Behavior, 1957

Nationwide patterns of metropolitan and nonmetropolitan fiscal behavior hide hitherto unanalyzed major regional differences, as shown in Table 3-3. In general, regional differences in metropolitan expenditures are greater than the nationwide differences between metropolitan and nonmetropolitan expenditures.

Three distinct factors appear to account for most of the interregional fiscal differences. First, regions differ in their income and tax base characteristics; second, they differ in the extent of local government responsibility for expenditures and taxes; and third, they differ in the role state aid plays in the fiscal system of each region. The effect of these different forces will be analyzed first with respect to per capita local general expenditures and then with respect to local taxes and state aid.

Although there are distinct differences in per capita local general expenditures among the regions, such expenditures in metropolitan areas exceeded those in the nonmetropolitan areas in every region. The absolute per capita expenditure differences between metropolitan and nonmetropolitan areas within each region, however, are less than the differences across regional lines.

TABLE 3-3: *Per Capita Local General Expenditures for all Functions by Region and for SMSA and NonSMSA Portions of these Regions, 1957*

Region	Entire region	SMSA portion	Non-SMSA portion
National	$157.23	$175.49	$126.88
Northeast	179.63	187.98	148.02
North central	160.83	169.50	147.34
South	107.11	128.33	90.02
West	206.10	214.79	191.13

SOURCE: U. S. Bureau of the Census, *Local Government Finances* (1957).

These differences across regional lines are accounted for primarily by the South. That the South should bring down the national average of local expenditures is to be expected; not only is average personal income lower in the South, but the expenditure and tax responsibility assigned to local government is considerably below that assigned elsewhere in the nation. These two forces are summarized in Tables 3-4 and 3-5.

On the basis of expected values, therefore, per capita local expenditures should be lowest in the nonmetropolitan South and highest in the metropolitan areas of the Northeast and the West. The nonmetropolitan South has the lowest level of expenditures, and the West, followed by the Northeast, has the highest level of metropolitan expenditures. Somewhat surprising on the basis of assignment and income is the very high level of local expenditures in the nonmetropolitan West. The factor accounting for this last phenomenon, in addition to state aid, is the high per capita property tax base in the nonmetropolitan West.

TABLE 3-4: *Per Capita Income by Region and by Metropolitan and Nonmetropolitan Portions of Those Regions, 1959*

	Total	Metropolitan	Nonmetropolitan
National	$1,850	$2,113	$1,388
Northeast	2,086	2,182	1,675
North central	1,905	2,176	1,480
South	1,420	1,771	1,130
West	2,121	2,282	1,700

SOURCE: U. S. Bureau of the Census, *County and City Data Book: 1962.*

TABLE 3-5: *Local Proportion of State and Local Expenditures and Taxes by Region: 1957*

	Expenditures	Taxes
National	65.8%	49.5%
Northeast	69.9	56.9
North Central	67.9	52.8
South	56.4	35.6
West	67.6	47.2

SOURCE: U. S. Bureau of the Census, *Local Government Finances* (1957).

Local taxes, like local expenditures, exhibit important inter-regional differences and, within each region, differences between the metropolitan and nonmetropolitan portions (Table 3-6). The expectation that the South would show even greater relative differences in taxes than it does in expenditures is borne out. There is little difference in per capita taxes in nonmetropolitan regions other than in the South, which causes the lower national figure.

Although regional fiscal differences are closely related to the regional income differences, the exact relationship varies from region to region. The ratio of local taxes to income is highest in the Northeast, followed by the North Central and West, and then by the South. In general, this follows the assignment of tax responsibility, except for the West which shows a slightly higher ratio relative to income than expected.

There is a rough uniformity outside the Northeast in the absolute differences between SMSA and non-SMSA taxes. The difference in the Northeast is $42.70, compared to differences of $23.20 (West), $28.55 (South), and $27.42 (North Central) in the other regions. In contrast to the absolute differences, the largest relative difference between metropolitan and nonmetropolitan areas is in the South where metropolitan taxes equal 187.2 per cent of those of non-metropolitan areas; in the West the equivalent relationship is 127.8 per cent.

The principal reason for the much smaller relative difference for expenditures than for taxes is state aid, which is consistently higher for nonmetropolitan areas than for metropolitan areas, both nationally and for each region (Table 3-7).

TABLE 3-6: *Per Capita Local Taxes by Regions and for SMSA and NonSMSA Portions of these Regions, 1957*

	Total	SMSA	Non-SMSA
National	$ 83.52	$ 98.88	$57.18
Northeast	109.34	117.03	74.83
North central	88.67	97.99	75.01
South	45.16	61.28	32.73
West	100.10	106.62	73.42

SOURCE: U. S. Bureau of the Census, *Local Government Finances* (1957).

The differences between expenditures and taxes not explainable by state aid are a result of greater fees, charges, and borrowing in metropolitan than in nonmetropolitan areas.

Just as there were clear-cut regional patterns for taxes and expenditures, there are patterns, but of a different kind, for state aid. The expenditure and tax patterns showed metropolitan area governments spending and collecting more tax monies than their nonmetropolitan counterparts; the opposite is true for all regions in the case of state aid. Nonmetropolitan areas clearly get larger absolute aid, and hence larger amounts of aid, relative to income than do metropolitan areas.

Just as aid tends to support higher expenditure in nonmetropolitan areas than taxes in those areas do, it also tends to overcome some of the income differences between metropolitan and nonmetropolitan areas. Table 3-8 shows the relationships between aid and income. The substantially higher percentage that aid is of income in nonmetropolitan areas is a measure of both the lower income and higher aid in these areas.

TABLE 3-7: *Per Capita State Aid to Local Governments by Regions and by SMSA and Non-SMSA Portions of these Regions, 1957*

	Total	SMSA portion	Non-SMSA portion
National	$42.42	$39.90	$46.92
Northeast	41.02	38.80	51.27
North central	40.89	36.00	48.03
South	32.29	26.69	38.62
West	66.01	64.30	74.42

SOURCE: U. S. Bureau of the Census, *Local Government Finances* (1957).

TABLE 3-8: *Per Capita State Aid to Local Governments (1957) as a Per Cent of Income (1959)*

	National (48 states)	SMSA portion (45 states)	Non-SMSA portion (45 states)
National	2.29%	1.89%	3.38%
Northeast	1.97	1.78	3.06
North central	2.15	1.65	3.25
South	2.27	1.51	3.42
West	3.11	2.82	4.58

SOURCE: U. S. Bureau of the Census, *Local Government Finances* (1957).

This counterbalancing role of aid is further illustrated by its relationship to the differences in taxes and expenditures between metropolitan and nonmetropolitan areas. Although the higher aid in nonmetropolitan areas does not completely offset the expenditure and tax difference, it does cut in that direction. Table 3-9 illustrates these relationships.

In summary, the differences in local fiscal patterns between metropolitan and nonmetropolitan areas are a result of several consistent regional patterns of tax and expenditure assignment, income, and state aid. There are in each region a few large metropolitan areas whose behavior tends to dominate the overall results. As shown in the previous chapter and as indicated in the regional analysis just completed, the state unit is the dominant one from a decision-making point of view. Its dominance is based on both the role of state aid and the nature of fiscal assignment.

Metropolitan/Nonmetropolitan Analysis by State

In conducting any analysis that uses metropolitanism as the organizing framework, there is always difficulty in determining which system of governmental jurisdictions are the appropriate building blocks. Population movements and social and economic interaction are relatively uninfluenced by jurisdictional boundaries. This characteristic of metropolitanism causes many studies to ignore governmental boundaries and to use only national and regional averages in explaining the character of metropolitanism.

TABLE 3-9: *Absolute Differences in Per Capita Fiscal Behavior Between Metropolitan and Nonmetropolitan Areas by Regions, 1957*

	Difference between expenditures	Difference between taxes	Difference between state aid
National	+ $48.61	+ $41.70	− $ 7.02
Northeast	+ 39.96	+ 42.70	− 12.47
North central	+ 22.16	+ 27.42	− 12.03
South	+ 37.41	+ 28.55	− 11.93
West	+ 23.66	+ 23.20	− 10.10

SOURCE: U. S. Bureau of the Census, *Local Government Finances* (1957).

Although for many purposes the ignoring of governmental jurisdiction may be appropriate, it certainly is not when the public sector is being analyzed. Decisions in this sector are made by governmental jurisdictions and it is, therefore, necessary to take such jurisdictions into account. One of the dominant jurisdictions in the whole governmental system of metropolitan areas is states. It is, therefore, necessary to analyze metropolitan fiscal behavior within the context of state boundaries. The first step is to determine the differences in such behavior between metropolitan and nonmetropolitan portions of states.

This use of state units makes the findings about metropolitan/nonmetropolitan fiscal behavior comparable to those already presented for overall state-local and local fiscal behavior. Although reduced slightly, the overwhelming importance of the assignment of expenditure and tax responsibility as between state and local government, which was demonstrated in the discussion of total local fiscal behavior by state, plays a similar role in the analysis of the metropolitan and nonmetropolitan portions of states. The 1957 data are presented in Appendices A-1, A-2 and A-3. They can be made directly comparable to the data included in the 1962 Census of Governments.[4]

Since both expenditure and tax assignment refer to the entire local sector rather than to the metropolitan and nonmetropolitan portions of a state, the observed relationships between metropolitan and nonmetropolitan fiscal behavior are likely to appear weaker than they in reality are. This assumption is based on the belief that local assignment is higher within the same state in metropolitan than in nonmetropolitan areas. Unfortunately, the method of reporting state fiscal data and conceptual difficulties involving less than a statewide assignment figure makes it impossible to calculate the overall distribution of state expenditures between metropolitan and nonmetropolitan portions of a state.

TABLE 3-10: *Per Capita Local Fiscal Behavior Metropolitan and Nonmetropolitan Portions of 45 States with Metropolitan Areas, 1957*

Fiscal category	METROPOLITAN			NONMETROPOLITAN			
	Mean	Standard deviation	Coefficient of variation	Mean	Standard deviation	Coefficient of variation	Coefficient of correlation
Expenditures							
General	$147.92	$37.09	25.1%	$134.12	$47.13	35.1%	.879
General (excluding outlay)	111.11	26.92	24.2	108.33	39.11	36.1	.903
Education	62.24	13.88	21.9	68.92	17.83	25.9	.752
Education (excluding outlay)	48.76	9.08	18.8	55.20	14.28	25.9	.844
Noneducation	83.75	28.44	34.0	66.02	33.71	51.1	.795
Noneducation (excluding outlay)	62.32	21.82	35.0	53.92	28.94	53.7	.857
Highway	15.27	7.23	47.3	19.85	10.65	53.7	.692
Highway (excluding outlay)	7.80	2.73	35.0	14.14	7.52	53.2	.684
Health and hospital (excluding outlay)	7.34	4.86	66.2	5.55	4.27	76.9	.687
Public welfare	6.67	8.06	120.8	7.73	11.96	154.7	.954
Revenues							
Total taxes	81.01	25.47	31.4	64.76	33.61	51.9	.903
Property taxes	71.10	25.04	35.2	60.27	32.75	54.3	.832
State aid	30.98	15.09	48.7	47.42	22.67	47.8	.852

SOURCE: U. S. Bureau of the Census, *Local Government Finances* (1957).

[84]

A comparison of metropolitan and nonmetropolitan expenditures using the state as the unit of analysis can be contrasted to the same comparison where national averages were employed. In the latter case metropolitan expenditures exceeded those in nonmetropolitan areas by $48.69 or 38.3 per cent. However, when each of the 45 states is taken as a unit, metropolitan area expenditures exceeded those in their nonmetropolitan areas by only $13.80, or 10.3 per cent. As shown in Table 3-10, expenditures were $147.92 in the metropolitan portion of the average state and $134.12 in the nonmetropolitan portion. However, the coefficient of variation in nonmetropolitan portions of states is considerably higher than in the comparable metropolitan portions, indicating that the nonmetropolitan portions are much more dissimilar.

The difference between local government expenditures in metropolitan areas and those in nonmetropolitan portions of the average state as indicated in the national pattern, is the product of entirely different expenditure patterns in the two areas. The patterns are composed of different combinations of education and noneducation expenditures. For the year 1957 total educational expenditures per capita in metropolitan portions were less than those in nonmetropolitan areas: $63.24 as compared to $68.92, a difference of only $5.68, or 8.2 per cent. As was the case in the national picture, per student expenditures are higher in the metropolitan areas due to their lower enrollment ratios. The coefficients of variation for educational expenditures are lower in both metropolitan and nonmetropolitan portions than for noneducational expenditures. When capital outlay is excluded, the coefficient of variation is even lower—only 18.8 per cent in the metropolitan portion. In other words, there is great uniformity in per capita educational expenditures both between metropolitan and nonmetropolitan areas and within these areas.

Noneducational expenditures show the opposite pattern:

metropolitan expenditures were $17.73, or 26.9 per cent, higher than nonmetropolitan expenditures. However, the coefficient of variation is considerably higher for these expenditures in nonmetropolitan portions: 51.1 per cent, as compared to 34.0 per cent in metropolitan portions. Thus, there is substantially more uniformity in noneducational expenditures among metropolitan portions of states than among nonmetropolitan ones.

The differences in the state average pattern of expenditures reflect the two principal revenue sources: local taxes and state aid. In metropolitan portions of states, state aid was only two-thirds as high as it is in nonmetropolitan ones: $30.98, as compared to $47.42. The coefficients of variation do not show any significant difference between metropolitan and non-metropolitan portions of states, although both are high. These high coefficients of variation for state aid are a reflection of the local expenditure assignment system for the welfare function that tends to be an either/or operation—either state operated or locally operated, but very highly state aided (with federal funds). The coefficients of variation are 120.8 and 154.7 per cent for metropolitan and nonmetropolitan areas, respectively.

If the heavily aided functions are excluded—i.e., education, highways, welfare, and health-hospitals—both the average and relative differences between metropolitan and non-metropolitan portions are larger: $21.58 and 65.5 per cent compared to $13.80 and 10.3 per cent when they are included. In other words, state aid acts as a greater equalizer of fiscal levels between metropolitan and nonmetropolitan portions when analyzed on a state basis than was true on a national basis.

On a stage-weighted basis, metropolitan and nonmetro-politan taxes show greater uniformity than they do on a national basis: for the metropolitan portions of the state, per capita taxes were $81.01, for the nonmetropolitan portions $64.76, as compared to the comparable national average figures of $98.88 and $57.15.

Metropolitan and Nonmetropolitan Fiscal Relationships by State

What factors determine the levels of local behavior in metropolitan and nonmetropolitan areas? Are they responding to the same forces or to different ones? Further, does the level in one type area influence the level in the other? In other words, does the level of fiscal activity in metropolitan areas influence the level in nonmetropolitan areas, or does causation run in the opposite direction, or do they respond to different forces?

In analyzing causation, the state averages for metropolitan and nonmetropolitan behavior are used. If the assignment system is as important as has been suggested, there should be a significant association by state between metropolitan and nonmetropolitan fiscal behavior—not only in their totals but even more so on a functional basis. In the case of the analysis of individual or groups of functions, the assignment variables, in general, are held constant.

The basic assumption is that similarities in metropolitan and nonmetropolitan behavior within a state should be clearly detectable, and the more clear-cut the effect of assignment, the higher should be the observed correlation between fiscal behavior of the metropolitan and nonmetropolitan portions of a state.

As shown in Table 3-10, there is a very significant correlation between metropolitan and nonmetropolitan behavior in every category analyzed. As measured by the coefficients of correlation, the values range from .684 in the case of highways (excluding capital outlays) to .954 in the case of public welfare. The results clearly demonstrate the importance of the state as a unit of analysis and the relevance of the assignment variable.

The correlations are high, but do not show unique relationships between the metropolitan and nonmetropolitan areas;

TABLE 3-11: *Simple Correlations of Selected Fiscal and Socioeconomic Variables in Metropolitan Portions of States, 1957 (All Variables in Per Capita Terms Unless Otherwise Noted)*

	State aid	Per capita income	Expenditure assignment per cent local	Tax assignment per cent local	Metropolitan population per cent state	Population per government	Nonwhite per cent total population
Total expenditures	.658	.733	.683	.543	.506	−.261	−.368
Total, less capital	.671	.746	.689	.558	.559	−.246	−.391
Total education	.538	.643	.483	.433	.422	−.315	−.450
Education, less capital	.525	.684	.404	.379	.389	−.338	−.511
Total noneducation	.613	.656	.675	.518	.478	−.181	−.289
Noneducation, less capital	.614	.649	.688	.539	.540	−.197	−.296
Total highways	.079	.178	.328	.501	−.224	−.425	−.291
Highways, less capital	.020	.081	.318	.536	−.224	−.436	−.310
Health and hospital, less capital	.537	.445	.616	.233	.411	−.103	−.092
Public welfare	.504	.419	.579	.461	.370	−.108	−.275
Total taxes	.232	.655	.668	.869	.352	−.403	−.536
Property taxes	.182	.581	.579	.854	.292	−.448	−.599
State aid	1.000	.381	.467	−.108	.477	.048	.017
Income		1.000	.390	.469	.586	−.163	−.451
Expenditure assignment per cent local			1.000	.584	.405	−.199	−.117
Tax assignment per cent local				1.000	.162	−.472	−.584
Metropolitan population per cent state					1.000	.146	−.059
Population per government						1.000	.549
Nonwhite per cent total population							1.000

In order to be significant at .05 level, r must be > ±.295
In order to be significant at .01 level, r must be > ±.384

therefore, there must be other influences, in addition to the role of the state, at work. What are the factors that account for the fiscal behavior variations among the metropolitan portions of the 45 states that have metropolitan areas, and for the variations among nonmetropolitan portions of the states? Stated another way, are the factors that explain variations among metropolitan portions the same as those that explain the variations among nonmetropolitan portions?

Although a multiple regression analysis will be applied to total expenditures and taxes, a simple correlation analysis is used on a more detailed functional basis for several of the major functions. From these analyses it is quite clear that the factors accounting for variations in local fiscal behavior in metropolitan areas do not differ in kind from those operating outside metropolitan areas. In other words, the same basic variables are operative in both type areas.

The results of a simple correlation analysis of the major fiscal categories for metropolitan and nonmetropolitan areas are summarized in Tables 3-11 and 3-12. In these tables the principal independent variables used earlier in the statewide analysis of state-local and local finances are used again— namely, per capita income, state aid, the two fiscal assignment measures, with the addition of the metropolitan proportion (population) of the state, the percentage nonwhite, and population per government.

The general picture of the observed behavior among metropolitan portions is that each of these factors except population per government shows a significant association as hypothesized with all expenditure categories, with the one exception—expenditures for highways. As has often been noted, the forces responsible for the per capita variation in local highway expenditures are considerably different from those influencing other functions, although the use of the assignment variable does provide some explanation for this function. On the tax side, state aid is not negative, as expected,

TABLE 3-12: *Simple Correlations of Selected Fiscal and Socioeconomic Variables in Nonmetropolitan Portions of States, 1957 (All Variables in Per Capita Terms Unless Otherwise Noted)*

	State aid	Per capita income	Expenditure assignment per cent local	Tax assignment per cent local	Metropolitan population per cent state	Population per government	Nonwhite per cent of population
Total expenditures	.612	.684	.576	.513	.409	−.576	−.491
Total, less capital	.597	.671	.553	.496	.400	−.567	−.479
Total education	.557	.703	.362	.348	.416	−.609	−.512
Education, less capital	.537	.640	.332	.323	.322	−.620	−.470
Total noneducation	.516	.617	.621	.564	.360	−.472	−.420
Noneducation, less capital	.549	.602	.608	.519	.416	−.435	−.396
Total highways	.349	.391	.551	.534	.010	−.673	−.494
Highways, less capital	.367	.436	.619	.586	.128	−.637	−.503
Health and hospital, less capital	.431	.251	.390	.100	.195	−.229	−.043
Public welfare	.545	.315	.489	.380	.292	−.277	−.317
Total taxes	.064	.659	.452	.819	.169	−.583	−.616
Property taxes	.063	.654	.440	.817	.159	−.590	−.634
State aid	1.000	.250	.320	−.229	.453	−.155	−.003
Income		1.000	.274	.536	.507	−.425	−.640
Expenditure assignment per cent local			1.000	.584	.405	−.302	−.341
Tax assignment per cent local				1.000	.162	−.539	−.669
Metropolitan population per cent state					1.000	.063	−.170
Population per government						1.000	.609
Nonwhite per cent total population							1.000

In order to be significant at .05 level, r must be $> \pm .295$
In order to be significant at .01 level, r must be $> \pm .384$

but the populations per government and nonwhite per centage of the population are both negative and significant, as expected.

In the case of nonmetropolitan fiscal activities all the variables, including population per government, are significant on the expenditure side. The reason for the government variable having a significant negative relationship with fiscal levels in nonmetropolitan portions, which it does not have in metropolitan portions, is undoubtedly its strong association with the South, where local fiscal activity is lower than in the rest of the country and where the number of governments relative to population is low.

It should also be noted that in nonmetropolitan areas the variable representing metropolitanism—i.e., the proportion of each state's population in metropolitan areas—is positively and significantly correlated with each fiscal category except highway expenditures, and in that case no relationship is demonstrated.

Overall, the general picture at the level of simple association shows no substantial differences in the forces influencing fiscal behavior patterns in metropolitan and nonmetropolitan portions of the states. Even the correlations between the independent variables do not show wide variations.

It is important to note that more refined variables, such as expenditure assignment and state aid by function, would probably sharpen the findings for both metropolitan and non-metropolitan areas in the same way as they improve the explanation of state-local expenditures by functions.[5]

Multiple Regression Analysis

Turning now to the multiple regression analysis, the same basic variables, with some modifications, used throughout this study are considered together. The modifications are the exclusion of the federal aid variable and the substitution of the metropolitan portion of the state's population for the density and urbanization variables. The results are presented below for local expenditures and taxes in the metropolitan portions of the 45 states with metropolitan areas.

$$P.\ C.\ Exp._M\ (1957) = \ -.021\ \text{Metro. Per Cent of State}$$
$$(.016)$$
$$+.078^{**}\ P.\ C.\ \text{Income}$$
$$(.013)$$
$$+.844^{**}\ P.\ C.\ \text{State Aid}$$
$$(.210)$$
$$+1.457^{**}\ \text{Loc. Exp. Assign.}$$
$$(.327)$$
$$-\$106.85$$
$$\bar{R} = .896 \qquad \bar{R}^2 = .802$$

$$P.\ C.\ Exp._{NM}\ (1957) = \ -.053^*\ \text{Metro. Per Cent State}$$
$$(.022)$$
$$+.099^{**}\ P.\ C.\ \text{Income}$$
$$(.015)$$
$$+.902^{**}\ P.\ C.\ \text{State Aid}$$
$$(.173)$$
$$+2.098^{**}\ \text{Loc. Exp. Assign.}$$
$$(.421)$$
$$-\$142.89$$
$$\bar{R} = .884 \qquad \bar{R}^2 = .780$$

$$P.\ C.\ Taxes_M\ (1957) = \ -.004\ \text{Metro. Per Cent State}$$
$$(.014)$$
$$+.020^*\ P.\ C.\ \text{Income}$$
$$(.008)$$
$$+.445^{**}\ P.\ C.\ \text{State Aid}$$
$$(.114)$$

$$+ 1.680^{**} \text{ Loc. Tax Assign.}$$
$$(.135)$$
$$- \$44.13$$
$$\bar{R} = .939 \qquad \bar{R}^2 = .882$$

$$\text{P. C. Taxes}_{NM} (1957) = -.037^* \text{ Metro. Per Cent State}$$
$$(.014)$$
$$+ .036^{**} \text{ P. C. Income}$$
$$(.012)$$
$$+ .417^{**} \text{ P. C. State Aid}$$
$$(.131)$$
$$+ 2.158^{**} \text{ Loc. Tax Assign.}$$
$$(.249)$$
$$- \$83.57$$
$$\bar{R} = .893 \qquad \bar{R}^2 = .797$$

As in the analysis of the statewide totals of local fiscal behavior per capita income, per capita state aid and local expenditure as a proportion of total state-local expenditures are positive and highly significant in explaining variations in per capita expenditures. The same relationships are found when taxes are analyzed and when the local assignment of taxes is substituted for the expenditure assignment variable. The exclusion of federal aid is the result of the absence of data, rather than the result of any alteration in the underlying model.

Of considerably greater interest is the fact that state aid continues to be positively related to per capita taxes in both metropolitan and nonmetropolitan areas as it was on the analysis of statewide variations in per capita local taxes. In fact, on the tax side there is a remarkable consistency both over time and between the metropolitan and national state-local totals with respect to the relationship between state aid and local taxes. For every dollar of state aid, local taxes increased by somewhat more than $0.40, taking into account tax assignment, income, and the metropolitan portion of the state's population.

This finding is consistent with the mandating of a local contribution contained in most aid programs, but it may also be due to other factors or a combination of mandated contributions and other factors.[6] On the other hand the finding is completely inconsistent on a metropolitan/nonmetropolitan and statewide basis with the notion that state aid is inversely related to the level of local taxes—that it acts as a substitute for local taxes.

As in the case of the national picture, the most important and significant single variable explaining variations in local taxes among the metropolitan and nonmetropolitan portions of states, as it is throughout the analysis, is the tax assignment variable. A more complex set of relationships, including the local expenditure assignment variable, explains the expenditure patterns with income as the single most important determinant both in the metropolitan and nonmetropolitan portions of states.

Table 3-13 summarizes the determinants of metropolitan and nonmetropolitan fiscal behavior. When these findings are contrasted to those for state-wide local totals, as presented in the previous chapter, the important difference relates to the role of the assignment variables. Although these variables remain important for metropolitan and nonmetropolitan behavior, they lose some of their power to state aid and possess,

TABLE 3-13: *Coefficients of Relative Importance (Beta Weights) for Metropolitan and Nonmetropolitan Per Capita Expenditures and Taxes and Selected Independent Variables, 1957*

Per capita	% Population metropolitan	Per capita income (1959)	Per capita state aid	Expenditure assignment	Tax assignment	R	R²
Metropolitan Expenditures	−.128	.537	.343	.375		.896	.803
Nonmetropolitan Expenditures	−.256	.595	.434	.426		.883	.780
Metropolitan taxes	−.037	.195	.267		.815	.939	.881
Nonmetropolitan taxes	−.253	.299	.281		.793	.893	.797

as would be expected, somewhat less overall explanatory power. This reduction results from the fact that these variables relate to entire states rather than to their component parts. A similarity of findings for entire local systems and the metropolitan/nonmetropolitan division relates to the higher explanatory power of the model for taxes than for expenditures.

Summary of Findings

Metropolitan United States is characterized by a considerably higher level of fiscal activity than is indicated by the high concentration of the nation's population within its boundaries. On the basis of the most recent data (1962), with 63.6 per cent of the population, local governments in metropolitan areas made 70.0 per cent of all direct general expenditures, raised 74.0 per cent of all local taxes, and had 76.2 per cent of all local debt, but received only 60.7 per cent of total state aid. When converted into per capita terms, this meant that direct local general expenditures were $235.92 per capita, or 33.6 per cent more than the $176.65 in nonmetropolitan areas. On the reverse side, metropolitan areas raised 62.9 per cent more per capita in taxes, had 70 per cent more debt per capita, and received 11.6 per cent less state aid.

It appears, however, that the relative position of metropolitan areas vis-a-vis nonmetropolitan areas has been declining, secularly, although the precise evidence is difficult to get because of an absence of reliable data. The apparent decline in the difference is due to the spread of the influence of metropolitanism beyond metropolitan area borders. This influence is perhaps most clearly seen in the case of education and highways, where the nonmetropolitan fiscal levels are clearly a response to metropolitanism. The fiscal tool that plays the dominant role in reducing the metropolitan and nonmetropolitan differences is state aid. The role of aid in the fiscal system of the United States is of fundamental importance to understanding the dynamics of fiscal behavior. The use of the metropolitan framework for analyzing fiscal behavior shows more clearly than ever before this crucial role of state aid.

The increases in state aid are associated with the enormous increases in the scope of the three highly aided functions—education, highways, and public welfare—whereas the remainder of the functions have had to be taken care of primarily from locally raised funds. The result (excluding the aided functions) is that the relative expenditure level of local government is considerably higher, almost twice as high on a per capita basis, in metropolitan areas than in nonmetropolitan areas. Local taxes in metropolitan areas were more than one and a half times as high as in nonmetropolitan areas.

Analyses of local fiscal behavior show basic differences by region. Some of these differences reflect differences in income, and some are a function of the assignment of local fiscal responsibility. As a result of this combination of factors the largest relative differences between metropolitan and nonmetropolitan areas exist in the South, where the absolute differences are also very great.

Analyzing the metropolitan/nonmetropolitan patterns of finance by state, a number of important conclusions consistent with the nationwide and regional analyses emerge. First, there is a significant correlation for every function between the level of local fiscal activity inside and outside metropolitan portions of states. These reflect the common statewide assignment systems and is the reason why the state must be included in the analysis.

Second, although the metropolitan level of fiscal activity is higher than the nonmetropolitan level of fiscal activity, increases in the former level are reflected in the latter. And in the case of state aid, even though it is higher in nonmetropolitan areas than in metropolitan areas, the same relationship exists.

The multiple regression analysis indicates that there are no basic differences in the forces and determinants influencing total expenditure and tax behavior of the metropolitan and non-metropolitan portions of the 45 states with metropolitan areas.

This chapter contains no surprises but it does clarify and expand some of the findings of earlier studies. The importance of the assignment systems are clearly demonstrated, as are the relationships between the other independent variables, particularly income and state aid, and taxes and expenditures. The nature of the state aid pattern reflects the nonmetropolitan locus of political power in state legislatures as of 1957.

The metropolitan portion of the state is an aggregate measure. In the following two chapters individual metropolitan areas will be considered in terms of their constituent central city and outside central city components, as well as integrated economic units.

References

1. U. S. Bureau of the Census. *Census of Governments: 1962.* Vol. V; *Local Government in Metropolitan Areas.* (Washington: U. S. Government Printing Office).

2. *Local Government Finances and Employment in Relation to Population: 1957.* Washington: U. S. Government Printing Office, 1961 (hereafter cited as *Local Government Finances* (1957)).

3. *Census of Governments: 1962.* Vol. V: *Local Government in Metropolitan Areas,* 11.

4. U. S. Bureau of the Census, *Census of Governments: 1962.* Vol. V. *Local Government in Metropolitan Areas* (Washington: U. S. Government Printing Office, pp. 188–195.

5. Yong Hyo Cho, *State-Local Governmental Systems: Their Determinants and Fiscal Implications* (Ph. D. dissertation, Syracuse University, 1965).

6. H. Thomas James, *School Revenue Systems in Five States* (Stanford University Press, 1961); and, with J. Allen Thomas and Harold J. Dyck, *Wealth, Expenditures, and Decision-Making* (Stanford University Press, 1964).

CHAPTER 4

Local Fiscal Patterns Within
and Among Metropolitan Areas

Most analyses of metropolitan fiscal behavior have centered on individual metropolitan areas rather than on metropolitanism in general (nationally, regionally, and by state), as was done in the previous chapter. This emphasis on individual metropolitan areas, the traditional unit of analysis, is in many ways the correct unit. It is the unit that is economically, politically, and governmentally interrelated even though it does not constitute a unified decision-making governmental jurisdiction.

Despite the advantages of using the metropolitan area as the prime unit of analysis, most studies to date have failed to provide information that has usefulness beyond the area being analyzed. This failure results from failing to place the metropolitan area being analyzed in its state-local context and to explicitly take into account its local governmental subsystem.

A more generalized approach to analyzing metropolitan fiscal behavior has been suggested, but its contribution has not been very useful. It has been an attempt to apply a spatially conceived model of welfare economics to urban areas.[1] In this model "the consumer-voter may be viewed as picking that community which best satisfies his preference pattern for public goods."[2] This application of the private-market model to the public sector requires assumptions that, in the real world, just cannot be made. First, there is the requirement that there be enough communities from which to choose; other necessary assumptions include: "full mobility, including the absence of restraints associated with employment opportunities; full knowledge on the part of 'consumer-voters'; no intercommunity external economies or diseconomies are associated with local public services; some factor limits the optimum size (the size at which its services can be provided at lowest average cost) of each community, given its set pattern of services; and communities are constantly seeking to reach or maintain this optimum size."[3]

Actually, this model does not present "a 'true' map of the real world of balkanized urban areas" not because of an absence of "empirical information about human behavior in the urban areas,"[4] but because it is the set of discontinuous responses to the vertical and horizontal balkanization that is at the heart of the metropolitan (urban) problem.

The problems of local finance must be phrased in terms that recognize them as governmental. The traditional analysis of individual metropolitan areas has merit in that it deals with the correct problem area, whereas the Tiebout model is a generalized model of choice not specifically urban in content. Although Tiebout deals with local expenditures, his is a unique (nonrelevant) model that has all local services provided by one jurisdiction (single government) with all revenues raised by that jurisdiction. It is precisely this lack of autonomous local jurisdictions that is at the heart of the metropolitan fiscal problem. Federal and state aid, and the sharing of the benefits of governmental expenditures and the costs among the various local governments that overlie our metropolitan areas, is the reality that must be analyzed.

The purpose of this chapter is to present a generalized

[99]

model drawn from those more traditional analyses that have used the local jurisdictions in metropolitan areas as their units of analysis. The aggregative analyses developed in the last chapter perform the function of providing the guidelines for drawing a useful model appropriate to this form of generalization.

Metropolitan analyses have centered almost universally around the most important problem area: the question of the relationship of the central city government to its related metropolitan hinterland. The central city or cities is not only an indissoluble part of the metropolitan area, as the definition of these areas emphasizes, but through its socioeconomic and formal governmental ties with its related metropolitan hinterland innumerable spillovers of benefits and costs are produced.

There are, of course, the relationships among the overlying governments outside central cities, but at the present time these appear to be of secondary importance to the primary problem, namely, the relationship of the central city areas to their related yet governmentally separate outside central city areas. Crucial to the analysis is the recognition that in each area there is a local governmental subsystem providing services, raising taxes, and receiving aid from other governments, or having the state, and to a much lesser extent the federal, governments provide the service directly. The emphasis is not on numbers of governments, 1400 or otherwise, but on the much smaller number of layers of interrelated governments and their expenditure and tax assignments— operating primarily in their broader state-local context.

The assumption underlying this analysis is that metropolitan fiscal behavior may be interpreted usefully as the product of the complex of decisions made by local governments that make up the central city area and the decisions of all local governments that make up the outside central city area—an area that may be entirely or only in part suburban in its characteristics. The model further assumes that the metropolitan fiscal behavior is the product of two different populations and has little meaning outside this context; that is, the responses to the needs and resources (including aid from state and federal governments) will vary insofar as the central city and outside central city populations vary.

The Central City-Suburbia Phenomenon

In the decade following World War II public attention concentrated on the "suburban" portions of metropolitan areas rather than on their central city parts. The phenomenal growth of these outside areas caused most students to analyze these areas rather than the cities from which most of the people came. Of particular concern was the impact of this suburban growth on the provision of public services in the newly built-up areas, as well as its presumed significances for changes in life styles. As a result scholars, journalists, and novelists poured out reams of copy about suburbia.[5]

More recently attention has shifted back to the central city. The new emphasis, however, is not simply on the city and the processes of urbanization that created it, as had been the concern in the prewar period; but instead is on the interrelations between city and suburb. This emphasis results not only in examining, for example, who moves to suburbia, but who stays in the cities and who replaces those who leave. Further attention is given to the shift in economic activities. Retail service and commercial activities, it has been discovered, follow their customers to the suburbs. Manufacturing moves outward, also, as it searches for more space—space appropriate for a rapidly changing technology.

With all this movement, what is left for the central city? What are its functions to become?[6] A debate has developed between pro- and anti-central city forces. The debate centers on two issues: what is, in fact, happening and what "ought" to happen. The first issue focuses on the question of whether the cities are in a condition of irreversible decline. Central city population stability and in many cases decline, particularly when annexations are taken into account, is cited as evidence that a new form of urban settlement is in the making. It is a spread rather than a compact one. Both residential and economic activities will no longer be concentrated in the central cities but will be distributed throughout larger and larger metropolitan areas. There is no single center but, instead, many subcenters. Technological changes in transport and communications, plus the peoples' preference for this pattern of living, are given as the reasons for the change.

This interpretation of what is happening and why has not gone unchallenged. The central city has its champions, too. Both the facts of population redistribution and its social and economic implications are debated. There is agreement that population is shifting, although some argue that its amount has been overstated and that the outward movement may be, in part, reversible. There are, it is claimed, certain functions that can be most efficiently performed in the central city. Central office activities, certain industrial activities, and specialized services are among them. In addition, if the central city environment is cared for properly many people, it is argued, will prefer to live there; some may even return from suburbia.

In addition to the empirically based argument about whether the central city will survive is the normatively based one about whether it ought to. If it is to survive, what kind of public policies should be directed to this end? The "ought" argument, which favors survival, has two parts. One part is based on the vital economic function of the central city and the other on its cultural significance. The first emphasizes several economic activities as "belonging" in the central city, placing the greatest stress on the advantage of a central city location for the country's chief business decision-makers. It is claimed that top executives and their staff aids, both internal and external to their companies, need to engage in face-to-face confrontation. This kind of relationship is possible only in a compact center. Therefore, if the center is lost, economic efficiency declines.

Other economic arguments on behalf of the central city center on retail, service, and manufacturing activities. In the case of retail and service activities, stress is placed on the greater variety of goods and services available in a central city than in a suburban shopping center; in the case of manufacturing, emphasis is placed on the advantage of a central city location to certain specialized manufacturing activities and to firms of small size.[7]

Finally, there is the claim that the quality of the nation's cultural life depends on cities. Only in cities, it is insisted, is it possible to have fine symphony orchestras, great libraries, dynamic museums, quality educational institutions, and first-rate theatres. Without prosperous, dynamic cities these activities will die or disperse, and dispersion will inevitably lower quality and availability. Related to this cultural advantage is the belief that the heterogeneity of the city has social advantages in contrast to the presumed dull, unimaginative conformity of the suburbs.

Whatever the merit of these opposed positions, recent public policy innovations have been designed, in part, to "save our cities." Most significant is the federal urban renewal program; originally designed as a slum removal and housing program, it has become, more and more, a general "save the city" or "save downtown" program. The expectations of the sponsors of the program are that the economic vitality of the central city will be aided and, as a result, more middle-income people will stay in the city and perhaps some will be attracted back from the suburbs. Simultaneously the revenue base of the city will be improved, making it possible for the city to provide the kinds of public services demanded by middle-income people: better education, a cleaner environment, less traffic congestion, and more parks. Other federal programs, including financial assistance for mass transit, planning, open space acquisitions, education, and antipoverty are designed to help save the city.

Another assignment for the central city is made by Paul Ylvisaker of the Ford Foundation, whose concern for central cities has prompted that foundation to sponsor both city-oriented research and action programs. Mr. Ylvisaker argues that "if the city has any mission at all, it is to turn out first-class citizens. This is a mission too often and too easily lost sight of in the scramble to secure new offices, new industries, new houses, and new sources of tax revenue. In a real sense our grants will have succeeded if they merely serve as a reminder of what our separate urban functions and civic enterprises are all about."[8]

Despite these public and private programs many factors, some controllable, others not, will determine the future distribution of people and the pattern of their economic and social activities. Whether the result will bring a halt in the decline in central cities only time will tell. Among the factors partially controllable are the public resources the city has available and its willingness to use them to attack the problems that beset it.

Among those problems confronting the central city is the salvaging and enhancing of its human resources. Although, as Ylvisaker suggests, these problems have an urgency that new offices, new industries, new houses, and new sources of tax revenue do not have, these latter concerns are not unrelated to the city's ability to solve its human problems. Whether or not any of these needs are to be met will depend, in part, on the ability of the cities to find the necessary material resources. These resources will have to come from either internal tax sources or external aid. Also important is the use to which the resources are put. It is within this context that an analysis of the fiscal behavior of central cities takes on its greatest importance.

Metropolitan Fiscal Behavior: Units of Analysis

Because of massive data problems it is not possible to analyze the fiscal behavior of all metropolitan areas. Instead it is necessary to use a sample of such areas. To be useful such a sample must be representative of metropolitan America, representative not only of metropolitan areas as units, but also of the component parts of such areas—central cities and outside central cities. The present analysis differs from that of Stephens and Schmandt[9] (the only predecessor analysis that dealt with metropolitan fiscal behavior on a national scale) in that the sample is not designed to determine the fiscal behavior of the average metropolitan county, but of a sample of metropolitan areas that has roughly the observed demographic and socioeconomic characteristics of metropolitan America.

As has already been demonstrated, there are significant fiscal differences between metropolitan and nonmetropolitan areas, whereas Stephens and Schmandt found that, "when the overall revenue patterns of metropolitan and nonmetropolitan county areas are compared, surprisingly little difference is found between the two—less than $4 per capita in terms of total revenue."[10] Further, they state that "the variances between the counties containing the central city and subsidiary counties are likewise not as great as might be anticipated. Central counties receive on the average 15 per cent more revenue per person than the outlying aggregates."[11]

But perhaps most basic is the fact that the average pattern they found bears little relationship to the nationwide patterns, which, in fact, show considerable differences between the metropolitan and nonmetropolitan areas. Their conclusion was, of course, a product of the choice of units used in the analysis. Metropolitan fiscal behavior can be measured in a number of ways: as an aggregate phenomenon, the total amount spent by local governments in metropolitan areas divided by the total population living in these areas; as the average behavior of the metropolitan portions of states; or by using lesser governmental units such as metropolitan and nonmetropolitan countywide aggregates. Each approach serves its own purpose and must be interpreted accordingly.

The results of measuring metropolitan and nonmetropolitan fiscal behavior by nationwide averages used earlier show a considerable difference from the results obtained when unweighted county averages were used. In contrast, there was no basic difference in the nonmetropolitan areas, whether weighted or unweighted averages were used. Specifically, the average metropolitan county has considerably lower fiscal activity in terms of its per capita measures, using per capita total general expenditures as a proxy for revenue, than the nationwide per capita averages for all metropolitan areas; however, there is no such difference between the average nonmetropolitan county and the nationwide average for all nonmetropolitan fiscal behavior.

No attempt was made by Schmandt and Stephens to compute nationwide estimates of total general revenue; however, nationwide metropolitan and nonmetropolitan estimates for total general expenditures were computed. These general expenditure and revenue figures are sufficiently alike to permit comparisons (Table 4-1). Comparable data for taxes and state aid were also computed.

TABLE 4-1: *Comparison of Per Capita Fiscal Activity in Metropolitan and Nonmetropolitan Areas, 1957: Alternative Definitions*

	Average metropolitan county	Average metropolitan county	Nation-wide metropolitan	Nation-wide Non-metropolitan	Average metropolitan area (the 36 area sample)
	(A)	(A)	(B)	(B)	(B)
Total general expenditure	n.a.	n.a.	$175.49	$126.88	$172.63
Total general revenue	$132.44	$128.61	n.c.	n.c.	n.c.
Total taxes	73.73	62.15	98.88	57.18	97.56
Total state aid	35.86	48.93	39.90	46.92	38.23

n.c. not computed
n.a. not available

SOURCE: (A) Stephens and Schmandt, *op. cit.*, 435. (B) U. S. Bureau of the Census, *Local Government Finances* (1957).

Thus, although the difference between general revenues in the average metropolitan county is only $3.83 greater than that of the average nonmetropolitan county, the metropolitan/ nonmetropolitan difference for nationwide expenditures (which, as has been noted, may be used as a good proxy for general revenues) is $48.61 greater; or put in another way, whereas the difference between the average nonmetropolitan county and the nationwide average for nonmetropolitan areas is $1.73, the comparable difference between the average metropolitan county and the nationwide average for metropolitan areas is $43.05.

Since these two fiscal measures (total general expenditures and general revenues) are not exactly the same (although they are very close), it is useful to analyze two other measures that are the same: taxes and state aid. Taxes in the average metropolitan county are $25.15 less than the nationwide average for local governments in all metropolitan areas. The average nonmetropolitan county has taxes $4.97 higher than the nationwide average for all nonmetropolitan areas. The differences reflect the importance of the large metropolitan counties in the nationwide metropolitan pattern.[12]

The picture of a much higher rate of local fiscal activity in metropolitan areas than in nonmetropolitan areas when nationwide averages are used is far more in conformity with our assumptions about such behavior than that shown by an analysis based on average metropolitan county behavior, which is heavily weighted by southern and small midwestern counties. It is from the nationally weighted metropolitan pattern showing fundamental differences between metropolitan and nonmetropolitan fiscal behavior that the sample used in the remainder of this analysis has been drawn.

Metropolitan Fiscal Behavior: 36 Sample Areas

The sample areas were selected to be as representative as possible of the total metropolitan portion of the nation in 1960 (or where necessary, 1957) as reported in the 1960 Census. Not only was the aggregate designed to be representative, but the central city and outside central city areas were also chosen to be representative of the universe from which they were drawn. Detailed data on each metropolitan area in the sample are given in Appendix B-1.

The 36 sample areas constituted 17.0 per cent of all Standard

TABLE 4-2: *Selected Socioeconomic Characteristics for the Sample of 36 SMSAs Compared to All SMSAs*

	SMSA U. S.	SMSA (sample)	Central cities U. S.	Central cities (sample)	Outside central city U. S.	Outside central city (sample)
Per capita Income, 1959	$2,113	$2,138	n.a.	$1,999	n.a.	$2,281
Median family Income, 1959	6,324	6,344	$5,940	5,816	$6,780	n.a.
Density	364	1,222	5,336	5,646	183	790
Population as per cent of SMSA (1957 est.)	100.0%	100.0%	53.6%	50.6%	46.4%	49.4%
Population 1957 as per cent of 1950	118.4	124.5	101.5	105.1	134.0	142.1
Per cent living in same house in 1960 as in 1955	48.6	52.0	47.4	51.6	49.7	52.7
Per cent nonwhite, 1960	10.8	10.7	16.8	17.0	4.6	5.1
Public school enrollment as per cent population, 1960	18.2	18.4	16.4	16.2	20.8	20.7
Per cent owner occupied	61.8	61.3	n.a.	48.5	n.a.	74.6
Sample population as per cent of total	100.0	33.2	100.0	36.3	100.0	30.5

SOURCE: U. S. Bureau of the Census, *U. S. Census of Population: 1960. Selected Area Reports. Standard Metropolitan Statistical Areas.* Final Report PC(3)-1D.

Metropolitan Statistical Areas (1960 definition), but they had 33.2 per cent of all metropolitan population (1957 estimates), 36.3 per cent of all central city population, and 30.5 per cent of all the population outside the central cities.

The single most important determinant of fiscal behavior, aside from the assignment variable, is generally conceded to be income. The second most important determinant for the analysis of local fiscal activity, property valuation, is not available. In this analysis two measures of income have been used: the median family income in 1959 and the per capita income in 1959, the latter based on the aggregate income figures of the 1960 Census of Population. The per capita figure for all SMSAs was $2,113 as compared to $2,138 for the sample areas. Median family income shows the same pattern. Central city income was lower than the outside central city income by both measures. No national measures of variation within each class are available; however, such measures are available for the sample areas and are discussed in detail below. The sample results confirm the existence of differences, but not statistically significant differences, between central city and outside central city areas on an individual metropolitan area basis. For the individual metropolitan area this phenomenon is due primarily to a rural component in the outside central areas, which depresses outside central city income, rather than to high income in central cities, supplemented by regional and size considerations.

The income pattern of the sample metropolitan areas is clearly representative of the national pattern, but that for density is not. The areas chosen in the sample have a higher density than for all metropolitan areas—1,222 per square mile as compared to 364 persons per square mile. The result is not a function of any difference between the densities of the central city areas included in the sample and the national average for central cities, but of the much higher density of the outside central city areas included in the sample. This is because none of the very low density metropolitan areas, such as San Bernadino, Reno, Las Vegas, which have such a large effect on the national totals, have been included in this sample. The result is that the density of 790 persons per square mile in the outside central city areas contrasts sharply with the national figure of 183 and therefore is probably much more "suburban" in character than the average of all outside central city areas.

Much has been made of the size of the central city relative to the total population of the SMSA. The studies of Hawley, Brazer, Woo Sik Kee, and other observers have found a relationship between the level of expenditures and this population proportion. The populations of the central city and outside central city areas were estimated, using the same straight line interpolations as the Governments Division used in estimating county populations for 1957. On this basis it is estimated that central city areas had 53.6 per cent of all metropolitan area population in 1957; for the sample it was slightly lower at 50.6 per cent. The different result is reasonable in that metropolitan areas included are larger than the average, and the larger the area the smaller the central city proportion of population. Nevertheless, the pattern is clearly close to the national one.

Another characteristic that has an effect, although its precise nature has never been completely described, is population growth. This problem becomes especially difficult when the analysis is in terms of per capita values rather than aggregates. In general it is assumed that the capital outlays and interest payments (repayment of principal being explicitly excluded) will be differentially responsive to population growth. Again using straight-line population estimates for 1957, it was found that the areas chosen grew slightly more rapidly than SMSAs for the nation as a whole, but central city growth for the sample was slightly higher than the national growth for central cities. But the national picture of much greater growth outside central city areas than inside is clearly evident in the sample, as is the relationship between outside central city and central city growth.

The greater growth in all three categories for the sample areas is reflected in the higher mobility of the population in these areas as measured by the proportion of persons over five years of age residing in the same house in 1960 as they did in 1955. Far more important, however, the data show that in terms of *movement* rather than *growth* the central city and outside central city areas were relatively indistinguishable; both areas were characterized by an enormous amount of movement in that only 50 per cent of the population were in the same house in 1960 as they had been in 1955. The lower rate of growth in central city areas, therefore, was not in any way associated with an absence of movement within the cities.

In metropolitan areas there is a much larger nonwhite population in the central city areas than in the outside central city areas. The proportions in the sample areas match the national patterns almost exactly, although as will be shown below there is considerable variation in each category.

The proportion of the total population enrolled in public schools has important effects on the aggregate demand for public services. The public school enrollment ratio outside of central city areas is considerably higher on the average than in the central city areas, both in the nationwide figures and in the sample areas.

The final characteristic for which detailed comparisons are presented is in the per cent in owner-occupied houses. On the basis of available data the sample proportion, 61.3 per cent, is very close to the nationwide metropolitan average of 61.8 per cent. And although national data are not available for central city and outside central city areas, it appears reasonable that the difference in the sample area data would hold up nationally.

The overall picture is thus of a sample very much in conformity with a priori considerations concerning the differences between the central city and outside central city areas and with the national averages taken as separate component areas or as metropolitanwide totals. What emerges is in general and in specific conformity with the general picture of the metropolitan areas, demonstrating the elements of difference between the central cities and outside central city areas, as well as the differences among central cities and among outside central city areas.

Government in Metropolitan Areas

Before turning to the analysis of the fiscal packages characteristic of the central city, outside central city areas, and metropolitan areas as a whole, it is necessary to make a brief survey of the local governmental systems that generate them. Unlike the socioeconomic characteristics, there is no relevant, typical system of local government providing services in metropolitan areas to which the sample areas may be compared. There are, however, basic groupings that provide a standard of reference.

As noted earlier, the emphasis in this analysis is on the systems of governments providing local services rather than on individual governments. First, there is no single local government encompassing any metropolitan area, either in the sample or in any of the areas excluded from the sample. The closest to this ideal type is Meriden, Conn., with one city and one independent special district. Further, there are few areas apart from such special cases as Meriden or Honolulu in which a single government is providing the entire range of local services to even a part of the entire metropolitan area (geographic but not functional fragmentation). Closest to this situation of general inclusive governments providing a full range of services to part of a metropolitan area are New England cities and towns. These jurisdictions have few, if any, overlying governments and comparatively few special disricts; the county is either nonexistent (as in Connecticut and Rhode Island) or unimportant and special districts are little used. There are also central cities with few or no overlying governments (New York City and Baltimore are examples) in which nearly the entire range of public services are performed by the city government.

Thus the Hartford and other Connecticut areas represent relatively simple governmental structures throughout their entire area because there are no governments overlying the basic city and town structure apart from a few special districts. The New England metropolitan area comes closest to the simple structure in which all local decisions are made by a single jurisdiction for a given area, although such areas are considerably smaller than the entire metropolitan area.

In outside central city areas the southern counties are, in fact, very like the New England towns in functional inclusiveness. Of the sample areas Baltimore City and several of the counties surrounding it approximate on much larger geographic scope the functional inclusiveness of the town system of New England. In addition to the inclusiveness of a single government such as New York City, there may be areas in which all the governments are conterminous. Hence New York City, Port of New York Authority, and the Waterfront Commission of New York Harbor all possess a single constituency, although the decision-making bodies are several in number.

Outside of these New England towns, southern counties, and a few central cities, the general characteristic of metropolitan areas is overlapping jurisdictions consisting of counties, school districts, municipalities, and special districts. The results are important spillovers as these jurisdictions share responsibility for the raising and spending of monies for some functions but not for others. The result may be the sharing of the cost of a service by a larger area than where the service is geographically concentrated. One example of this phenomenon

is where welfare services are performed by the county
The recipients may be heavily concentrated in the centra
city, whereas the service is supported countywide. Th
financing of highway services often has the opposite com
plexion. The service is concentrated outside the central cit
but the financing is shared by central city residents.

In the central city area the dominant governmental uni
throughout is the municipal government. Other than for th
usual overlying county, the central city generally has a
independent conterminous school district, but in a few impor
tant cases, such as New York City and Baltimore, the schoo
system is dependent. There are a few cases in which centra
cities directly provide services outside their boundaries.

Outside the central city the structure of government i
more complex. School districts and counties outside of Nev
England are the only "universals" involved. Municipal-typ
services are provided not only by municipalities and town
ships, but by counties and special districts as well. There are
with variations, two general patterns in the provision of th
municipal type of services; the first involves the municipalitie
and the second involves special districts in various combina
tions with towns and counties providing these services.

Tables 4-3 and 4-4 give some quantitative measure
through the use of fiscal data, of the degree of geographi
inclusiveness. Table 4-3 shows the degree of central cit
functional inclusiveness by showing the proportion of tota
local government expenditures made in the central city are
by the city government itself. The range is from around 9
per cent inclusiveness (Washington, Boston, and Baltimore
to a low of 29.5 per cent for Los Angeles.

Another way of examining the degree of geographi
inclusiveness is to measure the allocation of taxes to differer
governmental jurisdictions collected in a particular are
Table 4-4 provides such data for the cities, villages, an
urban towns of over 50,000 population in the New Yor

metropolitan area. In the most inclusive jurisdictions all taxes go to the general jurisdiction itself; in other cases it is divided among the jurisdictions operating in that area. As is shown in the geographic inclusive jurisdictions of Connecticut, all of

TABLE 4-3: *General Expenditures Per Capita in Central City Areas Made by the Central City Governments and Other Overlying Governments and Their Relative Proportions in the 24 Largest Metropolitan Areas, 1957*

City	Total general expenditures including overlying Governments in central city area (per capita)	Central city expenditures (per capita)	Central city expenditures as a per cent of total general expenditures in central city area (per cent)
Atlanta	$158	$ 72	56.6%
Baltimore	199	189	95.0
Boston	273	258	94.5
Buffalo	193	142	73.6
Chicago	203	96	47.3
Cincinnati	246	138	56.1
Cleveland	180	88	48.9
Dallas	175	86	49.1
Detroit	202	111	55.0
Houston	155	61	39.4
Kansas City	157	86	54.8
(Los Angeles)	261	77	29.5
(Long Beach)	320	122	38.1
Milwaukee	229	101	44.1
(Minneapolis)	182	80	44.0
(St. Paul)	189	125	66.1
New York	257	237	92.2
Newark	243	181	74.5
(Paterson)	160	132	82.5
(Clifton)	141	113	80.1
(Passaic)	166	138	83.1
Philadelphia	165	109	66.1
Pittsburgh	188	88	46.8
St. Louis	147	91	61.9
San Diego	191	65	34.0
(San Francisco)	218	146	67.0
(Oakland)	231	89	38.5
Seattle	174	73	42.0
Washington, D.C.	234	224	95.7

SOURCE: U. S. Bureau of the Census, *Local Government Finances in Standard Metropolitan Areas.* Vol. III, No. 6: *1957 Census of Governments* (Washington: U. S. Government Printing Office, 1959).

it goes to the municipality; in New York State it may all go to the municipality (New York City, since neither the Port Authority nor the Waterfront Commission has taxing powers) or may be shared by municipality, county, and school district.

TABLE 4-4: *Allocation Among Governmental Jurisdictions of Taxes Collected in Municipalities and Urban Townships of Over 50,000 Population in the New York Metropolitan Region, 1962*

	ALLOCATION OF TAXES COLLECTED IN THE MUNICIPALITIES AND URBAN TOWNSHIPS			Per capita total local
	Municipality	County	School district	taxes
Cities/Villages				
New York				
Mt. Vernon	44.1%	14.4%	41.5%	$163.42
New Rochelle	41.6	15.4	43.0	225.69
New York	100.0	—	—	219.87
White Plains	38.4	15.8	45.8	278.43
Yonkers	83.1	16.9	—	148.77
Connecticut				
Bridgeport	100.0	—	—	126.74
Norwalk	100.0	—	—	162.80
Stamford	100.0	—	—	192.55
New Jersey				
Bayonne	71.0	29.0	—	172.37
Clifton	77.3	22.8	—	139.08
East Orange	80.3	19.7	—	176.51
Elizabeth	89.1	10.9	—	144.15
Jersey City	82.4	17.6	—	191.47
Newark	85.2	14.8	—	194.89
Passaic	88.2	11.8	—	165.03
Paterson	88.5	11.5	—	130.95
Union	81.8	18.2	—	182.01
Urban Townships				
Connecticut				
Greenwich	100.0	—	—	221.76
New Jersey				
Bloomfield	74.9	25.0	—	167.34
Irvington	76.6	23.4	—	147.93
Union	23.7	19.9	56.5	155.50
Woodbridge	19.2	18.3	62.6	142.60

SOURCE: U. S. Bureau of the Census, *Compendium of City Government Finances in 1962.* (Washington: Government Printing Office, 1963). New Jersey Taxpayers Association, *Financial Statistics of New Jersey Local Government,* September 1962.

Central City—Outside Central City Fiscal Differences

Governmental fragmentation and overlapping makes difficult
the measurement of fiscal differences between central cities
and their outlying areas. Because many governments are usually
involved in both type areas, it is necessary to aggregate the
fiscal behavior of all the governments for each type of area.
Such aggregation, however, does not solve the entire problem
because some governments overlie all or parts of both central
cities and their outside areas. When such is the case, it is
necessary to allocate the fiscal output of the governments
between the two types of areas. In this analysis such allocation is done on the basis of population.

Such an allocation was made for this study of the 36 sample
areas already described (Table 4-5). Using the national
metropolitan fiscal characteristics as control totals, it is found
that the sample areas are quite close in their overall fiscal
behavior, as they are in their demographic and socioeconomic
characteristics.

Central city fiscal behavior differs from outside central city
behavior not only in the aggregate as measured by per capita
figures, but in the composition of the public services provided
as well. Metropolitan fiscal behavior shows very different
packages of public services for inside and outside the central
city areas.

As shown in Table 4-6, central city per capita expenditures
are $185.49, 16.04 per cent higher than the average of $159.83
for outside central city areas. Before examining this overall
difference in detail, it is useful to explore the similarities and
differences in the services provided in these two types of areas
(Table 4-7).

TABLE 4-5: *Fiscal Behavior of All SMSAs Compared to 36-SMSA
Sample, 1957*

Fiscal behavior (per capita)	National SMSA average	36-SMSAs sample average
Direct general		
Expenditures	$178.49	$172.63
Taxes	98.88	97.56
State aid	39.90	38.23

[117]

Specifically, the single most important function inside and outside the central city areas is education. However, in the outside central city areas it comprises 53.7 per cent of total expenditures, whereas in the central city areas it comprises but 31.3 per cent of the total local fiscal package. Or put in another way, noneducation expenses play a far more minor role in outside central city areas than is true in central cities.

This importance of noneducation functions in central cities is brought out even more when the three older highly aided functions—highways, health-hospitals (current), and public welfare—are excluded and the "all other" nonaided functions are analyzed. The striking similarity in the proportions for

TABLE 4-6: *Fiscal Characteristics of Central City and Outside Central City Areas, 36 Sample SMSAs, 1957*

Per capita	Central city	Outside central city	Differences CC-OCC
Total general expenditure	$185.49	$159.83	25.66*
Education expenditure	58.02	85.84	−27.82**
current	49.16	61.72	−12.56**
capital	8.86	24.12	−15.26**
Noneducation expenditure	127.48	73.95	53.53**
Total highways	16.55	14.41	2.14
Health and hospitals (current)	14.84	7.09	7.55**
Public welfare	10.22	8.34	1.88**
All other	85.70	43.80	41.90**
Taxes	109.07	85.78	23.29**
Property tax	92.06	78.58	13.48
Non-property tax	17.01	7.20	9.81**
Proxy variables			
Nonaided education exp. (education taxes)	42.24	56.43	−14.19**
Nonaided Noneducation exp. (noneducation taxes)	108.33	60.39	47.94**
Total aid	34.65	39.72	− 5.07
Education aid	16.12	28.43	−12.31**
Noneducation aid	18.60	11.83	6.77*
Exhibit:			
Per capita income	1,998.86	2,280.50	−281.64*

Notes: Totals do not add because of unallocated aid. All figures in per capita terms unless otherwise indicated.

* Significant at .05 level of confidence
** Significant at .01 level of confidence

highways and welfare brings into sharp focus the fact that the "all other" category makes up 46.2 per cent of all central city expenditures and only 27.4 per cent outside the central city.

Detailed data for these residual functions are not available, but it is clear that they include not only the general overhead, control, and interest on general debt categories, but the traditional municipal functions—police, fire, sewerage, refuse collection—as well. In addition, the new housing and urban renewal activities and a variety of commercial ventures not

TABLE 4-7: *Functional Expenditures and Revenues as a Per Cent of Total Expenditures; Central City as a Per Cent of Outside Central City for 36 SMSAs and Central City and Outside Central City Areas, 1957*

Function	SMSA	Central city	Outside central city	Central city as per cent of outside central city
Total direct general Expenditure, per capita	$172.63	$185.49	$159.83	116.05%
Total direct general Expenditure	100.0%	100.0%	100.0%	
Education Expenditure				
total	40.3	31.3	53.7	67.59
current	31.4	26.5	38.6	79.65
capital	8.9	4.8	15.1	36.73
Noneducation expenditure (total)	59.3	68.7	46.3	172.36
Total highways	9.5	8.9	9.0	114.80
Health-hospital (current)	6.6	8.0	4.4	114.85
Public welfare	15.6	8.5	5.2	122.54
All Other	37.5	46.2	27.4	195.36
Taxes (total)	56.5	58.8	53.7	127.10
Property	49.4	49.6	49.1	117.15
Nonproperty	7.1	9.2	4.5	236.25
State aid (total)	22.1	18.7	24.9	87.21
Education aid	12.9	8.7	17.7	56.70
Noneducation aid	9.3	10.0	7.4	157.22
Exhibit:				
Education aid/ education expenditure	32.0	27.8	33.1	
Noneducation aid/ noneducation expenditure	15.7	14.6	16.0	

Figures may not add because of rounding.

explicitly classified as utilities are involved. The relatively minor role of these activities in outside central city areas is consistent with the absence of municipal government or reasonable substitutes for it in some portions of outside central city areas. The causality, however, is not necessarily the lack of municipal jurisdictions for it may be that governments providing municipal-type services will come into being when the functions performed by these jurisdictions are needed.

For education, a function important to both types of areas, not only is the relative proportion much greater for outside central city areas, but the per capita amount is also significantly higher. The difference is due in about equal degree to current and capital expenditures. On a per student basis, however, the greater outside central city total education expenditures were due almost entirely to the capital portion of those expenditures; current education expenditures per student were actually slightly higher in central cities (Table 4-8).

If the per capita measure is taken roughly as an index of effort and the per student measure as an indicator of quality, the observed pattern indicates that at this point in time (1957) central city schools have a slightly higher quality of education but that the population outside the city is trying harder. The greater effort on the part of the outside city dwellers has generally been an effort to construct schools.

It must be emphasized that this finding is valid only at this point in time (1957). There is, in fact, reason to hypothesize that these patterns are undergoing rapid change. Central city expenditures per pupil (which have historically been higher) may be losing relative to that for outside central city schools. As the outside schools are built, resources are freed and are being devoted to current education expenditures as teachers are hired to complement the new buildings. Thus it can be

TABLE 4-8: *Education Expenditures and Aid Per Student in Central City and Outside Central City Areas of 36 SMSAs, 1957*

	Central city	Outside central city
Education expenditure per student	$366.17	$419.13
Current	312.27	303.17
Capital	53.90	114.86
Education aid per student	100.37	133.58

hypothesized that the observed 1957 pattern merely represents the point where the increasing expenditure curve of the outside central cities crossed the central city curve.

This hypothesis, implicit in the 1957 data, that central city schools are slipping behind their suburban neighbors is substantiated by 1962 data. Table 4-9 presents per pupil expenditures for the 37 largest metropolitan areas for which data are available. In only two cities (Detroit and Kansas City) do total per student expenditures in central cities exceed those in the outside central city areas, and in the case of current expenditures this situation is true for only five metropolitan areas (Detroit, New Orleans, Denver, Kansas City, and Rochester). On the average the differences are substantial; $144.96 for total expenditures per student and $65.66 for current expenditures.

In Table 5-1 noneducation expenditures show greater variation than those for education for both central city and outside central city areas. Where there is the possibility of direct state participation (welfare and hospitals, for example) the coefficients of variation are high with no basic difference in the relative variation in the two areas. However, the "all other" category appears to have much less variation than the other functions, even though it contains a very mixed combination of services. This combination of services varies much less than expected, both inside and outside central city areas.

Given the variation in each of the expenditure categories, are the differences between central city and outside central city areas significant in a statistical sense? On the basis of the 1957 average per capita total, expenditures in central cities, as compared to the outside areas as shown in Table 4-6, are significantly higher on .05 level of probability. However, as already implied this was due to the very different patterns of educational and noneducational expenditures. In the former case average outside central city expenditures were significantly higher both on a current basis and, to a greater extent, a capital basis. Indeed, total education expenditures were higher in outside central city areas in 32 of the 36 sample areas.

TABLE 4-9: *Total and Current Expenditures Per Pupil for Central Cities and Outside Central City Areas, 1961–62*

Cities	Total exp. per student -CC-	Total exp. per student -OCC-	Differ-ence	Current exp. per student -CC-	Current exp. per student -OCC-	Differ-ence
✓New York	$603.95	$869.32	− $265.37	$536.88	$684.34	− $147.36
✓Chicago	479.78	567.24	− 87.46	408.51	473.69	− 65.18
✓Los Angeles	482.62	802.88	− 320.26	437.14	554.54	− 117.40
✓Philadelphia	438.20	577.32	− 139.12	397.75	492.90	− 95.15
Detroit	543.81	528.50	+ 15.31	461.67	434.10	+ 27.57
✓Baltimore	431.95	577.28	− 145.33	366.07	427.61	− 55.54
Houston	290.62	555.25	− 264.63	290.09	450.35	− 160.26
Cleveland	412.70	585.21	− 177.51	370.59	459.50	− 88.91
✓St. Louis	391.33	527.68	− 136.35	386.58	423.73	− 37.15
Milwaukee	451.54	570.85	− 119.31	377.96	469.38	− 91.42
✓San Francisco	550.50	701.69	− 151.19	466.77	546.29	− 79.62
✓Boston	385.46	545.80	− 160.34	385.46	465.36	− 79.90
Dallas	383.36	445.60	− 62.34	301.96	325.40	− 23.44
New Orleans	278.89	341.66	− 62.77	271.87	233.05	+ 38.82
Pittsburgh	417.85	511.78	− 93.93	368.00	450.98	− 82.98
✓San Diego	547.65	697.98	− 150.33	414.63	538.95	− 124.32
Seattle	492.97	505.79	− 12.82	409.89	415.72	− 5.83
Buffalo	451.27	660.16	− 208.89	447.03	561.20	− 114.17
Cincinnati	411.16	745.91	− 334.75	373.11	577.74	− 204.63
Memphis	235.17	356.00	− 120.83	227.58	245.71	− 18.13
Denver	426.67	579.97	− 103.30	418.30	380.74	+ 37.56
Atlanta	276.86	352.63	− 75.77	272.52	287.80	− 15.28
Minneapolis	417.86	626.36	− 182.98	414.31	441.45	− 27.14
Indianapolis	365.29	650.24	− 284.95	352.87	467.92	− 115.05
✓Kansas City	468.23	460.94	+ 7.29	409.19	350.67	+ 58.52
Columbus	331.31	398.08	− 66.77	327.40	332.06	− 4.66
Newark	575.65	612.41	− 36.76	496.21	522.23	− 26.02
Louisville	301.46	658.04	− 356.58	301.44	477.73	− 176.29
Portland, O.	431.30	602.31	− 171.01	421.59	480.14	− 58.55
Long Beach	460.58	802.88	− 342.30	426.33	554.54	− 128.21
Birmingham	239.83	247.64	− 7.81	194.43	223.84	− 79.41
Oklahoma	279.33	367.88	− 88.55	269.23	291.67	− 22.44
Rochester	602.71	732.76	− 130.05	580.05	573.07	+ 6.98
Toledo	489.71	676.09	− 186.38	377.71	511.85	− 134.14
St. Paul	427.91	626.36	− 198.45	415.51	441.45	− 25.94
Norfolk	271.17	363.30	− 92.13	265.43	288.65	− 23.22
Omaha	293.08	522.74	− 229.66	282.58	394.90	− 112.32
Mean	414.46	559.42	− 144.96	376.33	441.99	− 65.66

SOURCE: Seymour Sacks and David Ranney, "Suburban Education: A Fiscal Analysis," *Urban Affairs Quarterly* (September, 1966). (Revised)

The opposite is true of noneducation expenditures; the central city area governments spent a significantly higher amount than the outside central city areas in 35 of the 36 areas. Because higher expenditures are not the case for the highway and welfare functions, the differences apart from those associated with health and hospitals were in the "all other" category. This last category contains the same functions that showed large expenditure differences between metropolitan and non-metropolitan areas—i.e., police, fire, refuse collection, parks and recreation, housing and urban renewal, airports, and other miscellaneous activities.

The financing of the expenditures also shows considerable difference between the two types of area. Taxes in central cities are significantly higher than in outside central city areas. About half of the $24 difference is accounted for by the much greater use of nonproperty taxes in central cities, whereas the higher property tax levels in the central city were a function, in part, of the greater relative importance of nonaided functions in the cities and the smaller amount of state aid.

This ability of central cities to sustain higher property tax levies with lower income levels brings the analysis to its most important omission, one typical of nearly all studies of this type: the exclusion of relevant (property) tax base data. It is the general contention of this study that the multiple correlation and regression analysis will have an upper limit insofar as it can explain variations in fiscal behavior because of this necessary omission. Income and tax base data become less related the smaller the governmental unit of analysis.

Although comprehensive data on the tax base are not available, the central cities have apparently been able to tap nonresidential property tax bases to a much greater extent than the communities surrounding them. Very rough guesses based on a small sample indicate that the residential proportion of the property tax base may average around 55 per cent in central city areas and 72 per cent in outside central city areas.

This difference means that cities are obtaining more of their locally raised revenues from nonresidential properties than the outside central city areas are. As a result the relationship between taxes and income may not be as different between these two types of area as it appears, if only taxes paid on residential property are taken into account.

Just as taxes are higher in central cities than outside, state aid is lower; total state aid is $5.09 per capita less in central cities. The underlying components of this difference are made clear when aid is separated into its parts, education and non-education. This division of aid, done for the first time in this study, provides an improved basis for understanding the role of aid in the fiscal systems of these two type areas. Education aid to outside central city areas is $12.31 per capita higher than to central cities, whereas the central cities receive $6.71 more per capita than their outlying areas for noneducation functions

Summary

The picture that emerges from this analysis is one of substantial differences between the central city and outside central city areas, both in their socioeconomic characteristics and in their fiscal responses. The governmental structure of central cities reflects both their needs as municipalities and the dominance of traditional municipal services. In outside central city areas municipal-type services play absolutely and relatively a smaller role, and the heavy concentration on education in these areas is demonstrated.

The meaning of metropolitan area finances now comes more clearly into focus. The differences in fiscal totals are the result of two divergent patterns of services. The fiscal dynamics of the two component areas were not different in 1957 and 1962 and later data indicates that there have been no major changes except that the differences in education expenditures are probably becoming greater. The next step in the analysis is to determine the factors responsible for the variation between and among the central cities, outside central cities, and among metropolitan areas.

References

1. Charles M. Tiebout, "A Pure Theory of Local Expenditures," *Journal of Political Economy*, LIV (October 1956), 416–424.
2. *Ibid.*, 418.
3. Harvey E. Brazer, "Some Fiscal Implications of Metropolitanism," in *Metropolitan Issues: Social, Governmental, Fiscal*, ed. Guthrie S. Birkhead, (Maxwell Graduate School, February 1962), 65–66.
4. David Davies, "Financing Urban Functions and Services," *Law and Contemporary Problems*, XXX (Winter 1965), 137.
5. For example, see Robert C. Wood, *Suburbia* (Boston: Houghton Mifflin Company, 1959); William M. Dobriner, *Class in Suburbia* (Englewood Cliffs: Prentice-Hall, Inc., 1963), and *The Suburban Community* (New York: G. P. Putnam's Sons, 1958); William H. Whyte, Jr., *The Organization Man* (New York: Doubleday Book Co., 1956); J. R. Seeley, R. A. Sems and E. W. Loosley, *Crestwood Heights* (New York: John Wiley & Sons, 1956).
6. Edgar Hoover and Raymond Vernon, *The Anatomy of a Metropolis* (Garden City, N.Y.: Doubleday Cook Co., 1962); Edgar Hoover, *Region in Transition* (Pittsburgh: University of Pittsburgh Press, 1963); Benjamin Chinitz, *City and Suburb* (Pittsburgh: University of Pittsburgh Press, 1964); Raymond Vernon, *Metropolis 1985* (Garden City, N.Y.: Doubleday Book Co., 1962).
7. Raymond Vernon, *The Changing Economic Functions of the Central City* (Committee for Economic Development, New York), and "Production and Distribution in the Large Metropolis," Annals, CCCXIV, (November 1957), 15–30.
8. *American Community Development*. Preliminary Reports by Directors of Projects Assisted by the Ford Foundation in Four Cities and a State. (Ford Foundation, 1963), 7.

9. G. Ross Stephens and Henry J. Schmandt, "Revenue Patterns of Local Governments," *National Tax Journal*, XV (December 1962), 432–437.

10. *Ibid.*, 435.

11. *Ibid.*, 435.

12. See also, Harvey Shapiro, "Economies of Scale and Local Government Finance," *Land Economics* (May 1963), 175–186.

CHAPTER 5

The Determinants of Metropolitan Fiscal Behavior

The central focus of this study is on the determinants of the fiscal behavior of local governments in metropolitan areas. In the last chapter emphasis was placed on the patterns of fiscal behavior; in this chapter the emphasis will be on the determinants of that behavior. Not only is considerable variation found within each of the classes of units analyzed (central cities, outside central cities, and metropolitan areas taken as a whole), but there are significant differences between the central city and outside central city areas as well. The purpose of this chapter is to analyze in a comparable and systematic fashion the determinants of the variations in fiscal behavior among the units within each class—central city, outside central city, and metropolitan areas as a whole—and to analyze the determinants of the differences in fiscal behavior between the central cities and their outside areas.

This effort to generalize about metropolitan fiscal behavior has not been tried before. The bulk of the work about metropolitan fiscal behavior that has been done to date can be divided into two kinds: *a.* those studies dealing with specific metropolitan areas, and *b.* those concerned with certain classes of governmental jurisdictions—i.e., cities, school districts, and so on. Most, if not all, fiscal analyses of individual metropolitan areas are restricted to the area being analyzed; the findings have not been tested to determine whether they can be generalized. It is fair, however, to assume that they cannot be generalized beyond the borders of the state in which the metropolitan area being analyzed is located, unless expenditure and tax assignment systems are taken into account. However, they are useful from an heuristic point of view as is indicated by the work done on the San Francisco,[1] St. Louis,[2] Cleveland,[3] Hartford,[4] Philadelphia,[5] and New York Metropolitan Areas.[6]

Analyses that have covered specific types of jurisdiction include studies of cities,[7] counties,[8] and school districts.[9]

In this analysis a group of independent variables has been selected for intensive analysis. These variables are tested relative to specific dependent fiscal variables for each type of area within metropolitan areas—i.e., central cities and outside central cities—and for entire metropolitan areas. As in the analysis of metropolitan and nonmetropolitan portions of the states, the aim is to see how given variables operate in different areas. An attempt to maintain a continuity with the previously used variables has been made, but it has been necessary to drop some entirely (such as urbanization and federal aid), to modify others (the substitution, for example, of a welfare dummy variable for the expenditure and tax assignment variables),[10] and to introduce a number of variables considered specifically applicable to each type area.

The second part of this chapter will stress the factors that determine the differences in the fiscal behavior of the central cities and their own outside areas. This approach stresses the relationships, not between like areas such as central cities, outside central cities, and entire metropolitan areas, but rather the effects of differences in income, state aid, the relative size of the central city, and a few other variables on the observed differences in fiscal behavior between central cities and the rest of their own metropolitan area.

Relating the first and second parts of this chapter are a set of fiscal variables whose dual role has not been adequately recognized. These variables, although they are considered as dependent for a given area, may act as independent variables for another part of the same area or for another fiscal variable in the same area. Thus, the effect of education on noneducation expenditures within a given area may be studied. So may the effect of the reverse. Finally, relating the component parts to the total, the effects of education expenditures outside the central city on that of the central city may be traced, as may that of the noneducation expenditures. It might be contended that both are a function of a common set of factors; however the results are sufficiently at variance with that contention to require their explicit introduction into the analysis.

The Dependent Variables

The dependent variables with which some combination of the independent variables just described are tested for the 36 sample Standard Metropolitan Statistical Areas and their component parts, sample Central Cities (CC) and sample Outside Central Cities (OCC) are as follows:

a. Per capita total direct general expenditures (P. C. Total Exp.)

b. Per capita total education expenditures (P. C. Ed. Exp.)

c. Per capita total noneducation expenditures (P. C. Non-Ed. Exp.)

d. Per capita total taxes (P. C. Total Taxes)

and the following tax proxy variables:

e. Per capita total nonaided education expenditure (this variable may be used as a proxy for local school taxes) (P. C. Ed. Taxes)

f. Per capita total nonaided noneducation expenditures
this variable is used as a proxy for local nonschool taxes)
(P. C. Non-Ed. Taxes).

The relationships to be examined in this chapter are shown
in Table 5-1. The variance explained in the first part of the
chapter is shown in the coefficients of variation in the first
three columns of the table. The fourth column gives the
coefficient of variations for all SMSAs in 1962. The remarkable
similarity between these and the coefficients for the 36-area
sample for 1957 gives further evidence of the stability over
time of the relationships being analyzed.

The division of expenditures into education and noneducation categories, as well as the effort to get at the local
division in taxes for these two broad categories, is designed
to divide the expenditures of local governments into their
most meaningful categories. Education and noneducation

TABLE 5-1: *Coefficients of Variation and Differences, Selected Fiscal
Variables Central City, Outside Central City, and Standard Metropolitan
Statistical Areas, 1957*

	COEFFICIENTS OF VARIATION (PER CAPITA)			
	(36-AREA SAMPLE)			
Per Capita:	SMSA	CC	OCC	All SMSAs: 1962
General expenditures (a)	21.28%	20.97%	29.11%	28.15%
Education (b)	24.50	19.99	30.28	26.98
Education excluding capital	20.43	17.37	36.18	24.76
Noneducation (c)	28.80	26.97	48.58	37.08
Highway	42.02	46.89	54.82	54.06
Health and hospitals	52.75	68.32	64.60	125.88
Public welfare	92.28	89.23	97.48	116.49
All other expenditures	27.95	25.38	45.12	n.c.
Taxes (d)	30.45	30.53	42.16	38.85
Proxy variables				
Nonaided education (education taxes)	32.85	27.96	45.13	n.a.
Nonaided Noneducation (noneducation taxes)	25.59	26.96	44.18	n.a.
Total state aid	54.77	51.41	58.03	54.79
Education aid	59.87	48.32	62.18	n.a.
Noneducation aid	90.33	81.24	98.48	n.a.

SOURCE: Appendix B.

expenditures are quite different from central city to central city and between central cities and their outside areas. Education expenditures, for example, made up 33.3 per cent of total expenditures in central city areas in 1957 as compared to 53.7 per cent in the areas outside central cities. Nonaided education expenditures, the proxy for education taxes, are 28 per cent of total taxes in central cities and 48 per cent in the outside central city areas.

The Independent Variables

Insofar as possible the independent variables used throughout this study will also be employed in this chapter, with some additions for specific types of areas and specific independent variables. Income and state aid are used throughout and need no further explanation except to point out that education and noneducation aid variables appropriate to the dependent variable are used as required. Education aid, for example, is used for analyzing both educational expenditures and education taxes, whereas noneducation aid is used with its appropriate expenditure and tax variables.

A new variable introduced in this part of the analysis is one that indicates whether welfare is a local or state function. Welfare can be divided this way because it is predominantly performed by either the state or local level of government and serves, therefore, as a substitute for the assignment variables used in the state-local and local analyses. This substitution of the welfare dummy for the assignment variable is made necessary by the impossibility of computing an exact assignment variable on less than a statewide basis. The usefulness of average statewide expenditure or tax assignment variable is reduced somewhat for part of a state because it is likely that assignment varies from one part of a state to another. The use of a statewide average assignment, therefore, might be quite far off the mark for any specific central city/outside central city area, or even for an entire metropolitan area. Welfare, on the other hand, is either a state or local expenditure responsibility throughout a state, and it plays a large role in determining the overall assignment proportion.[11]

Welfare assignment is conceptually, therefore, a better variable for determining the impact of differences in assignment on less than a statewide basis. Despite this conceptual advantage it should be noted that the assignment and welfare variable were tested in regression runs and were found to play substantially the same roles.

Another characteristic of the welfare assignment variable must also be taken into account in interpreting its impact on fiscal variations. Because welfare is a highly aided function, it follows that these two variables—state aid, particularly the noneducation portion thereof, and welfare assignment—will interact in a way that necessitates their being interpreted together. When welfare is assigned to local jurisdictions, it is invariably highly aided by the state, with considerable amounts of this aid coming in the first instance from the federal government and being passed on by the state to its local jurisdictions. In other words, when welfare is assigned to local government, it inevitably follows that substantial welfare aid, even if this only means the channeling of federal aid, will also be received by those governmental units (counties, municipalities) performing the welfare function. These variables, therefore, will act together, and probably in the same direction. Since there is usually substantial aid provided to local governments for purposes other than welfare, both the aid and welfare assignment variables must be used.

Another new variable introduced in this part of the analysis is the proportion of education expenditures in the total expenditures. As has already been pointed out, this proportion is one of the striking differences between central cities and outside central city areas. Those few central cities with a high proportion of their expenditures devoted to education are more like their outside areas than is the case of those cities where this is not the situation. In other words, this variable may be interpreted as a proxy measure of the suburban characteristics of the central city areas.

Political scientists have frequently suggested that home ownership tends to hold down tax levels, particularly at the local level, where property taxes· predominate. To test this proposition, the proportion of owner-occupied housing units in the total housing units is introduced as an explicit variable. It is assumed that its relationship with expenditures and taxes will be negative. The variable is only used to test central city fiscal behavior because it has very little variance in the outside central city areas.

Another variable introduced into the analysis at this point is the rural proportion of the population outside central cities. The Census Bureau's definition of SMSAs makes it inevitable, because of the use of entire counties for defining metropolitan areas, that some rural population will be included in most metropolitan areas. Because it is anticipated that the fiscal patterns of these rural portions of metropolitan areas will be more like nonmetropolitan areas than their suburban neighbors, it is necessary to take account of this dichotomy within the outside central city areas. The variable used is the proportion of rural population in the total outside central city population. On a nationwide basis the average percentage of population in the rural farm and rural nonfarm categories in metropolitan areas outside central cities is approximately 25 per cent. For the outside central city areas of the 36 sample metropolitan areas used in this study the rural portion varies from none in the Jersey City area to over 50 per cent in the Memphis and Utica-Rome metropolitan areas. The average pattern of the 36-area sample is summarized by the mean value of 25.7 per cent, which is almost exactly the national average for outside central city areas.

Finally, a set of variables designed to determine the

relationship of one category of expenditures or taxes to another is used. The effort is to determine the extent to which the level of noneducation expenditures per capita, for example, influences the levels of per capita education expenditures in the same type area. For each dependent variable an independent variable of this kind is used to check the interrelationship between the broad functional categories of education and noneducation on both the expenditure and tax sides.

The interrelationships between these independent and dependent variables will be examined for each dependent fiscal variable in turn. In each case the impact of the various independent variables on the dependent variables will be examined for each type area—entire SMSAs, central cities, and outside central city areas.

The presentation for each independent variable will follow the same format. First, the hypothesis made about the relationship of each relevant independent variable to the dependent variable under examination for each type area is presented: central city, outside central city area, and entire SMSA. Following this set of hypotheses the estimating equation showing the actual relationships is given. This equation is then followed by a brief statement of the most significant findings for that fiscal variable.[12]

Per Capita Total General Expenditures

The model used to explain variations in per capita total direct general expenditure for the sample central city, outside central city, and SMSAs is basically the same throughout. This model is in essence the same as that used in explaining variation in metropolitan and nonmetropolitan expenditures with the substitution of the welfare dummy for the expenditure assignment variable. The differential effect on the correlation of education expenditures as a proportion of total expenditures is examined, as is the impact of the proportion of owner-occupied housing. Finally, the per cent of population outside the central city living in rural areas is introduced as an explicit variable.

The signs of the coefficients of the independent variables as they are expected in the final regression equations for each dependent variable in each area are shown in the text table at the beginning of each section. For 36 observations, given five variables, there are 29 degrees of freedom. To be significant at the five per cent level, the regression coefficient must be 2.045 times the standard error; to be significant at the o.1 level it must be 2.756 times its standard error.[13] The hypotheses with respect to per capita total general expenditures (P. C. Exp.), 1957, are in Table 5 - H1.

TABLE 5 - H1.

	Per capita income	Per capita total state aid	Welfare dummy	Ed. exp. as per cent of total Expenditures	Per cent housing owner-occupied	Per cent OCC population rural
Central city	+	+	+	0	0	
Outside CC	+	+	+	0		−
SMSA	+	+	+	0	0	

The estimating equations for this variable are as follows:

P. C. Exp. (CC)   = + .036* P. C. Income
               (.014)
           + .755* P. C. State Aid
               (.350)
           + 20.43 Welfare Dummy
               (11.63
           − 1.29 Education as Per Cent
               (.878)   Total Expenditures
           − 1.00* Per Cent Housing
               (.474)   Owner-Occupied
           + 167.20

$$\bar{R} = .831 \qquad \bar{R}^2 = .690$$

$$P. C. Exp. (OCC) = + .025^{**} \text{ P. C. Income}$$
$$(.007)$$
$$+ 1.111^{*} \text{ P. C. State Aid}$$
$$(.245)$$
$$+ 26.28 \text{ Welfare Dummy}$$
$$(12.98)$$
$$- .002 \text{ Education Exp. Per Cent}$$
$$(.050) \qquad \text{Total Expenditures}$$
$$- .760^{*} \text{ Rural Population Per Cent}$$
$$(.339) \qquad \text{Outside Central City}$$
$$\text{Population}$$
$$+ 76.90$$
$$\bar{R} = .883 \qquad \bar{R}^2 = .779$$

$$P. C. Exp. (SMSA) = + .036^{**} \text{ P. C. Income}$$
$$(.007)$$
$$+ .846^{**} \text{ P. C. Total Aid}$$
$$(.196)$$
$$+ 25.03^{**} \text{ Welfare Dummy}$$
$$(8.75)$$
$$- .743 \text{ Education Exp. Per Cent}$$
$$(.508) \qquad \text{Total Expenditures}$$
$$- 1.010^{*} \text{ Per Cent Housing}$$
$$(.393) \qquad \text{Owner-Occupied}$$
$$+ 143.55$$
$$\bar{R} = .911 \qquad \bar{R}^2 = .830$$

Once again the asterisks indicate significance, * at the .05 level, ** at the .01 level.

Using virtually the same model, the total explanatory power of all these variables acting together is greatest for the SMSAs as a whole and lowest for central cities. In part, this result is assumed to be due to the technical problem of allocating expenditures of overlying governments to the component parts of each metropolitan area. The use of population proportions for such allocation undoubtedly overstates and understates, depending on the function that must be allocated to each of the parts. There is not, however, any single allocation device that could do the job better.

Income is more important to variations of outside central city areas than it is for variations among central cities. Aid is important in both places. The proportion of education expenses to total expenditures is significant in central cities but not outside these cities. In both central cities and outside central city areas (but primarily in the former) there is a negative relationship between the level of total expenditures and the educational proportion. This decrease in total expenditures as the education proportion increases is indicative of an interrelationship between education and noneducation expenditures in central cities. As the proportion of education expenditures increases, noneducation expenses decrease.

These findings contain no major surprises and are consistent with the hypothesis. The forces influencing variations in total per capita expenditures are not substantially different among the component parts of metropolitan areas. Variations among outside central city areas can be more completely explained than those among central cities, but the difference in the former is not great. In large part, the same forces apparently are operative in both type areas and therefore for entire metropolitan areas.

Per Capita Education Expenditures

As has been noted throughout this study, by far the largest component of local expenditures are those made for education. In both cities and outside central cities educational expenditures are larger than those for any other function, and in many outside central city areas educational expenditures amount to more than those for all other functions combined. There is, nevertheless, a considerable amount of variations among both central cities and outside central city areas in these expenditures measured in per capita terms.

The hypotheses with respect to per capita education expenditures (P. C. Ed. Exp.), 1957, are in Table 5 - H2.

TABLE 5 - H2.

	Income	Education aid	Per cent housing owner-occupied	Non-education expenditures	Public school enroll-ment ratio	Per cent population rural OCC
Central city	+	+	+	−		
Outside CC	+	+		−		−
SMSA	+	+			−	

The estimating equations for this are as follows:

P. C. Ed. Exp. (CC) $= .020^{**}$ P. C. Income
(.005)

$+ .421^{*}$ P. C. Education Aid
(.194)

$+ .131$ Per Cent Housing
(.154) Owner-Occupied

$+ .079$ P. C. Noneducation
(.051) Expenditures in
Central Cities

$- 4.46$
$\bar{R} = .727$ $\bar{R}^2 = .529$

P. C. Ed. Exp. (OCC) $= .022^{**}$ P. C. Income
(.005)

$+ .876^{**}$ P. C. Education Aid
(.209)

$- .051$ Rural Population
(.265) Proportion Outside
Central Population

$$+ .083 \text{ Outside Central}$$
$$(.117) \quad \text{Noneducation}$$
$$\text{Expenditures}$$

$$+ 6.41$$
$$\bar{R} = .746 \qquad \bar{R}^2 = .556$$

$$\text{P. C. Ed. Exp. (SMSA)} = + .024^{**} \text{ P. C. Income}$$
$$(.004)$$

$$+ .750^{**} \text{ P. C. Education Aid}$$
$$(.160)$$

$$+ .027 \text{ Enrollment ratio}$$
$$(.086)$$

$$- 4.89$$
$$\bar{R} = .789 \qquad \bar{R}^2 = .621$$

The total explanatory power of these variables in combination for per capita education expenditures is less for each type of area than it is for total expenditures in like areas. The overall lower explanatory power in the case of education expenditures is probably due to the omission of a variable of particular relevance to the education functions—perhaps ethnic composition. Income is significant throughout, reflecting its influence on both the demand and supply side.

In relation to the hypothesis it is clear that education aid is more significant and important in the outside central city areas than it is in central cities. This finding is undoubtedly related to variations in the much larger amounts of aid these areas receive than central cities do. As expected, the proportion rural in the outside central city areas does not affect education expenditures as strongly as it does total expenditures.

Of particular interest is the role of owner-occupied housing. In the case of total expenditures the influence of this variable is to hold down expenditures; not so with education expenditures, where the variable is not negative, but rather more in accord with the original null hypothesis.[14]

Another variable of interest but used only in the regression for the entire SMSA sample is the enrollment ratio—i.e., the proportion of students in the public schools as a proportion of total population. Contrary to expectations this variable does not show a relationship of any significance with per capita expenditures for education for any of the type areas under analysis. For each of the areas neither the age distribution nor private school enrollment reduces the per capita expenditures for the public schools. Other studies of educational expenditures being done at the Metropolitan Studies Center of Syracuse University do indicate that there is a positive relationship between proportion of students in private schools and expenditures *per student* in the public schools.[15]

Noneducation Expenditures Per Capita

Noneducational expenditures show much greater relative variation than do educational expenditures, a result that is partly a function of the differential assignment of the welfare function. Thus, while the standard deviations are about the same the coefficients of variations are vastly different because the remainder of the noneducation package differs so greatly.

As is indicated in the statement of the hypothesis, the income variable is not considered in this case. Its exclusion is based on the hypothesis that it is of negligible importance. This was brought out by simple correlations of + .105 for central cities, + .231 for outside central cities, and + .099 for SMSAs. Instead, a number of other variables were introduced. These are summarized in the text table below. The hypotheses with respect to per capita noneducation expenditures (P. C. Non-Ed. Exp.), 1957, are in Table 5-H3.

TABLE 5-H3.

	Per capita income	Per capita non-ed. aid	Welfare dummy	Per cent housing owner-occupied	Per cent rural pop. outside CC	Per capita ed. expenditures	Per capita non-ed. expenditures
Central city	n.c.	+	+	−		−	+(OCC)
Outside CC	n.c.	+	+		−	−	+(CC)
SMSA	n.c.	+	+	0			

The estimating equations for this variable are:

$$\text{P. C. Non-Ed. Exp. (CC)} = \underset{(.314)}{1.069^{**}} \text{ P. C. Non-Ed. Aid}$$

$$- \underset{(12.16)}{5.26} \text{ Welfare Dummy}$$

$$- \underset{(.317)}{1.189^{**}} \text{ Per Cent Housing Owner-Occupied}$$

$$+ \underset{(.174}{.424^{**}} \text{ P. C. Non-ed. Expenditures (OCC)}$$

$$+ \underset{(.306)}{.293} \text{ P. C. Ed. Exp. (CC)}$$

$$+ 119.82$$

$$\bar{R} = .868 \qquad \bar{R}^2 = .753$$

$$\text{P. C. Non-Ed. Exp. (OCC)} = \underset{(.339)}{.249} \text{ P. C. Non-Ed. Aid}$$

$$+ \underset{(8.91)}{24.10^{*}} \text{ Welfare Dummy}$$

$$- \underset{(.170)}{.475^{**}} \text{ Per Cent of Population Rural}$$

$$+ \underset{(.110)}{.345^{**}} \text{ P. C. Non-Ed. Exp. (CC)}$$

$$+ \underset{(.114)}{.155} \text{ P. C. Ed. Exp. (OCC)}$$

$$+ 13.03$$

$$\bar{R} = .885 \qquad \bar{R}^2 = .783$$

$$\text{P. C. Non-Ed. Exp. (SMSA)} = \underset{(.006)}{.006} \text{ P. C. Income}$$

$$+ \underset{(.260)}{.852^{**}} \text{ P. C. Non-Ed. Aid}$$

$$+ 22.53^{**} \text{ Welfare Dummy}$$
$$(.767)$$

$$- 1.328 \text{ Per Cent Housing}$$
$$(.3073) \quad \text{Owner-Occupied}$$

$$+ 146.36$$
$$\bar{R} = .876 \qquad \bar{R}^2 = .768$$

The rather high overall explanatory power of these variables for noneducation expenditures is rather surprising since these are made up of quite different baskets of services from place to place. It is interesting, too, that high results were obtained even with income excluded as a variable.

Most significant of the variables are noneducation aid and the welfare dummy, which, as already explained, do interact. It is their combined influence that must be taken into account. Of particular interest, too, is the role of owner-occupied housing in central cities. There is clearly a dampening influence on noneducation expenditures as the proportion of home ownership increases.

Total Taxes Per Capita

Although per capita income was excluded in the analysis of the total noneducation combination its inclusion in the analysis of total taxes is a necessity. Underlying the analysis of taxation is the question of its relationship to income. At this point the regrettable, but necessary, omission of the property tax base as an explicit variable must be noted. It is assumed that a considerable unexplained variance is attributable to the lack of a property tax base variable. The hypotheses with respect to per capita total taxes, 1957, are in Table 5 - H4.

TABLE 5 - H4.

	Per capita income	Per capita state aid	Welfare dummy	Per cent housing owner-occupied	Per cent population rural: OCC
Central cities	+	−	+	−	
Outside CC	+	−	+		−
SMSA	+	−	+	−	

The estimating equations for this variable are as follows:

P. C. Taxes (CC) $= + .036^{**}$ P. C. Income
$\qquad$ (.011)
$\qquad$ $- .481$ P. C. State Aid
$\qquad$ (.267)
$\qquad$ $+ 35.584^{**}$ Welfare Dummy
$\qquad$ (9.534)
$\qquad$ $- 1.488^{**}$ Per Cent Housing
$\qquad$ (.312) $\quad$ Owner-Occupied
$\qquad$ $+ 106.49$
$$\bar{R} = .836 \qquad \bar{R}^2 = .699$$

P. C. Taxes (OCC) $= + .026^{**}$ P. C. Income
$\qquad$ (.006)
$\qquad$ $- .053$ P. C. State Aid
$\qquad$ (.197)
$\qquad$ $+ 32.966^{**}$ Welfare Dummy
$\qquad$ (8.742)
$\qquad$ $- .687^{*}$ Per Cent Population Rural
$\qquad$ (.264)
$\qquad$ $+ 29.49$
$$\bar{R} = .862 \qquad \bar{R}^2 = .744$$

P. C. Taxes (SMSA) $= + .035^{**}$ P. C. Income
$\qquad$ (.005)
$\qquad$ $- .361^{*}$ P. C. State Aid
$\qquad$ (.160)
$\qquad$ $+ 39.313^{**}$ Welfare Dummy
$\qquad$ (6.680)
$\qquad$ $- 1.178^{**}$ Per Cent Housing
$\qquad$ (.291) $\quad$ Owner-Occupied
$\qquad$ $+ 88.03$
$$\bar{R} = .905 \qquad \bar{R}^2 = .819$$

Because of the importance to local expenditures of inter-governmental flow of funds it follows that taxes raised locally should be more closely related to specific community characteristics than expenditures are. Further, it is assumed that aid will tend to be negatively related to local taxes because external funds should hold down the need for locally-raised revenues.

Personal income, a *local* characteristic, is highly significant for all types of areas in explaining variations in per capita taxes, but aid is only weakly associated with taxes. This finding about aid substantiates the characteristic of aid already found in the analysis of local and state-local fiscal levels. It dampens very little, if at all, local tax effort.

As anticipated, the proportion of owner-occupied housing in central cities and in entire SMSAs is negatively associated with local taxes. The same is true in the outside central city for the proportion of population, that is rural.

Per Capita Education Taxes (Proxy)

Total taxes, like expenditures, may be divided into groups: those for education and those for noneducation purposes. Direct information for taxes by purpose is obscured by the fact that in a number of instances the education function is carried on by a general purpose government. To deal with the problem it was necessary to develop an indirect measure of education taxes, and nonaided education expenditure was chosen as this measure. In a similar way noneducation taxes were also computed. Underlying the separate treatment of education taxes is the hypothesis that they are very highly related to income, perhaps more so than any other fiscal variable analyzed.

Perhaps even more significantly, it is assumed that the effects of state aid may be more clearly seen if the aid can be related to the purposes for which it is used. Thus, it is hypo-

hesized that education aid should lead to a significant reduc-
ion in local taxes for education. Further, it is assumed that
unlike taxes devoted to noneducation purposes, education
axes should be unrelated to the proportion of owner-
occupied housing.

Also introduced into the analysis at this time are the taxes
or noneducation purposes for the same types of area. Here,
he hypothesis is that on the tax side educational taxes are
alternatives for noneducation taxes and vice versa. Hence,
a negative sign is anticipated in the case of the noneducation
expenditures. The hypotheses with respect to per capita
education taxes (P. C. Ed. Taxes), 1957, are in Table 5 - H5.

TABLE 5 - H5.

	Income	Education aid	Proportion owner-occupied	Enrollment ratio	Noneducation taxes
Central city	+	−	0		− (CC)
Outside CC	+	−	0		− (OCC)
SMSA	+	−		+	

The estimating equations for this variable areas follows:

P. C. Ed. Taxes (CC) = .020** P. C. Income
$\qquad$ (.005)
$\qquad$ − .536* P. C. Ed. Aid
$\qquad$ (.203)
$\qquad$ + .218 Per Cent Housing
$\qquad$ (.185) Owner-Occupied
$\qquad$ + .119 P. C. Non-Ed. Taxes
$\qquad$ (.073) (CC)
$\qquad$ − 13.47
$\qquad\qquad \bar{R} = .687 \qquad \bar{R}^2 = .471$

P. C. Ed. Taxes (OCC) = .023** P. C. Income
$\qquad$ (.005)
$\qquad$ − .180 P. C. Ed. Aid
$\qquad$ (.193)

$$+ .427 \text{ Per Cent Owner-}$$
$$(.364) \quad \text{Occupied}$$
$$+ .059 \text{ P. C. Non-Ed. Taxes}$$
$$(.138) \quad \text{(OCC)}$$
$$- 26.11$$
$$\bar{R} = .733 \qquad \bar{R}^2 = .537$$

$$\text{P. C. Ed. Taxes (SMSA)} = \quad .025^{**} \text{ P. C. Income}$$
$$(.004)$$
$$- .265 \text{ P. C. Ed. Aid}$$
$$(.148)$$
$$+ .130 \text{ Enrollment Ratio}$$
$$(.789)$$
$$- 2.71$$
$$\bar{R} = .784 \qquad \bar{R}^2 = .615$$

Education taxes are more highly correlated with income than any other fiscal variable. Apparently in this instance income is not only a measure of the availability of resources for this function, but perhaps even more clearly a measure of the demand for it. Education aid does apparently hold down, to a limited extent, education taxes in central cities but possesses an insignificant influence in outside central city areas and for SMSAs as a whole.

As hypothesized, proportion of home ownership has little influence on education taxes. The significance of this variable obviously lies with its negative effect on the noneducation functions of government.

The hypothesis that education taxes would move inversely with noneducation taxes has not been substantiated; although not significant, it is nevertheless positive in both the central city and outside central city areas. There apparently is no significant relationship between these two sides of the public finance equation on the tax side. This generalization may somewhat overstate the case for central cities, where it appears that the relationship between education and noneducation taxes is positive but weak in contrast to the hypothesized negative relationship.

Per Capita Noneducation Taxes (Proxy)

This tax variable is the noneducation counterpart of the education tax proxy. In this case two additional independent variables are used in the analysis. A dummy variable representing the South is added because it is known that for outside central cities in the South very few noneducation municipal-type services are provided.

The other new variable is the education tax proxy. The substitute ability of one kind of tax for another is tested by this variable. It is hypothesized that high education taxes will act to hold down noneducation taxes.

The hypothesis about aid is based on the proposition that external funds will make it possible for jurisdictions to reduce their dependence on their own tax resources.

The hypotheses with respect to per capita noneducation taxes (P. C. Non-Ed. Taxes) are in Table 5 - H6.

TABLE 5 - H6.

	Per capita income	Per capita noneducation aid	South, non-South dummy	Density	Education tax proxy
Central city	+	−	−	+	− (CC)
Outside CC	+	−	−	+	− (OCC)
SMSA	+	−	−	+	− (SMSA)

The estimating equations for this variable are as follows:

$$\text{P. C. Non-Ed. Taxes (CC)} = -.006 \text{ P. C. Income}$$
$$(.016)$$
$$- 1.487^{**} \text{ Per Cent}$$
$$(.448) \text{ Housing Owner-Occupied}$$

$$+ .329 \text{ P. C. Non-Ed.}$$
$$(.285) \quad \text{Aid}$$
$$- 4.69 \text{ Regional Dummy}$$
$$(12.44)$$
$$+ .000 \text{ Density}$$
$$(.001)$$
$$+ .640 \text{ P. C. Nonaided}$$
$$(.472) \quad \text{Ed.}$$
$$+ 163.48$$
$$\bar{R} = .676 \qquad \bar{R}^2 = .457$$

P. C. Non-Ed. Taxes (OCC) =
$$.005 \text{ P. C. Income}$$
$$(.005)$$
$$+ .329 \text{ P. C. Non-Ed.}$$
$$(.342) \quad \text{Aid}$$
$$- 16.34 \text{ Regional}$$
$$(9.73) \quad \text{Dummy}$$
$$+ .007^{**} \text{ Density}$$
$$(.003)$$
$$- .086 \text{ Per Cent Housing}$$
$$(.598) \quad \text{Owner-}$$
$$\qquad \text{Occupied}$$
$$+ 50.79$$
$$\bar{R} = .697 \qquad \bar{R}^2 = .486$$

P. C. Non-Ed. Taxes (SMSA) =
$$.006 \text{ P. C. Income}$$
$$(.010)$$
$$+ .422 \text{ P. C. Non-Ed.}$$
$$(.214) \quad \text{Aid}$$
$$- 6.397 \text{ Regional}$$
$$(7.967) \quad \text{Dummy}$$
$$- .813 \text{ Per Cent Housing}$$
$$(.509) \quad \text{Owner-}$$
$$\qquad \text{Occupied}$$

$$+ .004^* \text{ Density}$$
$$(.002)$$
$$- .167 \text{ P. C. Nonaided}$$
$$(.282) \quad \text{Ed.}$$
$$+ 123.16$$
$$\bar{R} = .740 \qquad \bar{R}^2 = .548$$

A great variety of kinds of services are supported by nonschool taxes. The particular services provided in any type of community result from many different and elusive forces. These characteristics of nonschool taxes account for the rather low overall explanation of the variables used in this analysis. Nevertheless some rather interesting findings do emerge. Again, as with noneducation expenditures, income is not important—in fact, it has a slightly negative relationship with central city nonschool taxes. In this instance income apparently acts on neither the supply nor demand side. Although aid was hypothesized to be negatively related with these taxes, it is not; the relationship is weak but positive. Aid does not reduce local tax effort.

A variable that recognizes the special characteristics of the South is used here for the first time. Its use is based on the knowledge that the South has relatively little activity at this level of its governmental system. To the extent that the services represented in this fiscal category are provided at all in the South, they are provided by the state. The expected negative relationships are found.

The density variable is reintroduced for this category of fiscal activity because of the belief that if density is to play any role in explaining fiscal variables it will be with this category of services. This belief is borne out by the positive relationships found.

In contrast to the weak but positive relationship of education taxes to noneducation taxes, the opposite is true with the impact of education taxes on noneducation taxes. In this case

TABLE 5-2: *Elasticity Coefficients: Dependent Fiscal Variables—Central City, Outside Central City, and SMSAs in Relation to Selected Variables, 1957 (Based on Log Transformed Variables)*

	Income	Appropriate aid	Ed. exp. as per cent of total	Ed. exp.	Noned. exp.	Ed. taxes	Noned. taxes	Per cent owner occupied	Per cent rural	Enroll. ratio
Total expenditures		*Total*								
Central city	.488**	.150**	−.250					−.251**	−.077*	
Outside CC	.615**	.384**	−.214					−.215		
SMSA	.660**	.186**	−.176							.122
Education expenditures		*Ed.*								
Central city	.728**	.113*			.154			.062		
Outside CC	.893**	.264**			.113				.023	
SMSA	1.017**	.209**								
Non-ed. expenditures		*Non-ed.*								
Central city	n.c.	.110**		.032	.226*occ					
Outside CC	n.c.	.011		.372	.890**cc			−.335**		
SMSA	.095	.035						−.548**	−.114	
Taxes		*Total*								
Central city	.927**	−.136						−.666		
Outside CC	.839**	−.028								
SMSA	.931**	−.152*						−.411*	−.133*	.076
Education taxes (proxy)		*Ed.*								
Central city	.993**	−.177**					.201	.078		
Outside CC	1.219**	−.066					.009	.259		
SMSA	1.348**	−.110								
Non-ed. taxes (proxy)		*Non-ed.*							*Density*	
Central city	.161	.044				.090		−.559**	.004	
Outside CC.	.127	.070				.106		.050	.197*	
SMSA	.193	.035				−.016		−.716**	−.007	

the relationship is still weak but negative. In other words, except for the central city, education taxes seem to hold down, if but slightly, noneducation taxes.[16]

Elasticities of Variables

The results of this section are summarized through use of their constant value elasticities, with the log transformed variables, in Table 5-2. Using the models developed in this chapter, the responsiveness of each of the dependent variables to income and to the appropriate aid variables, as well as a number of other variables, are shown. No attempt has been made to find the elasticities of the dummy variables as distinguished from the assignment variables for which the elasticities were very much in conformity with expectations.

The responsiveness of the fiscal variables to income is clearly greater (and significant) when education is included in the total than when education and noneducation fiscal variables are viewed individually. This is a uniform phenomenon. Further, the income elasticity of taxes is clearly higher than that for expenditures. Finally, it appears that the more comprehensive the area the higher the income elasticity.

Education aid shows a higher elasticity in the case of education expenditures than noneducation aid does in the case of noneducation expenditures. In addition outside central city areas show a greater responsiveness to aid than do the central city areas, thus implying a more complete and comprehensive set of noneducation requirements in the central city than outside.

The elasticities of taxes in response to changes in aid are as expected in the case of total aid and education aid; they are not as expected in the case of noneducation aid. Specifically, total taxes are reduced by 0.15 for every one per cent increase in total aid for central cities. In the outside central city area the reduction is virtually nil; for every one per cent increase

TABLE 5-3: *Coefficients of Relative Importance (Beta Weights)—Central City, Outside Central City, and SMSAs in Relation to Selected Variables, 1957*

	Income	Appro-priate aid	Welfare dummy	Ed. exp. as per cent of total	Ed. exp.	Non-ed. exp.	Taxes	Per cent owner occupied	Per cent rural	Enroll. ratio	R^2
Total expenditures											
Central city	.293	.344	.262	−.225				−.307			.690
Outside CC	.389	.550	.287	−.060					−.271		.779
SMSA	.425	.482	.341	−.151				−.235			.830
Education expenditures											
Central city	.541	.287				.233		.135			.529
Outside CC	.602	.588				−.099			−.032		.556
SMSA	.622	.586								.040	.621
Non-ed. expenditures											
Central city		.468	−.076		.091cc	.382occ		−.413			.753
Outside CC		−.094	.389		.133occ	.381occ			−.254		.783
SMSA	.084	.417	.382			n.a.		−.385			.768
Taxes											
Central city	.350	−.259	.539					−.538			.699
Outside CC	.510	−.034	.455								.744
SMSA	.716	−.254	.660					−.338			.819
Education taxes (proxy)							*Noned. taxes*				
Central city	.562	−.365					.296	.223			.471
Outside CC	.652	−.126					−.062	.161			.537
SMSA	.716	−.227						.021			.615
Non-ed. taxes (proxy)			*Regional*						*Density*		
Central city	.028	.155	−.073					−.580**	.071		.457
Outside CC	.129	.144	−.278					−.030	.485*		.486
SMSA	.003	.264	.115					.304	.290		.543

in state aid there is a reduction of less than 0.03 per cent in education taxes. In the case of the nonschool tax proxy the pattern is reversed, for aid is associated, if at all, with an increase in taxes.

The only other elasticities on which specific comment will be made are those involving the proportion of owner-occupied housing and the rural proportion of the population residing in the outside central city area. What is very clear is that for every increase of one per cent in the proportion of owner-occupied housing, the total expenditures are reduced by 0.26 per cent in the central city and by 0.38 per cent in the entire SMSA. The rural proportion operates in the same direction outside the central city, as a one per cent increase in the rural proportion leads to a reduction of 0.12 in total expenditures and 0.17 per cent in noneducation expenditures. Education expenditures are reduced, too, but only by 0.02 per cent for every increase of one per cent in the rural proportion of population.

Overall the results of this part of the study can be summarized through an examination of the beta weights of the independent variables. Table 5-3 presents these weights for each major independent variable relative to the dependent variables for each type of area.

As is shown in the table, income has a significant positive influence in all types of areas on each of the fiscal variables, except for noneducation expenditures and nonschool taxes. In the case of central cities the relationship of income to nonschool taxes is negative rather than positive.

As has been stressed throughout this study, intergovernmental flows of funds play a crucial role. As expected, state aid tends to be positively associated with all types of expenditures, but surprisingly it is also associated positively with nonschool taxes and has only a slight negative association with both total and school taxes.

The welfare dummy, used as a substitute for the assignment

variable, is positively associated with expenditures, as would be expected, and with total taxes. The combination of the findings about the welfare dummy in this instance, and its positive association (shown in Chapter 2) with total state-local taxes, is one of the major and surprising findings of this entire study. The proportion of owner-occupied housing has a significant influence on variations in central city expenditures; however, it is positively associated with education and negatively with noneducation.

As expected, the higher the proportion of rural population in outside central city areas, the lower the noneducation fiscal levels, but the influence is not significant for education expenditures. Again, the uniformity of education expenditures across metropolitan lines and within these lines is illustrated.

The South, as a region, influences nonschool taxes and so does density—but in opposite directions. The South as a region is low on the noneducation side and accounts for some of the variation within this category for all metropolitan areas and their parts. Density is positively associated with nonschool taxes.

The level of one type of fiscal activity (education expenditures and taxes) and of the other type (noneducation expenditures and taxes) seem to move together in all types of areas except for nonschool taxes in outside central cities, and in this instance high levels of school taxes seem to hold down nonschool taxes—a not unexpected result, considering the priority given to education in many suburban communities.

The influence of each of the variables in different areas is about as predicted. In summary it seems fair to suggest that by and large the same forces are operative in both central cities and outside central cities. Income is important, with the exceptions already noted throughout, as is aid and the welfare dummy. The differences are with variables, which tend to be related to specific types of areas—e.g., home-ownership in central cities and rural population proportion in outside central city areas.

The Metropolitan Area: Central Cities and Their Outlying Areas—Relationships and Differences

The analysis of the determinants of metropolitan fiscal behavior up to this point has concentrated on the variations among central cities and among outside central city areas that make up the metropolitan area, as well as among the entire areas taken as units. Major policy concern, however, relates to the relationship of individual central cities to their own outlying areas. The absence of analyses appropriate to this focus is the result of the absence of data, on the one hand, and of a conceptual model relating the central city to its outlying area on the other. Insofar as the fiscal relationships of central city areas to their surrounding outside central city areas have been considered, it has been done either indirectly or by case studies—i.e., on an individual area basis.

The only work directly relevant to the analysis done here is that of Harvey Brazer in his study of *City Expenditure in the United States* and the predecessor analysis done by Amos Hawley.[17] Brazer analyzes, among other categories of cities, 40 large cities and their overlying governments for which expenditure data was available. This group of cities exhibits virtually the same characteristics as the central city areas of the sample metropolitan areas considered in this study. The analysis here of both central cities and outside central cities provides a basis for generalizing the Brazer results to encompass not only central city areas, but their outside areas and entire metropolitan areas as well.

The Brazer finding of most significance for the analysis of central city/outside central city patterns is the relationship of the level of central city expenditures to the central city's proportion of total SMSA population. The smaller the proportion of the population in the central city, the higher its per capita expenditure. An earlier related finding by Hawley showed "that per capita costs of government (computed on the population residing within the city) are more closely related to population living outside the city ($r = .554$) than with the population occupying the city ($r = .398$)."[18]

The usual explanation given for this finding is one of exploitation of central cities by their suburbs. The greater the relative size of the outside central city area, the greater the exploitation.

Although this finding about the relationship of per capita fiscal levels for central cities relative to their proportion of total SMSA population is confirmed in the present study, the same finding is also true for the outside central city areas for noneducation expenditure and taxes. The larger the outside central city proportion of population, the higher *its* per capita noneducation expenditures and taxes. Specifically, as shown in Table 5-4, the smaller the ratio of the central city population to that of the SMSA, the higher the per capita noneducation expenditures outside the central city, just as is true for the central city.

Another check on the validity of the influence of population proportion on both central city and outside central city expenditures is to examine the influence of population proportion on entire SMSA variations. If the influence runs in only one direction, that is if its influence is only on the central city expenditures, the effect should disappear when the entire SMSA is examined. Such is not the case; the population proportion in the central city is also negatively related to non-

TABLE 5-4: *Simple Correlation Coefficients Between Selected Fiscal Variables and the Proportion of SMSA Population in Central Cities (36-SMSA Sample), 1957*

	Central cities	Outside central cities	SMSAs	All SMSAs (1962)
Per capita expenditures				
Total per capita	−.440	−.189	−.268	−.179
Education	−.204	+.067	−.249	−.240
Noneducation	−.429	−.339	−.147	−.104
Per capita taxes				
Total per capita	−.550	−.315	−.359	−.144
School taxes (proxy)	−.142	+.122	−.165	n.a.
Nonschool taxes (proxy)	−.514	−.547	n.c.	n.a.

education expenditure levels for entire SMSAs. This finding for entire SMSAs confirms the finding for both central cities and outside central city areas.

The Brazer-Hawley hypothesis, if it is to hold at all, must be a much more complex phenomenon than that originally suggested. For if the central city has its noneducation expenditures and taxes increased because of the burden of services imposed upon it by the size of its outside area, the outside area also has its level of noneducation expenditures and taxes influenced by the small relative size of the central city. And indeed the level of expenditures and taxes is higher for the entire SMSA.

This behavior is obviously caused by some other characteristic of metropolitan areas that possess a relatively smaller proportion of its population in the central cities—probably a combination of size and regional influences. It is in the North, particularly the Northeast, that central city boundaries have responded least to the outflow of population. The larger areas also tend to contain less of their population in the central city, and these areas, too, allowing for regional differences, have higher levels of fiscal behavior than the smaller areas.

These findings about the influence of the proportion of SMSA population in central cities reduces the value of this variable as an explanatory factor in central city/outside central city fiscal differences. The explanation will have to be sought in conjunction with other variables.

The Influence of Central City Fiscal Behavior on Outside Central City Behavior

Another approach to the relations between central city and outside central city fiscal behavior is to examine the extent to which changes in the levels in one type of area are associated with changes in the other type. Table 5-5 shows the relationships between central city and outside central city at given levels of central city fiscal behavior. The method used is to raise and lower the level of central city fiscal activity by one standard deviation and then to examine what happens on the average to the outside central city fiscal level. Two questions can be answered in this manner: *a.* what happens to the absolute difference, *b.* what happens to the relative difference?

If the assumption is made that the higher the level of central city expenditures, the lower the level of outside central city expenditures, this is clearly not the case. In other words, the level of fiscal activity of the central city area and its overlying government is always positively and significantly correlated with the fiscal activity of its outlying area. The reason for this is the overwhelming importance of the assignment systems to both the central city and outside central city areas, which is intensified by the fact that the two areas are normally within the same state.

If the assumption is made that the absolute and relative

TABLE 5-5: *Outside Central City Fiscal Behavior at Various Levels of Central City Fiscal Behavior, 1957 (36-SMSA Sample)*

Local per capita fiscal variables		Central city level	Outside central city level	Absolute difference (CC−OCC)	Relative difference (CC as per cent of OCC)
Total expenditures	+	$224.38	$186.98	+ $37.40	120.0%
	mean	185.49	159.83	+ 25.66	116.1
	−	146.60	132.67	+ 13.93	110.4
Education	+	69.62	100.26	− 30.64	69.4
expenditures	mean	58.02	85.84	− 27.82	67.6
	−	46.42	71.42	− 25.00	65.0
Noneducation	+	161.87	96.07	+ 65.80	168.4
expenditures	mean	127.48	73.95	+ 53.53	172.3
	−	93.09	51.83	+ 41.26	179.6
Taxes	+	141.95	113.99	+ 27.96	124.5
	mean	109.07	85.78	+ 23.29	127.1
	−	76.19	57.57	+ 18.62	132.3
State aid	+	52.81	58.70	− 5.89	90.0
	mean	34.65	39.72	− 5.07	87.2
	−	15.89	20.14	− 4.25	78.9
Education aid	+	23.99	43.59	− 19.60	55.0
	mean	16.12	28.43	− 12.31	56.7
	−	8.25	13.27	− 5.02	62.1
Noneducation aid	+	34.49	21.51	+ 12.98	160.3
	mean	18.60	11.83	+ 6.77	157.2
	−	2.71	2.15	+ .56	126.0

differences between the central city and outside central city areas change in the same direction as the level of changes in central city fiscal activity, the picture is not clear. First, as per capita total central city expenditures change, the absolute and relative differences between central and outside central city areas move in the same direction. The higher the level of central city expenditures, the greater the absolute and relative differences. In the case of education expenditures, the same is true for absolute differences but not for the relative difference, which declines. As noneducation expenditures increase in the central city, absolute difference between central city and outside central city increases; but the relative difference decreases, although only slightly.

On the down side, as central city total expenditures decline, the absolute and relative differences also decline. The same is true for education expenditures, but not for noneducation expenditures. In this latter case, the absolute difference declines, but the relative difference increases. In other words, low noneducation expenditures in the central city means even lower expenditures, relatively, for this category outside the central city. Again, the difference in the behavior of education and noneducation expenditures is demonstrated.

Turning to the revenue side, taxes and state aid show varying patterns. Insofar as taxes are concerned the pattern resembles, as it should, noneducation expenditures; that is, the higher the level of central city taxes, the greater the absolute differences and the smaller the relative differences. Although this is the expected result following from changes in the size of the index number base, it does not hold in the analysis of state aid. At the outset, the important thing to note is that the absolute difference between the outside central city and central city state aid is relatively invariant. On the average, the difference is somewhere between $4 and $6. However, this is the result of two very different aid patterns with important tax consequences.

First, it is quite clear that as the level of education aid in the central city increases, the level outside increases more than proportionately. The higher the level of education aid in the central city, the higher the absolute level of education aid outside the central city and the greater the relative gap between central city and its outside area. As noneducation aid increases in the central city, both the absolute and relative differences increase. The offsetting effect of education and noneducation aid is retained, therefore, regardless of the level of aid.

The interrelationships between the fiscal behavior of central cities and their outside areas is demonstrative of their response to common determinants. They tend to move together. The differences, whatever the level of central city fiscal behavior, remain although in some instances the relative differences decline.

Determinants of Central City/Outside Central City Differences

The hypothesis underlying the analysis of differences is that the factors responsible for differences between central city and their outside areas are the same as those responsible for variations among central cities, among outside central city areas, and among entire SMSAs.

Specifically, differences in per capita income, per capita total state aid, per capita education and noneducation aid, and enrollment ratios will be considered, as will be the already discussed ratio of the central city population to that of its SMSA. On the basis of the findings for variations among like areas, it is presumed that differences in income and state aid should be both significant and important. Further, it is assumed that the effects of the two should be cumulative.

Generally speaking, the results of the simple correlation analysis, as shown in Table 5-6, are as expected. Income differences are significant in explaining differences in expenditures, but even more significant in explaining differences in taxes. Differences in state aid are also significant in explaining differences in expenditures, but they are not significant in explaining differences in taxes. A phenomenon noted earlier appears once again in the analysis of taxes and of the school tax and nonschool tax proxies. First, greater differences in education aid are associated with lower differences in taxes, especially school taxes. Secondly, higher aid for nonschool purposes is, in fact, associated with higher differences in taxes.

Differences in enrollment are not only reflected in higher education expenditures per capita, but in higher school aid per capita. The results again are reasonable and as expected.

TABLE 5-6: *Simple Correlation of Differences in Independent and Dependent Variables for Central City and Outside Central City Areas, 1957 (36-SMSA Sample)*

	Income	Total state aid	Education aid	Non-education aid	Enroll-ment	Central city popula-tion as per cent of SMSA	Central city employ-ment as per cent of SMSA
Differences in per capita expenditure	.441	.559	.261	.426	.309	−.176	.304
Education expenditure	.293	.437	.326	.198	.467	−.202	.157
Noneducation expenditure	.434	.429	.093	.450	.038	−.113	.348
Taxes	.528	.077	−.130	.243	.027	−.282	.438
School tax (proxy)	.559	.041	−.237	.351	.173	−.234	.211
Nonschool tax (proxy)	.324	.271	.180	.133	.043	−.173	.356
Total aid	−.101	1.000	.715	.471	.471	.114	−.012
Education aid	−.462	.715	1.000	.257	.540	.043	−.088
Noneducation aid	.444	.471	−.257	1.000	−.107	−.005	.153
Income	1.000	−.101	−.462	.444	−.206	.044	.492

To be significant at .05 level, r must be > ±.330

To be significant at .01 level, r must be > ±.425

Multiple Regression Analysis

It is presumed that the basic differences between the central city and outside central city areas are a function of both socio-economic and fiscal factors. The fiscal factors are partly "political" and partly "governmental-structural" in nature. The socioeconomic factors are measured by differences in income and the enrollment ratios; the fiscal factor is summarized by the differences in state aid. Other structural factors to be considered are the existence of metropolitan (i.e., county-wide welfare and education) districts, which by their basic nature preclude differences. Finally, the significance of the central city proportion of the total SMSA population is again considered.

Using the same format as was used earlier in the analysis of the separate areas the following were the hypotheses concerning the differences between the several independent variables and the dependent variables as in Table 5 - H7.

TABLE 5 - H7.

Per capita differences	Income	Relevant state aid	Enrollment ratio	CC population as per cent of SMSA population
Total expenditures	+	+	n.c.	−
Education expenditures	+	+	+	−
Noneducation expenditures	0	+	n.c.	−
Taxes	+	−	+	−
School tax (proxy)	+	−	+	−
Nonschool taxes	0	−	−	−

The estimating equations for differences in per capita expenditure are as follows:

$$\text{P. C. Exp. (CC-OCC)} = \underset{(.007)}{.035^{**}} \text{ Differences in P. C. Income}$$

$$+ \underset{(.344)}{2.080^{**}} \text{ Differences in P. C. State Aid}$$

$$- .736^* \text{ Central City}$$
$$(.272) \quad \text{Proportion of SMSA}$$

$$+ \$85.49$$
$$\bar{R} = .799 \qquad \bar{R}^2 = .639$$

P. C. Ed. Exp. (CC-OCC) = $.020^{**}$ Differences in
$\quad (.005) \quad$ P. C. Income

$\quad + .687^*$ Differences in
$\quad (.316) \quad$ P. C. Ed. Aid

$\quad + 2.854^*$ Differences in
$\quad (1.174) \quad$ Enrollment Ratio

$$- .44$$
$$\bar{R} = .676 \qquad \bar{R}^2 = .457$$

P. C. Non-Ed. Exp.
$\quad$ (CC-OCC) = $.009$ Differences in
$\quad (.008) \quad$ P. C. Income

$\quad + .846$ Difference in
$\quad (.436) \quad$ P. C. Non-Ed. Aid

$\quad - .168$ Central City
$\quad (.249) \quad$ Proportion of SMSA

$\quad + .310$ Difference in
$\quad (.191) \quad$ P. C. Ed. Exp.

$$+ 68.11$$
$$\bar{R} = .587 \qquad \bar{R}^2 = .345$$

Using these variables, the first equation explains 63.9 per cent of the observed variation in total expenditures. Variation in per capita state aid and variations in per capita income are roughly of the same order of importance. For every dollar of difference in state aid the difference in total per capita expenditures is + $2.08; for every dollar of difference in income the difference is + $.035. On the other hand, the greater the central city population is as a proportion of the SMSA population, the smaller the expenditure difference between central city and its outside area. For every one per cent difference in the central city's proportion of total SMSA population, the difference in total expenditures is reduced by $0.736.

The fact that as much as 63.9 per cent of the variation in the differences in per capita total expenditures in central city and outside central city expenditures can be explained by these factors, is of considerable interest. The results are surprising because it would be presumed that variations in the combinations of governmental services would have the effect of obliterating the differences. But it appears that in terms of per capita expenditures they are not of such importance as to overwhelm the significance of state aid, income, and the proportional population share of central city areas.

Turning now to the components of total expenditures, both education and noneducation expenditures will be analyzed. Differences in education expenditures are explained by the model to a greater extent than the differences in noneducation expenditures, although to a lesser extent than the explanation of differences in total expenditures. As in the case of total expenditures, the variables that are associated with the variations among cities are also associated with the differences between central cities and outside central city areas.

Differences in education aid, enrollment ratio, and income are significant in explaining the differences in education expenditures. In contrast, noneducation expenditures taken as a whole are difficult to explain. Differences in functional responsibility, primarily for hospitals and welfare associated in a random manner with municipal governments, is probably the primary cause. The model is at its weakest when it deals with the differences in noneducation expenditures. This is due to the fact that no simple model can include such variables, for example, as whether fire and police protection and refuse and garbage collection are provided in the outside area by local governments or through private vendors.

The estimating equations for differences in per capita taxes between central cities and their outside areas are as follows:

$$
\begin{aligned}
\text{P. C. Taxes (CC-OCC)} = \ & .022^{**} \text{ P. C. Differences} \\
& (.005) \quad \text{in Income} \\[4pt]
& + .311 \text{ P. C. Differences} \\
& (.253) \quad \text{in State Aid} \\[4pt]
& - .475^{*} \text{ Central City} \\
& (.201) \quad \text{Proportion} \\
& \qquad\qquad \text{SMSA} \\[4pt]
& + 54.36 \\
& \bar{R} = .633 \qquad \bar{R}^2 = .401
\end{aligned}
$$

$$
\begin{aligned}
\text{P. C. Ed. Taxes (CC-OCC)} = \ & .021^{**} \text{ Differences in} \\
& (.006) \quad \text{P. C. Income} \\[4pt]
& + .049 \text{ Differences in} \\
& (.296) \quad \text{School Aid} \\[4pt]
& - 8.45 \\
& \bar{R} = .560 \qquad \bar{R}^2 = .313
\end{aligned}
$$

$$
\begin{aligned}
\text{P. C. Non-Ed. Taxes} & \\
\text{(CC-OCC)} = \ & .012 \text{ Differences in} \\
& (.007) \quad \text{P. C. Income} \\[4pt]
& - .094 \text{ Differences in} \\
& (.429) \quad \text{Nonschool Aid} \\[4pt]
& + .333 \text{ Employment} \\
& (.175) \quad \text{Ratio (CC)} \\[4pt]
& + 12.12 \\
& \bar{R} = .442 \qquad \bar{R}^2 = .196
\end{aligned}
$$

Finally, on the tax side, differences in total per capita taxes are mostly explained by income differences and to a minor extent by central city proportion of total SMSA population. Of greater interest is the fact that differences in state aid are positively correlated with differences in taxes, again demonstrating that state aid is not replacive of local tax effort. If variables indicating the assignment of the welfare function are included, the total explanatory power of the model increases from $\bar{R}^2 = .401$ to $\bar{R}^2 = .456$. The addition of these welfare assignment variables does not reduce the influence of income.

Neither school nor nonschool per capita tax differences can be as well explained as total tax differences. Income is again significant for school taxes but not for nonschool taxes. The aid variable is not significant in either case in reducing taxes.

It is these differences in fiscal behavior between central cities and their outside areas, and to a lesser degree between metropolitan and nonmetropolitan areas, that raise most of the public policy issues associated with metropolitanism. The contribution that this analysis has made to an understanding of these issues and to policy alternatives is discussed in the following chapter.

References

1. Herbert A. Simon, *Fiscal Aspects of Metropolitan Consolidation*, (Berkeley, California: Bureau of Public Administration, University of California, 1943); and Julius Margolis, "On Municipal Land Policy for Fiscal Gains," *National Tax Journal*, IX (September 1956).

2. The work of Werner Z. Hirsch, see especially *Paths of Progress for St. Louis*, and *Measuring Factors Affecting Expenditure Levels of Local Government Services* (St. Louis: Metropolitan St. Louis Survey, 1957).

3. Seymour Sacks and William F. Hellmuth, Jr., *Financing Government in a Metropolitan Area* (New York: The Free Press, 1961); and Jesse Burkhead, "Uniformity in Governmental Expendi-

tures and Resources in a Metropolitan Area: Cuyahoga County," *National Tax Journal*, XIV (December 1961).

4. Seymour Sacks, *Municipal Taxation and Regional Development* (East Hartford, Conn.: Capitol Regional Planning Agency, March 1963).

5. Oliver P. Williams, *et al. Suburban Differences and Metropolitan Policies* (Philadelphia: University of Pennsylvania Press, 1965).

6. Robert C. Wood, *1400 Governments* (Cambridge, Mass.: Harvard University Press, 1961); and Alan K. Campbell, "Taxes and Industrial Location in the New York Metropolitan Region," *National Tax Journal*, XI (September 1958), 195-218.

7. Harvey E. Brazer, *City Expenditures in the United States*, Occasional Paper #66, (New York: National Bureau of Economic Research, Inc., 1959); and Woo Sik Kee, "Central City Expenditures and Metropolitan Areas," *National Tax Journal*, XVIII (December 1965), 337-353.

8. Deil S. Wright, *Trends and Variations in Local Finances: The Case of Iowa* (Iowa City: Institute of Public Affairs, University of Iowa, 1965).

9. H. Thomas James, J. Allen Thomas, and Harold J. Dyck, *Wealth, Expenditures and Decision-Making* (Palo Alto, Calif.: Stanford University Press, 1964); Seymour Sacks and David C. Ranney, "Suburban Education: A Fiscal Analysis," *Urban Affairs Quarterly* (September, 1966); and Seymour Sacks, "Central City and Suburban Public Education: Fiscal Needs, Fiscal Resources, Fiscal Realities," *Education Yearbook, 1966* (Chicago: National Society for the Study of Education, to be published, Spring, 1968).

10. For an explanation of dummy variables see Daniel B. Suits, "The Use of Dummy Variables in Regression Equations," *Journal of the American Statistical Association*, Vol. LII (December 1957), 548-581.

11. This division of the welfare function is explicitly done by Selma Mushkin in her analysis of the impact of state and federal aid on local general expenditures and revenues in seventeen selected SMSAs. "Intergovernmental Aspects of Local Expenditure Decisions" in Howard G. Schaller, ed., *Public Expenditure Decisions in the Urban Community* (Washington: Resources for the Future, Inc., 1966), 37-61.

12. Many variables, both independent and dependent, were tested in the process of selecting those to be used in the final analysis. Other dependent variables originally used were: p. c. current Education expenditures, p. c. highway expenditures, p. c. health and hospital expenditures, p. c. public welfare expenditures, p. c. "all other" expenditures, p. c. property taxes, per pupil total education expenditures, per pupil current education expenditures, per pupil state aid for eduction.

Other independent variables originally used were: total population, population per square mile, 1957 population as per cent of 1950 population, per cent population residing in the same dwelling in 1960 as lived there in 1955; per cent of population nonwhite 1960, median family income, 1959, ratio of families with incomes over $10,000 to those under $3,000 in 1959, owner-occupied housing 1960, non-South/South "dummy" variables, area, population per government, and governmental fragmentation variable.

13. Because the signs of the coefficients have been predicted, it is appropriate to use a single-tail test rather than the two-tailed test used throughout. The significance of the results are thus understated where the signs are predicted.

14. It is interesting to contrast this finding with that made by Wilson and Banfield in their analysis of voting behavior on bond issues. They found a negative correlation between home ownership and "yes" votes on a selected set of welfare-oriented bond issues. This finding is not inconsistent with the negative correlation found here between home ownership and both total expenditures and noneducation expenditures. The findings here, however, would suggest that there might be a positive correlation between "yes" votes on education bond issues and home ownership. See James Q. Wilson and Edward C. Banfield, "Public Regardingness as a Value Premise in Voting Behavior," *American Political Science Review*, LVIII (December 1964), 876–877.

15. Seymour Sacks and David C. Ranney, "Suburban Education: A Fiscal Analysis," *Urban Affairs Quarterly*, (September 1966).

16. These findings relative to central cities are generally consistent with those of the one study to which they can be meaningfully compared. In Brazer's already cited study of the 40 largest central cities and their overlying governments, he used a number of

variables, both dependent and independent, that are consistent with the ones used in this analysis. Where consistent variables are used the findings are comparable. Harvey Brazer, *City Expenditures in the United States* (New York: National Bureau of Economic Research, Inc., 1959), 25–28.

17. *Op. cit.*, and Amos H. Hawley, "Metropolitan Population and Municipal Government Expenditures in Central Cities," in Paul K. Hatt and Albert J. Reiss, Jr., eds., *Cities and Society* (New York: The Free Press 1959).

18. *Op. cit.*, 775.

CHAPTER 6

Summary of
Fiscal Characteristics
and Policy Implications

Underlying this whole study is the proposition that metro-politanism provides a useful and necessary framework for examining both state-local and local fiscal behavior. Although metropolitanism is broader than any of the local parts of the governmental jurisdictional system, the concept does provide a means for analyzing fiscal behavior within a context that relates that behavior to interrelated political and socioeconomic areas.

Because these areas do not fit within any common local governmental jurisdiction, it is necessary to examine whether the jurisdictional system has an independent influence on fiscal behavior. The complexity of the system that governs metropolitan America is only partially described, however, by the fragmentation of local jurisdictions. In addition, every state divides both expenditures and tax responsibility differently as between the state and local parts of the governmental system. Alongside both jurisdictional fragmentation and differences in assignment systems are flows of external revenue into the fiscal coffers of both state and local governments. It is the impact of the combination of these complex governmental systems and socioeconomic characteristics on fiscal behavior that has been the focus of the study.

The primary concern of the study has been to determine and explain the causes of differences in fiscal levels among areas of the same type and the differences in such levels among different types of areas. Of particular interest for understanding the nature of metropolitanism are the findings about variations in fiscal levels and services for the component parts of a metropolitan nation.

For both total expenditures and taxes the highest fiscal levels are found in central cities. These totals, however, hide substantial differences among functions and revenue sources. The broad division of expenditure behavior into its education and noneducation components helps to explain the internal composition of the differences in total fiscal levels between both metropolitan and nonmetropolitan areas and between central cities and their outside areas.

Education possesses the greatest uniformity among different types of areas, whereas the noneducation package varies substantially from one type of area to another. Within the noneducation group of services it is the traditional municipal functions and the newer urban renewal and housing programs that show the greatest differences. This combination of services requires over twice as high expenditures on a per capita basis in metropolitan areas as it does in nonmetropolitan, and approximately the same relationship was found for this set of services between central cities and their outside areas.

Although education expenditures show greater uniformity than those for noneducation, there are some differences worth noting. On a per capita basis, using 1957 data, central cities have the lowest education expenditures, considerably below their own outside areas, but also lower than nonmetropolitan areas. When compared on a per student basis, the pattern is considerably different, with central cities showing a figure not too different from those of other types of areas, although this pattern seems to be undergoing change. From 1957 to 1962 the central cities clearly lost ground educationally to their outside areas, and today, with a few exceptions, indications are that substantially more is being spent on a per student, as well as on a per capita, basis in suburbs than in central cities.

On the revenue side there is a steady progression in local tax levels from nonmetropolitan areas to central cities, with central city taxes being nearly twice as high on a per capita basis as nonmetropolitan ones and 38 per cent higher than those for outside central cities. The tax differences are greater, proportionately, than expenditure differences, and the gap is largely explained by the pattern of intergovernmental aid. The least aid is received by central cities and the most by nonmetropolitan areas. The differential in aid between metropolitan and nonmetropolitan areas is consistent with the differences in resources, but such is not the case, especially when needs are taken into account, for the differences in aid between central cities and their outside areas. In this case it is the outside central city areas that do better despite the fact that their resources, as measured by income, are greater than those possessed by central cities.

The hypothesis on which this study has been based is that these differences among different type areas can be explained, at least in part, by the same forces that help to explain differences among like types of areas. The fiscal differences in total expenditures between central cities and their outside areas can be more completely explained than any other fiscal variable. The three variables—differences in income, differences in state aid, and central city proportion of total SMSA population—have a combined explanatory power of 0.639. Each of the three variables is statistically significant. In explaining differences in education expenditures, differences in income, education aid, and enrollment ratio are all significant but their total explanatory power is somewhat less than for total expenditures. Least explainable is the noneducation expenditure category. This finding is not surprising in view of the many different components which make up the noneducation combination in all type areas.

In the case of differences in taxes, total taxes are most explainable, but not to the extent that total expenditures can be explained. In the case of school taxes (nonaided educational expenditures) it is income that is significant, whereas for nonschool taxes (nonaided noneducational expenditures) the total explanatory power of the difference variables is as low as it is for noneducation expenditures.

In examining central city/outside central city fiscal differences, the behavior of the independent variables—income and state aid—is of special interest. Income is more highly correlated with expenditures than with taxes, indicating that income operates more strongly on the demand side than on the supply side. The greater the income differential, the greater the differential in services demanded. This influence of income is greater for education than for noneducation services.

As would be expected, state aid is strongly and positively associated with differences in expenditures, particularly education expenditures, but its lack of a significant negative association with taxes is surprising. It is clear, as has been pointed out many times in this study, that aid does not act as a replacement for local taxes but may be, in part, additive to them. This finding is especially true in suburban areas; however, for central cities there appears to be a small partial replacement of local taxes by external aid.

Overall, the differences between central city and outside central city areas fiscal behavior are significant, and this significance is greater when that behavior is divided into its major education and noneducation components. Undoubtedly other factors help to explain the differences, but the common variables used throughout this study make a significant contribution to explaining them. Many different government systems are involved for each type area, and with none possessing completely conterminous jurisdictional boundaries, it is surprising that the differences can be explained as well as they are.

Equally as important to the understanding of the nature of metropolitan fiscal behavior in explaining variations between different type areas, is trying to understand the variations among like type areas.

Table 6-1 summarizes the coefficients of multiple determination, $\bar{R}^2$s, found for each type area for the basic fiscal variables used in this analysis. In each case the figure is for the most comprehensive model utilized.

These findings are all a product of a basic explanatory model that uses as common independent variables income, appropriate state aid, and assignment or the welfare dummy as a proxy for assignment. In several instances additional variables were used for specific type areas. Home ownership, for example, was hypothesized and then found to be useful in explaining variations among central cities, whereas the rural proportion of population was likewise hypothesized and then found to be useful for outside central city areas.

TABLE 6-1: *Summary Table—Coefficients of Multiple Determination (R^2) All Classes of Areas,* * 1957*

Per capita	Total local (1962)	Nonmetro-politan portion of states	Metro-politan portion of states	36-SMSA SAMPLE		
				SMSAs	Outside central cities	Central cities
Expenditures						
Total	.914	.780	.802	.830	.779	.690
Education	.721			.621	.556	.529
Noneducation				.768	.783	.753
Taxes						
Total	.948	.797	.882	.819	.744	.699
Education (proxy)				.615	.537	.471
Noneducation (proxy)				.548	.486	.457

* Regression equations can be found in the appropriate chapters.

Two general points need to be made about the level of explanatory power found for various type areas. First, the more general the area being considered, the higher the level of the explanation as measured by the coefficients of multiple determination. In part, this result is a product of the role of assignment. The assignment of expenditure and tax responsibility to local government as measured by their statewide proportions is a dominating, if not the dominant, variable in explaining interstate variations in *local* fiscal behavior. Without these variables comparisons of variations in local fiscal behavior are extremely difficult because of the differences from state to state in the assignment of fiscal responsibilities between state and local governments.

Many errors of interpretation have been committed when due recognition has not been given to this phenomenon. In some studies an attempt is made to solve the problem of differences in state assignment by comparing only common functions across state lines—police, fire, and general control, for example. This method, although better than trying to compare total expenditures, has the weaknesses of omitting many functions and, more importantly, of ignoring the significance for fiscal behavior of the variation in the combination of local functions. Further, local taxes, because they are seldom tied to specific functions, cannot be compared across state lines by this common function method.

The use of the local assignment variables, therefore, makes possible interstate comparisons of local fiscal behavior with an exactitude never before accomplished. The power of the assignment variable and its proxy, welfare assignment, declines in importance when states are divided into metropolitan, outside central city, and central city areas. If an exact assignment proportion for each type area were available, the importance of these variables no doubt would have been greater for the less than statewide areas.

One further point needs to be made about the assignment

variables. It was not expected that these variables would have any influence beyond indicating the relative fiscal roles of the different levels of government. For tax assignment this assumption is *not* correct. The higher the local tax assignment, the higher state-local taxes are.

The other overall conclusion about these general findings is related to the fact that variations in total fiscal behavior in like types of areas, as represented by total expenditures and total taxes, can be better explained than their parts. This higher explanatory power for the broader fiscal categories, with the exception of noneducation expenditures, is true for all type areas. Apparently this phenomenon is a result of inter-action between the various components of these totals. To some extent there must be substitutability among the various functions of government.

Turning now to specific type areas, variations in the metropolitan portions of states are largely explained by the three common variables. The importance of assignment has been explained, and aid and income act at their most powerful at this level of analysis.

Variations among the 36 sample metropolitan areas cannot be as well explained as the variations among metropolitan portions of states, but the explanation is high—higher than for their component parts, central cities and outside central cities. Again, the three basic variables are the important ones.

For outside central cities the explanatory power is higher than for central cities. The addition of the rural proportion of population is important for the outside central city area, especially for noneducation fiscal behavior.

Central city fiscal differences are less explainable than the fiscal differences for other areas, and of these variables non-education fiscal variations are the least explainable. It is apparent that of all fiscal variables examined, tax support of the noneducation group of services is the most difficult to explain.

In the case of central cities the role of home-ownership is worthy of particular note. The education and noneducation services respond differently to this variable. The variable is not associated with education but has a significant negative association with noneducation expenditures and taxes.

There obviously are many other variables that could have been used in this analysis; in fact, many such variables not reported here were tested. All of those not reported were rejected because they did not show any significance for the broad nationwide analysis being done. Such variables as number of governments, degree of two-party competition, ethnic composition, employment patterns, and many others were tried. It is quite possible that in a more restricted framework they would have been found important. An already cited study of voting behavior on bond issues,[1] for example, has indicated that ethnic composition is related to attitudes about local spending. The present analysis, because of its aggregative character, may well have missed this type of influence.

It seems that perhaps the next appropriate step in this kind of analysis would be to concentrate on smaller areas and on a more detailed breakdown of fiscal outputs. More detailed data than now provided by the various data-collecting agencies will be necessary before such studies can be done. For example, it seems clear that federal aid will play a more important role in the state-local fiscal system in the future. For the significance of both federal and state aid to be tested, it is essential that the reporting detail, by function, recipient jurisdiction and the type area be improved.

A case in point was provided by the recent Senate hearings on the problems of large cities. The subcommittee involved requested both the federal administrative agencies and the mayors of several major cities to provide data concerning the amounts of federal aid cities receive. Great discrepancies existed in the various figures provided. Mayor Lindsay of New York City, for example, could come no closer to estimating the amount than to suggest it was "something over a half billion [dollars] and something under a billion."¹ Even the federal administrative agencies could not agree on how much aid cities were receiving, with the estimates ranging from $17 to $28 billion annually.²

The complex state-local government system is largely responsible for this lack of precision. Because the aid provided is by function, and because the same function is performed by different types of jurisdictions in different states, the records do not automatically show what types of areas receive aid. There is a need to total aid by area type (metropolitan, non-metropolitan, city, suburb, and so on) if useful analysis is to be done. The Governments Division of the U. S. Bureau of the Census took a giant stride in the 1957 *Census of Governments* by totalling fiscal behavior by a metropolitan/non-metropolitan breakdown. What is now needed is a further breakdown for the component parts of these area types.

Within the limitations of the data available, this study has been as inclusive, both fiscally and geographically, as possible; it is hoped that a contribution to understanding fiscal behavior has been made. From the findings certain public policy consequences emerge. The final section of this chapter is devoted to describing some of these policy implications.

Public Policy Implications

The public policy issues that surround metropolitanism can be divided into two broad categories. The set of issues that has been associated with this phenomenon for the longest period relates to the supposed need for local governmental reorganization: "The impression has long prevailed among political and civic reformers that the problems of growing metropolitan areas would be magically solved if only simple, symmetrical patterns of local government were established."³

The other set of issues is that associated with the level and quality of services provided to the residents of metropolitan areas. Of particular importance to this category of policy questions is the impact on service needs caused by the "sorting out" of population that is taking place within metropolitan areas. The resulting pattern of different kinds of service needs in central cities and their outside areas becomes one of the crucial metropolitan aspects of the service issue. Of most concern currently is the adequacy of those services for the poor who reside in increasing numbers in central cities. The long-term goal is to make adequate, from their individual and combined interests, the services rendered by both central cities and their outside central city areas.

The discussion of the policy implications of the findings of this study are divided into these two broad policy areas. Although there is some overlapping it is believed that the policy implications can be made clearer by the use of such a division.

Implications for Governmental Reorganization

The conventional wisdom in the metropolitan field stresses the necessity for the total reorganization of the governments of these areas. The argument is that the present governmental fragmentation and overlapping in metropolitan areas makes it impossible for what is otherwise a social and economic unit to rationally attack the problems that more and more tend to be area-wide rather than merely jurisdiction-wide. The local governmental organization variables used in this analysis—population per government and area per government—did not show any significant relationship to the fiscal variables. In other words, there does not seem to be any strong relationship between these measures of governmental fragmentation and differences in levels of fiscal activity.

This inability to find a meaningful relationship does not mean that none exists. It may be that the variables used to define fragmentation did not represent the significant governmental characteristics or that the other variables employed were sufficiently strong to hide the significance of fragmentation. It may be, too, that the significance of fragmentation lies not so much in fiscal levels as in policy and program coordination. Fragmentation is characteristic of all metropolitan areas in the country but it takes many different forms. As has been shown, one way of measuring and describing the degree of fragmentation as it relates to central cities is to compute the proportion of expenditures made in a central city area by the central government that supposedly governs the area. For the 24 largest metropolitan areas the range is from a low of 29·5 per cent for Los Angeles to a high of 95 per cent for Baltimore.

The Los Angeles situation was well illustrated by the testimony of Mayor Yorty of Los Angeles before a Senate subcommittee. He responded to many questions about the performance of government functions within his city by pointing out that many of the functions the subcommittee wanted to discuss were not the responsibility of the city government at all, but of a great variety of governments in the Los Angeles area, including the state, the county, school districts, and special districts. Whatever the impact this fragmentation has on fiscal levels for the area, it is clear that coordination of interrelated programs—welfare and education, for example—cannot be done effectively by the present system.

Fragmentation is also related to the inevitable division of the resource base. Because income is an important determinant of much fiscal behavior, it follows that this jurisdictional division has fiscal consequences.

The high correlations found between nearly all fiscal variables and income indicate that the division of metropolitan areas into sections that have different income characteristics results in different levels of fiscal activity. If a broader jurisdiction were adopted, particularly if it included the central city, the resulting higher average levels for central cities might produce higher fiscal levels in these areas. Simultaneously, of course, such levels might be reduced in the outside central city areas. In other words, the impact of income could be made to work differentially if the politically relevant levels of income were altered through changes in governmental boundaries.

It is also possible that the competitive situation caused by fragmentaion, which is particularly important among outside central city school jurisdictions, but also has some impact on central city school expenditures, may cause present per capita and per student expenditure to be higher than would be the case if a common area-wide school jurisdiction were established. In other words, the effort to acquire or maintain quality education in certain jurisdictions may well bid up the price of educational services for all the neighboring jurisdictions. The result could be a higher average educational quality than would be the case if there were a common jurisdiction for education.

The higher average school expenditure level that is caused by the present system, however, is not responsive to the nature of the education problem that has been produced by metropolitanism. The need is for the concentration of educational resources in the central cities. It is in these cities that the educational function is most difficult to perform adequately. Yet the present system distributes resources in exactly the opposite direction, less where the problems are most severe and more where the problems are relatively easy to cope with. Governmental reorganization would make it possible to plan education on an area-wide basis and could make a contribution to overcoming this paradox.[4]

Whatever may be the advantage of governmental reorganization, the findings of this study relative to the importance of external aid do indicate a means by which such reorganization could be encouraged. The carrot of state and federal aid could be used for this purpose. It is perfectly clear that the consolidation movement among school districts was accomplished primarily by the provision of extra aid for those districts that accepted consolidation. This example could be followed for other functions or sets of functions, and on the basis of the findings of this study, there need not be any significant reduction in local fiscal effort as a result. In other words, aid may be used as a means of accomplishing desired reorganization, and the side effect would not necessarily be a reduction in local fiscal effort.[5]

Implications for the Provision of Services

Of general importance to the overall level of services are the findings in this study related to the significance of the assignment variables. Although the assignment variables were developed as a means of making possible local fiscal comparisons across state lines, it was learned in the process that the character of assignment itself influences fiscal levels to the extent the local tax assignment is positively correlated with state-local tax levels. In other words, the higher the assignment of tax responsibility to the local level, the higher state-local tax totals are. If the policy goal, therefore, is to devote greater resources to the public sector, thereby generally raising service levels, it follows that high local tax assignment will help in accomplishing this end.

State aid plays a similar role. Because state aid is replacive only to a minor degree of local tax effort, at most, the addition of aid to local resources will increase local expenditures. A system, therefore, that combines high local tax assignment with large amounts of state aid will increase the level of local expenditures. Because both state aid and assignment are in practice variables that can be influenced by public action, it follows that their adjustment could be made to fit whatever public policy goal is sought. The alternatives available to any particular state depend on its present aid and assignment system. For some, emphasis should be placed on changing assignment (particularly true for the South); for others, more aid could be provided; and for still others, some combination of these two alternatives could be adopted.

A more specific service issue relates to the great amount of attention given recently to urban poverty. Concern has been expressed about the concentration of disadvantaged people in central cities, and policies have already been adopted that it is hoped will result in more resources being devoted to this metropolitan problem. Several findings in this study are relevant to how this might be accomplished.

Because state aid is found on the whole not to be replacive of local tax effort, it is possible to increase total resources devoted to fighting poverty by increasing state and federal aid. The present administration has already embarked on this route through its education aid and antipoverty programs. Those involved in these programs have already shown great interest in whether the resources supplied are replacive of local effort. The findings in this study indicate that care should be exercised in not allowing isolated examples or short-term responses, which may give the impression that local effort is being reduced, to obscure the long-run additive quality of aid in the solving of the poverty problem. The finding, however, that only in central cities is aid at all replacive of local tax effort does mean that this phenomenon needs to be closely watched as aid comes to play a larger and larger role in local finance systems.

Relative to central city poverty, great emphasis has been placed on the role of central city education. Much of this emphasis, especially in recent years, has been on the problem of educating the disadvantaged in central cities. The income-education relationship within the central city is one of the most important findings in this study because it is the only part of the fiscal picture in central cities that is income-related. The reason for this relationship is probably that aspiration levels are, to some degree, measured by income.

The raising of income levels in central cities, therefore, should cause a raising of educational standards. To the extent that urban renewal succeeds in attracting middle- and high-income people back to the central city, it may cause greater resources to be devoted to central city education. There is, however, a chicken and egg problem because urban renewal will not be likely to attract people back until educational quality is improved. It follows, therefore, that those who champion urban renewal should place much greater emphasis than in the past on improving educational quality in central cities.

Long term Implications

Since the Supreme Court decision insisting on "one man-one vote" as a principle for representation in the American governmental system, there has been much speculation about the significance of greater metropolitan representation in state legislatures. The uniformly higher aid levels outside of metropolitan areas, for example, is consistent with the present pattern of representation, with greater aid on a per capita basis going to nonmetropolitan than to metropolitan areas. The reason for greater aid to suburban than to city areas is less clear.

Although suburban areas are under-represented in state legislatures, even more so than central cities, they have done relatively well in terms of state aid. This result probably is related both to the historical situation when these areas were, in fact, rural and to the set of functions—education and highways—that state legislatures aid. The functions generally aided by the states make up a larger part of the services provided in suburban areas than of those provided in central cities. The suburban areas thus receive more total state aid relative to their fiscal burden than do central cities.

Because reapportionment will increase suburban more than central city representation, it follows that the present aid advantage of the suburban areas will be retained. On the other hand it is possible that a reapportioned state legislature will be sufficiently metropolitan-oriented to show concern for central city problems. The result could be a change in the group of services aided—the addition of police, fire, and sanitation, for example—which would help the cities, or central cities might be provided with more direct general aid. The evidence on this issue is not yet in, but past behavior would seem to point in the direction of the suburban aid advantage being retained.

If the states do not respond more generously to central city needs than they have in the past, it follows that equity in the system will result only from increased federal aid to cities. Even this possibility, however, does not guarantee that the fiscal outputs will match the program needs of the cities. This problem is at its greatest with the education function. Suburbs are today devoting more resources on a per student basis to education than cities. Further, there seems to be a determination on the part of many suburban school districts to stay ahead of cities. More federal aid to cities for education, therefore, may result in the suburbs simply tapping their own superior resources more extensively and manipulating state aid even more skillfully to maintain their education edge over the cities. Because the pool of education resources is limited, the result will be a rise in the cost of education services, but cities would continue to labor under a fiscal disadvantage.

It is difficult within the context of the present governmental system to see how any manipulation of the forces now operative can change the present pattern of responses to central city education needs. A redrawing of local governmental boundaries might help, but it does not seem that anything else will, unless it be a direct state or federal assumption of responsibility for the education function. Such an assumption of direct responsibility is merely an indirect means of changing the basic character of the governmental system.

Whatever the policy response to the present governmental system operating in metropolitan areas, the rapid growth of the state and local public sector described in the first chapter will continue. There is no reason to assume that there will be any basic change in that pattern, and all projections made over the past few years on the basis of substantive analysis of needs have underestimated the increase in these levels. The issue, therefore, is not whether fiscal growth will continue but whether the service patterns will consist of different combinations of services or whether the areas in which they are provided will be reconstituted. The first seems more likely than the latter.

It does seem clear that the present education/noneducation patterns of services in central city and outside central city areas is likely to change. The truly suburban areas will soon undergo rapid increases in their noneducation expenditures, whereas a renewed emphasis is being placed on education in some central cities. It is not clear, for reasons already given, that this emphasis will reduce the gap between central city and outside central city education expenditures. The big push, however, for new education expenditures in the central city is of very recent origin and its relative impact has not yet shown itself in the fiscal data.

As metropolitan expenditures increase, nonmetropolitan expenditures have increased more rapidly, thereby reducing the divergence. If metropolitanism is one of the dynamics causing increased expenditures, then as the country increasingly metropolitanizes, the fiscal levels in the nonmetropolitan areas will go up, too, and perhaps even more rapidly. It is therefore possible to predict that the greater relative growth in local fiscal activity over the next few years will be in the nonmetropolitan rather than the metropolitan areas, even though the absolute growth in metropolitan areas will continue to be greater.

The distribution of responsibility as measured by assignment and aid possesses great stability in the overall governmental system. Thus far federal aid, although it has increased substantially, has not basically altered the relative roles of the various parts of the system. Nor have increased state government fiscal totals increased their role in the total system. The lack of change in relative roles simply demonstrates that all parts of the system are growing rapidly; there is every indication that all will continue to grow. The only distinct possibility for an alteration in relative roles is for the federal aid proportion to increase, but such an increase will require a massive upward adjustment in such aid.

The growth in overall state-local fiscal activity is a clear reflection of the increasingly metropolitan nature of the United States. The emphasis of this study has been on the nature of the relationships between metropolitanism and fiscal behavior. Although the relationships are complex and interrelated, the metropolitan framework has been useful in understanding both the dynamics of local fiscal behavior and the policy consequences of this behavior. In turn, knowledge of the nature of metropolitanism has been expanded through an understanding of its fiscal dimension.

References

1. James Q. Wilson and Edward C. Banfield, "Voting Behavior on Municipal Public Expenditures: A Study in Rationality and Self-interest," in *The Public Economy of Urban Communities*, ed. Julius Margolis (Baltimore: Johns Hopkins Press, 1965), 74–91.

2. *New York Times*, August 23, 1966.

3. John C. Bollens and Henry J. Schmandt, *The Metropolis: Its People, Politics, and Economic Life* (New York: Harper & Row, 1965), 183. For a review of the arguments surrounding this issue and of the political problems associated with it, see Chapters 7 and 16.

4. The problem is being examined by a study now being done at the Metropolitan Studies Center, Syracuse University: *Large City Education Systems.* Some of the early findings of that study are reported in the following articles: Campbell and Meranto, *op. cit.,* Sacks and Ranney, *op. cit.* and Alan K. Campbell, "The Socio-Economic, Political and Fiscal Environment of Educational Policy-Making in Large Cities," presented at the 1966 Cubberley Conference, School of Education, Stanford University, July 1966.

5. The Intergovernmental Cooperation Act, which at this date has passed the Senate but not the House, represents a step in this direction of using federal aid to accomplish some governmental reorganization. Under this bill metropolitanwide planning agencies would be granted the right to review, but not veto, local government applications for federal funds for the building of physical facilities.

Appendix

Appendix A-1

Population, Income, and Race Inside and Outside Standard Metropolitan Statistical Areas, by State, 1957

	Est. pop. in 000 1957	Per cent pop. SMSA 1957	Per capita income: 1959		Median family income: 1959		Non white as per cent of total pop.	
			SMSA	Non-SMSA	SMSA	Non-SMSA	SMSA	Non-SMSA
NORTHEAST								
Maine	905	19.70%	$1,710	$1,439	$5,506	$4,706	.4	.6
N. H.	585	17.73	1,882	1,760	5,858	5,588		.4
Ver.	386	—	—	1,515	—	4,890	—	.2
Mass.	5,001	85.21	2,056	1,837	3,366	5,784	2.6	1.2
R. I.	839	86.19	1,840	1,716	5,625	5,300	2.2	4.2
Conn.	2,377	77.56	2,424	1,820	6,989	6,557	5.2	1.4
N. Y.	16,197	85.52	2,326	1,708	6,522	5,526	10.0	2.2
N. J.	5,697	78.92	2,299	1,954	6,854	6,543	9.4	6.1
Pa.	11,023	77.86	1,946	1,533	5,933	4,985	9.5	1.2
Del.	408	68.89	2,322	1,703	6,823	4,839	12.1	18.7
Md.	2,873	78.22	2,133	1,538	6,746	4,826	17.7	14.7
NORTH CENTRAL								
Mich.	7,388	73.12	2.071	1,583	6,368	5,329	12.0	2.4
Ohio	9,178	69.52	2,108	1,613	6,531	5,408	11.0	1.9
Ind.	4,441	33.83	2,005	1,673	6,330	5,333	10.7	1.4
Ill.	9,670	76.93	2,449	1,290	7,086	4,947	13.2	2.0
Wis.	3,797	46.28	2,176	1,558	6,819	5,146	4.3	.7
Minn.	3,284	51.34	2,120	1,326	6,629	4,349	1.7	.8
Iowa	2,717	33.21	1,984	1,480	6,206	4,486	2.5	.4
Mo.	4,210	57.87	2,089	1,286	6,152	3,591	13.1	3.7
N. D.	629	10.58	1,836	1,303	5,983	4,372	.4	2.3
S. D.	672	12.72	1,713	1,269	5,702	4.031	.7	4.5
Neb.	1,386	37.56	2,053	1,375	6,203	4,101	5.7	.7
Kans.	2,097	37.35	2,125	1,565	6,364	4,660	7.8	2.6
SOUTH								
Va.	3,772	50.94	1,981	1,201	6,139	3,857	19.9	21.7
W. Va.	1,904	30.91	1,750	1,212	5,620	5,078	4.2	5.1
Ky.	3,010	34.10	1,836	1,064	5,676	3,131	10.4	5.5
Tenn.	3,484	45.77	1,633	1,053	5,033	3,132	23.3	10.9
N. C.	4,408	24.56	1,730	1,096	5,244	3,583	23.1	26.2
S. C.	2,303	32.23	1,415	1,015	4,638	3,457	27.7	38.3
Ga.	3,794	46.01	1,743	1,032	5,238	3,325	25.6	31.0
Fla.	4,297	65.57	1,852	1,490	5,012	4,139	16.5	20.7
Ala.	3,205	45.55	1,530	1,008	4,936	3,136	32.0	28.4
Miss.	2,178	8.59	1,556	911	4,783	2,745	40.1	42.5
La.	3,085	49.96	1,679	1,060	5,160	3,335	30.9	33.3
Ark.	1,823	19.11	1,584	1,017	4,647	2,867	19.1	22.5
Okla.	2,300	43.88	1,935	1,360	5,575	3,806	9.5	5.3
Texas	9,019	63.39	1,821	1,289	5,492	3,784	12.7	12.4

Appendix A-1 (continued)

	Est. pop. in 000 1957	Per cent pop. SMSA 1957	Per capita income: 1959 SMSA	Non-SMSA	Median family income: 1959 SMSA	Non-SMSA	Non white as per cent of total pop. SMSA	Non-SMSA
WEST								
N. Mex.	870	27.57	1,943	1,469	6,252	5,002	3.1	9.6
Ariz.	1,136	71.36	1,909	1,403	5,833	4,859	5.7	21.2
Mont.	650	22.59	1,947	1,603	6,092	5,194	1.3	4.2
Idaho	645	—	—	1,608	—	5,259	—	1.5
Wyo.	318	—	—	1,888	—	5,877	—	2.1
Colo.	1,625	67.95	2,066	1,512	6,307	4,728	4.0	1.1
Utah	830	67.45	1,799	1,479	6,142	5,447	1.5	2.8
Wash.	2,711	62.12	2,172	1,796	6,574	5,662	4.2	2.5
Ore.	1,694	50.38	2,127	1,768	6,277	5,538	2.8	1.3
Nev.	248	74.23	2,505	1,905	7,086	5,812	7.5	8.1
Calif.	14,178	86.47	2,379	1,849	6,889	5,657	8.6	4.1

Appendix A-2

Summary of Local Fiscal Characteristics Inside and Outside Standard Metropolitan Statistical Areas, by State, 1957

	Per capita total general expenditures SMSA	Non-SMSA	Local expenditure assignment	Per capita total taxes SMSA	Non-SMSA	Local tax assignment	State aid SMSA	Non-SMSA
NORTHEAST								
Maine	$109.08	$ 96.90	49.3%	$ 92.51	$ 70.18	49.8%	$ 9.77	$ 7.60
N. H.	113.20	124.16	50.7	89.13	93.23	61.8	5.76	10.68
Ver.	—	115.60	48.8	—	77.53	46.2	—	25.56
Mass.	191.09	248.00	66.9	119.47	160.40	59.4	50.43	68.00
R. I.	118.55	104.22	54.2	83.95	62.10	51.9	19.26	15.06
Conn.	156.98	117.08	49.1	101.88	77.78	50.7	16.28	26.17
N. Y.	239.29	222.25	78.8	148.20	94.23	61.3	52.91	91.04
N. J.	175.40	154.51	74.9	126.12	112.23	71.7	20.71	26.58
Pa.	136.15	102.57	64.9	80.57	41.80	44.6	26.02	48.42
Del.	92.49	82.36	33.4	41.11	19.94	24.0	31.67	48.28
Md.	168.90	126.86	64.7	81.32	45.44	45.7	44.63	53.97

Appendix A-2 (continued)

	Per capita total general expenditures		Local expenditure assignment	Per capita total taxes		Local tax assignment	State aid	
	SMSA	Non-SMSA		SMSA	Non-SMSA		SMSA	Non-SMSA
NORTH CENTRAL								
Mich.	186.78	157.95	64.8	95.54	55.42	44.7	58.11	75.93
Ohio	166.06	144.38	71.3	89.09	56.92	51.8	35.82	55.23
Ind.	141.73	133.34	65.5	87.48	66.83	53.3	31.08	39.93
III.	170.14	135.29	71.4	114.46	85.81	60.1	23.89	26.50
Wis.	211.87	177.71	79.2	108.22	80.29	49.8	61.31	77.70
Minn.	195.02	183.15	71.2	103.73	82.58	51.2	42.22	60.67
Iowa	139.37	158.51	61.6	88.87	88.97	49.4	26.35	44.22
Mo.	135.50	89.21	60.1	85.28	46.14	51.9	16.17	26.67
N. D.	158.46	134.25	50.8	96.05	88.31	52.0	17.20	28.22
S. D.	131.54	131.61	51.5	98.16	105.18	62.2	9.85	14.04
Neb.	138.45	144.48	66.2	83.06	97.02	63.4	18.88	31.29
Kans.	161.45	171.45	61.8	88.23	106.99	57.1	31.29	47.63
SOUTH								
Va.	128.76	73.31	57.6	63.99	29.73	35.7	24.13	30.73
W. Va.	94.09	75.46	50.5	48.45	28.06	29.6	23.12	35.55
Ky.	117.90	65.09	53.0	70.54	26.90	38.1	13.02	25.52
Tenn.	114.17	89.82	62.7	55.44	25.56	33.5	27.91	44.99
N. C.	99.91	62.66	43.5	48.89	24.41	26.5	18.35	19.00
S. C.	100.56	84.08	56.7	33.80	23.44	25.0	36.72	42.64
Ga.	122.17	98.85	58.1	58.34	27.37	33.1	23.30	46.11
Fla.	149.86	127.31	61.4	77.60	49.65	43.7	25.62	45.39
Ala.	107.19	89.82	55.4	40.56	18.33	28.2	28.69	51.82
Miss.	107.83	83.63	56.5	62.95	31.34	31.5	21.47	36.60
La.	142.64	119.29	48.1	54.67	27.37	25.2	51.22	69.78
Ark.	81.33	68.71	49.0	40.11	26.84	29.9	16.61	26.69
Okla.	123.90	108.83	47.3	56.82	42.10	32.0	24.97	49.33
Texas	143.37	125.52	65.5	69.10	62.37	47.7	24.91	37.61
WEST								
N. Mex.	116.04	126.07	47.3	45.77	31.98	24.2	46.27	83.44
Ariz.	162.14	143.60	60.2	70.14	59.62	41.5	41.46	56.32
Mont.	190.55	151.40	54.2	107.83	114.24	58.2	16.17	22.67
Idaho	—	134.40	52.5	—	76.93	49.4	—	30.07
Wyo.	—	186.60	57.0	—	79.06	44.8	—	61.36
Colo.	183.16	224.79	68.8	99.04	99.31	51.3	47.84	102.05
Utah	136.73	139.36	58.5	76.87	62.34	43.9	30.18	49.10
Wash.	159.31	177.51	56.4	62.05	53.03	30.9	50.51	74.39
Ore.	165.72	167.98	58.8	99.81	83.80	44.5	34.96	45.76
Nev.	213.24	224.70	55.4	93.04	120.46	41.5	42.38	66.27
Calif.	237.90	246.17	73.1	119.31	110.02	50.6	74.41	97.86

Appendix

Appendix A-3

Per Capita Local Expenditures by Function Inside and Outside Standard Metropolitan Statistical Areas, by States, 1957

	Total education expenditure		Total noneducation expenditure		Total welfare expenditure		Total highway expenditure		Health and hospital expenditure for operation	
	SMSA	Non-SMSA	SMSA	Non-SMSA	SMSA	Non-SMSA	SMSA	Non-SMSA	SMSA	Non-SMSA
NORTHEAST										
Maine	$48.32	$48.98	$60.76	$47.92	$2.67	$3.46	$16.73	$18.71	$2.67	$1.56
N. H.	25.32	63.40	69.40	60.75	7.04	4.93	17.71	18.65	4.48	3.67
Ver.	—	59.62	—	56.08	—	3.16	—	28.66	—	2.00
Mass.	63.13	92.80	127.98	154.40	26.48	35.85	15.88	36.00	13.13	3.20
R. I.	48.79	60.63	69.76	43.65	5.54	1.47	10.00	8.93	2.82	.96
Conn.	78.95	66.35	78.01	50.80	2.35	.73	11.04	16.93	3.46	.88
N. Y.	80.63	102.80	158.77	103.99	22.31	18.64	19.51	36.82	18.57	6.58
N. J.	71.86	69.14	98.48	125.43	8.04	6.87	11.25	19.80	12.87	5.71
Pa.	61.11	64.48	75.08	37.96	3.54	2.69	11.49	12.17	2.79	.47
Del.	48.48	53.16	44.01	29.20	2.76	4.40	2.71	5.27	1.20	.13
Md.	68.46	73.78	100.44	53.08	9.16	9.81	17.00	15.37	6.19	4.04
NORTH CENTRAL										
Mich.	84.98	78.24	101.80	79.71	5.56	3.85	19.32	33.77	12.95	8.61
Ohio	69.40	77.02	96.67	67.33	10.61	8.81	18.33	23.19	7.90	5.12
Ind.	64.93	69.71	76.76	63.67	12.09	10.19	12.05	16.39	5.50	8.68
Ill.	64.68	77.73	105.44	57.60	5.49	4.90	25.02	17.75	6.91	27.5
Wis.	65.77	64.62	146.01	113.16	15.36	18.53	29.77	46.02	16.31	9.70
Minn.	78.50	84.86	116.56	98.25	19.89	24.03	19.31	32.02	16.79	8.12
Iowa	67.59	77.21	71.78	81.31	4.23	4.23	17.40	37.78	7.46	10.05
Mo.	56.96	57.67	78.58	31.51	.74	.48	13.93	9.71	10.08	3.94
N. D.	63.14	63.62	95.33	70.63	4.80	4.07	36.48	34.96	2.59	1.28
S. D.	70.13	67.78	61.41	63.83	2.08	2.76	21.04	28.08	2.44	3.70
Neb.	61.14	64.67	77.23	79.84	10.25	15.09	15.58	28.92	9.61	7.07
Kans.	73.42	72.80	88.02	98.65	12.47	24.89	20.13	31.98	3.73	6.66

SOUTH										
Va.	57.19	46.37	71.63	26.90	7.11	5.68	7.76	3.07	3.64	2.20
W. Va.	47.78	54.96	46.38	20.46	1.67	1.25	3.48	2.24	5.54	3.32
Ky.	55.25	42.87	62.68	22.22	2.67	.43	6.66	4.26	6.48	3.60
Tenn.	48.62	47.64	65.57	42.17	1.08	1.08	11.53	16.48	10.89	4.23
N. C.	31.14	24.47	68.70	38.21	11.14	11.21	8.04	3.52	6.70	4.84
S. C.	58.29	54.44	42.24	29.66	.52	.43	4.83	5.97	9.63	6.39
Ga.	48.02	49.07	74.22	49.73	2.10	1.78	12.32	14.82	12.03	7.90
Fla.	56.30	59.37	93.58	67.91	1.67	.90	11.03	12.49	10.30	10.65
Ala.	43.31	45.30	63.88	44.52	.32	.12	15.75	20.26	4.29	4.95
Miss.	48.65	38.35	46.27	46.14	.63	.38	19.58	19.46	1.68	5.29
La.	51.95	75.43	90.67	43.87	.27	.06	15.14	10.93	2.19	2.31
Ark.	41.33	37.88	39.94	30.84	.56	.24	8.50	10.56	1.28	3.75
Okla.	44.68	80.12	54.78	45.42	.66	.58	10.80	21.72	2.60	3.44
Texas	67.34	72.95	76.01	52.62	.77	.47	15.19	17.28	5.98	4.70
WEST										
N. Mex.	53.56	83.32	62.48	42.77	.25	.07	7.79	8.63	6.64	4.14
Ariz.	89.37	77.51	73.46	64.56	.02	.42	14.42	15.61	5.74	8.44
Mont.	73.44	83.67	117.01	67.75	5.03	4.60	38.35	21.25	3.19	4.15
Idaho	—	66.86	—	67.54	—	1.44	—	23.45	—	6.62
Wyo.	—	94.71	—	91.88	—	15.52	—	16.29	—	16.45
Colo.	74.75	83.89	108.39	140.89	34.57	60.93	16.11	32.57	6.58	7.52
Utah	77.89	86.77	58.83	52.56	.80	.36	10.75	15.04	5.81	4.34
Wash.	73.36	98.00	85.96	79.48	.16	.13	19.55	29.53	9.50	6.08
Ore.	80.52	91.31	85.22	76.66	4.38	3.46	20.55	30.16	4:40	3.08
Nev.	71.53	98.89	141.71	125.81	2.54	5.88	13.36	23.24	21.76	23.20
Calif.	95.10	97.10	142.82	149.00	27.59	36.08	13.87	24.95	12.89	18.73

Appendix

Appendix B

Fiscal, Socio-Economic and Governmental Characteristics, 36 Standard Metropolitan Statistical Area Sample, 1957

Standard metropolitan statistical areas	Total expenditures (per capita)			Educational expenditures (per capita)			Current expenditures (per capita)			Highway expenditures (per capita)			Health expenditures (per capita)		
	SMSA	CC	OCC	SMSA	CC	OCC	SMSA	CC	OCC	SMSA	CC	OCC	SMSA	CC	OCC
Albany-Schenectady-Troy	$180	$172	$188	$86	$63	$105	$66	$52	$77	$19	$16	$22	$6	$7	$6
Atlanta	133	158	100	54	55	53	44	51	39	15	22	9	12	14	12
Atlantic City	177	232	140	50	47	52	48	46	49	18	18	18	11	15	9
Baltimore	199	199	142	59	59	71	47	47	47	19	19	19	11	11	1
Binghamton	201	228	185	93	69	108	80	67	88	17	11	20	22	42	10
Bridgeport	147	145	149	62	41	90	51	40	64	8	6	10	8	11	6
Buffalo	203	193	210	78	52	99	61	45	73	19	17	21	12	12	12
Cleveland	186	180	186	67	50	85	52	44	60	20	19	22	14	11	6
Hartford	165	186	154	85	51	103	59	47	65	10	8	12	5	12	1
Houston	162	155	187	78	65	126	55	47	86	17	18	14	6	8	1
Jacksonville	133	175	91	56	56	56	43	43	43	9	16	3	8	10	6
Jersey City	214	237	194	51	50	52	50	50	51	7	6	8	31	47	18
Kansas City	146	186	112	59	63	55	43	55	34	18	25	13	7	19	5

Madison	215	241	177	75	71	81	58	57	59	36	38	38	9	11	7
Memphis	116	125	79	40	37	59	32	29	43	13	14	5	12	14	3
Miami	188	226	169	70	70	70	47	47	47	11	10	11	13	13	13
Milwaukee	222	229	210	65	51	89	45	40	53	30	32	26	23	25	17
Nashville	108	152	75	49	43	55	43	42	43	9	13	6	10	16	5
Newark	197	243	181	85	76	88	63	64	63	10	6	12	18	36	11
New York	257	257	260	82	63	140	60	50	89	19	18	22	23	28	8
Norwalk	160	145	195	98	81	139	69	53	108	20	6	10	2	2	1
Paterson-Clifton-Passaic	156	155	157	48	56	81	55	51	56	11	7	11	7	9	6
Rochester	199	200	196	70	53	92	54	48	63	18	17	18	13	16	10
Sacramento	216	256	189	96	83	104	68	66	70	11	17	8	17	17	15
St. Louis	134	149	124	61	46	71	48	41	52	13	10	15	11	21	5
San Antonio	112	113	104	53	48	87	38	35	60	15	17	3	5	6	0
San Diego	190	191	189	80	72	90	62	57	67	14	17	9	9	7	12
San Jose	209	226	203	100	74	108	65	61	67	14	19	12	12	16	11
Savannah	95	112	61	35	36	33	35	36	33	5	6	2	9	10	9
Seattle	159	174	142	71	57	87	56	48	66	23	26	11	11	5	6
Spokane	157	165	139	76	67	99	55	50	68	23	27	15	4	4	3
Stamford	176	151	205	88	64	115	71	62	81	13	10	16	4	2	6
Syracuse	200	198	201	75	54	90	65	51	75	30	28	32	7	8	7
Tampa-St. Petersburg	132	159	89	47	48	45	41	42	39	12	15	7	16	24	2
Toledo	167	172	155	67	58	88	56	54	59	14	15	11	10	11	3
Utica-Rome	205	192	216	96	62	127	71	53	87	30	28	32	11	15	8

Appendix

Appendix B (continued)

Standard metropolitan statistical areas	Public welfare expenditures (per capita)			All other expenditures (per capita)			Noneducation expenditures			Taxes (per capita)			Property taxes (per capita)		
	SMSA	CC	OCC	SMSA	CC	OCC	SMSA	CC	OCC	SMSA	CC	OCC	SMSA	CC	OCC
Albany-Schenectady-Troy	$16	$16	$15	$51	$71	$84	$95	$109	$84	$107	$114	$101	$104	$110	$98
Atlanta	3	3	2	48	64	48	79	103	48	68	98	44	61	84	41
Atlantic City	13	15	12	84	138	88	127	186	88	143	194	110	113	136	98
Baltimore	12	18	3	98	92	71	140	140	71	105	87	62	75	91	54
Binghamton	16	21	10	53	78	78	108	158	78	96	107	89	92	101	13
Bridgeport	1	2	1	67	87	59	85	105	59	98	99	97	93	97	96
Buffalo	17	19	16	77	95	111	125	141	111	114	116	112	99	98	99
Cleveland	12	12	11	73	88	101	119	130	101	103	106	98	100	103	95
Hartford	2	5	1	63	110	52	80	135	52	105	137	89	104	135	87
Houston	1	1	1	60	64	61	84	91	61	85	84	70	80	79	84
Jacksonville	1	1	1	59	93	35	77	120	35	58	79	38	45	55	36
Jersey City	11	12	11	112	121	142	162	187	142	160	162	158	144	149	140
Kansas City	4	1	6	57	78	56	87	123	56	85	105	69	71	79	64
Madison	17	18	17	77	104	96	140	170	96	99	104	70	97	101	90
Memphis	1	1	1	49	59	21	75	88	21	53	55	45	43	43	42

Miami	3	3	3	92	130	99	118	156	98	107	132	94	87	103	78
Milwaukee	15	17	13	90	104	121	157	178	121	118	126	104	114	122	101
Nashville	1	1	1	38	78	21	58	109	21	61	71	51	55	62	48
Newark	9	13	7	68	111	93	112	167	93	146	178	139	132	157	123
New York	24	28	11	109	119	119	175	193	119	164	167	153	120	111	148
Norwalk	1	1	1	52	56	56	62	65	56	112	98	148	112	98	147
Paterson-Clifton-Passaic	6	9	5	58	75	76	82	99	76	116	118	116	105	106	105
Rochester	28	23	23	76	91	104	130	147	104	121	122	119	86	87	86
Sacramento	30	30	30	63	110	85	121	173	85	98	128	75	83	102	70
St. Louis	2	1	3	47	72	53	73	103	53	84	98	75	67	65	68
San Antonio	0	0	1	32	42	17	59	65	17	51	54	26	48	51	25
San Diego	21	21	21	67	75	99	110	120	99	86	93	76	72	75	68
San Jose	24	24	24	59	94	95	109	153	95	109	145	97	99	123	91
Savannah	2	2	2	44	58	28	60	76	28	53	64	31	44	52	28
Seattle	0	0	0	55	86	54	88	117	54	66	81	48	51	59	41
Spokane	0	0	0	53	66	40	81	98	40	56	62	42	47	50	38
Stamford	3	4	3	69	72	91	89	87	91	146	131	162	143	129	159
Syracuse	21	20	21	67	88	112	125	144	112	103	121	91	92	99	88
Tampa-St. Petersburg	1	1	1	56	70	43	85	111	43	66	78	43	49	55	38
Toledo	9	9	9	66	77	67	100	113	67	86	94	66	62	62	63
Utica-Rome	16	18	15	52	70	90	109	130	90	87	93	81	83	88	79

Appendix

Appendix B (continued)

Standard metropolitan statistical areas	Nonaided expenditures (per capita)			Nonaided education expenditures (per capita)			Nonaided Noneducation expenditures (per capita)			Total aid (per capita)			Education aid (per capita)		
	SMSA	CC	OCC	SMSA	CC	OCC	SMSA	CC	OCC	SMSA	CC	OCC	SMSA	CC	OCC
Albany-Schenectady-Troy	$124	$131	$118	$55	$42	$65	$ 69	$ 89	$ 52	$57	$41	$70	$31	$20	$39
Atlanta	110	136	77	32	39	27	77	97	48	23	22	24	21	16	24
Atlantic City	145	204	107	36	39	33	110	165	74	31	28	33	14	7	18
Baltimore	139	127	109	47	54	54	93	72	56	60	48	32	13	9	17
Binghamton	125	155	107	41	30	47	84	125	60	76	73	79	52	40	60
Bridgeport	134	135	133	53	33	78	81	102	55	13	11	16	9	7	12
Buffalo	151	148	154	50	35	62	101	113	92	52	45	57	28	17	37
Cleveland	152	146	154	57	43	73	95	103	82	34	34	32	10	7	13
Hartford	149	174	137	75	44	91	75	130	46	16	13	18	10	7	12
Houston	139	137	125	55	47	84	84	90	42	23	18	41	23	18	42
Jacksonville	103	148	64	28	31	31	75	117	33	27	27	27	28	25	25
Jersey City	195	220	174	41	42	40	154	178	134	19	17	20	11	9	12
Kansas City	123	168	84	38	51	28	85	117	56	23	18	26	21	12	28
Madison	160	185	87	68	66	51	92	116	17	54	56	33	7	5	10

City															
Memphis	89	96	61	27	24	42	61	72	20	27	29	18	13	12	1
Miami	167	205	147	50	50	82	117	154	97	21	21	21	20	20	20
Milwaukee	160	165	149	61	42	40	99	123	67	63	64	61	5	9	6
Nashville	84	119	60	35	30	40	48	88	20	24	33	15	14	13	15
Newark	176	217	162	72	63	76	104	155	87	21	25	19	13	13	13
New York	205	204	210	60	44	107	145	160	103	52	53	50	22	19	33
Norwalk	145	133	174	87	71	126	58	62	48	15	12	21	11	10	13
Paterson-Clifton-Passaic	139	137	139	61	43	67	78	94	72	18	18	18	14	13	14
Rochester	148	165	140	46	37	58	103	122	82	47	42	55	24	16	34
Sacramento	132	208	90	43	63	31	90	144	59	84	67	91	53	30	66
St. Louis	116	135	104	49	35	58	67	100	46	18	14	20	12	10	13
San Antonio	90	95	71	34	31	54	57	65	15	22	18	33	20	18	33
San Diego	129	133	124	44	48	40	85	86	85	61	58	64	36	24	50
San Jose	138	168	129	56	48	58	82	118	71	71	59	74	44	25	50
Savannah	78	95	45	18	20	17	60	75	28	17	18	16	17	16	16
Seattle	109	126	88	32	35	28	77	91	54	51	48	54	39	22	54
Spokane	115	122	95	46	42	55	69	80	40	43	42	43	31	25	44
Stamford	162	140	186	79	56	104	83	84	82	15	12	19	9	8	11
Syracuse	133	150	121	30	33	27	103	117	93	68	48	81	46	21	62
Tampa-St. Petersburg	110	135	66	27	28	24	83	107	42	24	27	23	21	21	22
Toledo	132	137	119	55	50	66	77	87	53	35	35	36	12	8	22
Utica-Rome	131	137	125	47	33	59	84	104	66	74	55	91	49	30	66

Appendix B (continued)

Standard metropolitan statistical areas	Nonwhite population as per cent of total population			School enrollment as per cent of total population			Owner-occupied housing as per cent of total housing, 1959			Education expenditures as per cent of total expenditure			Population per government unit		
	SMSA	CC	OCC	SMSA	CC	OCC	SMSA	CC	OCC	SMSA	CC	OCC	SMSA	CC	OCC
Albany-Schenectady-Troy	3%	6%	1%	16%	12%	24%	61%	44%	90%	47%	36%	556%	2548	31662	1455
Atlanta	23	38	7	21	20	23	59	46	73	40	35	526	13100	106338	7423
Atlantic City	18	36	7	17	14	19	62	34	81	28	20	370	4232	21030	2704
Baltimore	22	35	7	18	17	18	64	54	76	30	34	498	70893	471115	28015
Binghamton	1	2	0	20	17	22	65	48	75	46	30	581	3192	25787	2047
Bridgeport	5	10	1	17	14	20	62	41	82	42	28	604	16417	78668	8117
Buffalo	7	14	2	17	13	19	61	44	74	39	27	470	9011	273486	4511
Cleveland	15	29	1	16	15	18	62	45	78	36	28	458	12666	147946	6276
Hartford	6	16	1	21	14	22	59	25	78	51	27	666	12463	55581	8870
Houston	20	23	10	21	20	24	65	60	80	48	42	672	11832	145333	2700
Jacksonville	23	41	9	21	20	22	66	50	82	42	32	611	37272	50519	25990
Jersey City	7	14	2	11	12	10	29	27	32	24	21	269	25906	94325	15398
Kansas City	11	18	6	19	16	21	65	54	77	41	34	496	4118	63015	2308
Madison	1	2	0	18	16	21	62	54	73	35	29	459	901	20000	380

Memphis	36	37	34	21	20	23	57	55	65	35	29	740	41688	160667	8469
Miami	15	23	11	17	14	19	59	42	69	37	31	416	25905	69741	18072
Milwaukee	6	9	0	15	14	17	58	48	76	29	22	422	8444	141800	3210
Nashville	19	38	5	19	17	20	61	40	77	46	28	728	34213	59667	21928
Newark	13	34	7	17	16	17	54	23	65	43	31	486	8870	103822	6710
New York	12	15	5	15	13	20	34	22	74	32	25	540	17881	2604992	4406
Norwalk	6	8	1	21	19	25	68	63	81	61	56	713	7286	10380	4193
Paterson-Clifton-Passaic	4	9	2	17	15	18	65	45	72	48	36	518	5849	45710	4502
Rochester	4	8	0	16	12	20	67	51	88	35	26	469	6550	161393	2785
Sacramento	8	13	4	23	19	25	66	58	73	44	33	551	3223	25190	2006
St. Louis	15	29	6	16	14	17	62	38	78	46	31	575	4585	195514	2780
San Antonio	7	7	4	19	19	18	64	64	63	47	43	839	19126	39500	3907
San Diego	6	8	3	20	19	23	59	53	67	42	37	478	7608	123550	3473
San Jose	3	3	3	23	20	24	69	64	71	48	33	531	5835	25513	4650
Savannah	34	36	28	21	20	23	51	47	69	37	32	544	16114	17535	10901
Seattle	5	8	1	20	16	24	67	57	79	44	33	616	4081	112200	1885
Spokane	2	3	1	19	17	24	69	66	75	49	41	715	2090	61667	620
Stamford	5	8	2	17	16	20	62	54	71	50	42	559	18373	29062	13028
Syracuse	3	6	1	19	13	23	67	49	80	38	27	445	1915	107126	1151
Tampa-St. Petersburg	12	16	6	17	17	18	74	70	80	36	30	510	15429	37135	7727
Toledo	10	13	2	18	16	22	70	64	87	40	34	567	10696	44812	3567
Utica-Rome	2	3	0	20	16	22	64	50	76	47	32	582	1545	50387	833

Appendix

Appendix B (continued)

Standard metropolitan statistical areas	State aid: Non-education			Personal income (1959)			Total population (000)			Population per square mile			Population growth: 1957 population as per cent of 1950		
	SMSA	CC	OCC	SMSA	CC	OCC	SMSA	CC	OCC	SMSA	CC	OCC	SMSA	CC	OCC
Albany-Schenectady-Troy	$26	$20	$31	$1982	$1987	$1984	637	285	352	287	7500	161	108%	95%	121%
Atlanta	2	7	0	1924	1934	1915	930	425	505	540	3320	316	128	128	128
Atlantic City	17	21	15	1795	1583	1921	152	60	92	265	5030	163	115	97	130
Baltimore	47	39	16	1967	1867	2086	1631	942	688	902	11930	398	116	99	151
Binghamton	24	33	18	2019	2118	1964	204	77	127	288	7040	181	111	95	122
Bridgeport	4	3	4	2191	1955	2531	279	157	122	1733	10490	834	116	99	139
Buffalo	23	28	20	2031	1910	2114	1242	547	695	782	14020	449	114	99	137
Cleveland	24	27	19	2332	1856	2784	1697	888	810	2467	10960	1334	116	97	147
Hartford	5	6	5	2400	2105	2531	486	167	319	946	9800	642	120	94	139
Houston	0	1	0	2031	2063	1934	1112	872	240	650	2660	174	138	146	114
Jacksonville	2	2	2	1725	1612	1815	410	202	208	528	6740	278	135	99	210
Jersey City	8	9	8	2039	1964	2101	622	283	339	13816	21770	10587	96	95	97
Kansas City	2	6	0	2161	2175	2151	972	598	531	592	4600	351	119	97	148
Madison	47	51	23	2059	2197	1874	206	120	86	172	3330	74	122	125	118

Memphis	14	16	1	1589	1650	1357	584	482	102	777	3770	163	121	122	119
Miami	1	2	1	2017	1832	2101	803	279	524	391	8210	259	162	112	213
Milwaukee	58	55	55	2273	2105	2505	1123	709	414	1413	7790	588	117	111	129
Nashville	10	21	0	1770	1281	2135	376	179	197	707	6170	392	117	103	134
Newark	8	12	7	2518	1793	2748	1623	415	1208	2325	1730	2548	111	95	117
New York	30	34	16	2422	2306	2733	10353	7815	2538	4818	24810	1384	108	99	153
Norwalk	4	2	8	3010	2574	4034	87	62	25	1214	2490	536	133	127	156
Paterson-Clifton-Passaic	4	5	3	2505	2046	2646	1094	274	819	2561	11930	2028	125	105	133
Rochester	24	26	22	2293	2066	2563	557	323	234	827	8970	367	114	97	151
Sacramento	31	41	25	2255	2464	2125	435	176	278	443	3920	296	157	138	199
St. Louis	5	4	7	2063	1801	2214	1958	782	1176	614	12820	376	114	91	136
San Antonio	2	0	15	1530	1425	2152	63	553	78	506	3430	72	126	136	85
San Diego	25	34	15	2190	2302	2050	890	494	396	209	2570	97	160	148	115
San Jose	27	34	25	2332	2206	2390	537	128	409	412	2320	328	185	135	209
Savannah	0	1	0	1516	1530	1462	177	123	55	402	2920	136	117	103	250
Seattle	12	26	0	2329	2522	2133	1028	561	467	2265	6300	1280	122	120	124
Spokane	12	17	0	1957	2066	1753	261	185	76	148	4300	44	118	108	143
Stamford	6	3	9	4042	2860	5527	165	87	78	1378	2290	954	123	118	128
Syracuse	22	27	18	2007	2153	1917	534	214	320	221	8570	133	115	97	131
Tampa-St. Petersburg	2	4	1	1768	1798	1725	663	409	255	509	2940	218	162	185	136
Toledo	23	27	14	2107	2013	2324	439	314	125	1278	6530	423	111	103	136
Utica-Rome	25	26	25	1822	1849	1799	317	149	167	119	1590	65	112	104	118

Appendix B (continued)

Standard metropolitan statistical areas	Population per governmental unit			Governmental fragmentation (SMSA)	Welfare dummy (SMSA)	Hospital dummy (SMSA)	Local expenditure assignment (SMSA)	Local tax assignment (SMSA)	Rural pop. in OCC as per cent of OCC total pop.
	SMSA	CC	OCC						
Albany-Schenectady-Troy	2548	31662	1455	2176	1	0	78.8%	61.3%	43
Atlanta	13100	106338	7423	1432	0	1	58.1	33.1	42
Atlantic City	4232	20130	2704	744	1	1	74.9	71.7	26
Baltimore	70893	471115	28015	1681	1	0	64.7	45.7	33
Binghamton	3192	25787	2047	1259	1	1	78.8	61.3	46
Bridgeport	16417	78668	8117	969	0	0	49.1	50.7	4
Buffalo	8011	273486	4511	6062	1	1	78.8	61.3	25
Cleveland	12666	147946	6276	2357	1	1	71.3	51.8	4
Hartford	12463	55581	8870	626	0	0	49.1	50.7	27
Houston	11832	145333	2700	5382	0	0	65.5	47.7	22
Jacksonville	37272	50519	25990	194	0	1	61.4	43.7	27
Jersey City	25906	94325	15398	612	1	1	74.9	71.7	0
Kansas City	4118	63015	2308	2730	0	0	60.1	51.9	20
Madison	901	30000	382	7853	1	0	79.2	49.8	43
Memphis	41688	160667	8469	1897	0	1	62.7	33.5	59

Miami	25905	69741	18072	385	0	1	61.4	43.7	6
Milwaukee	8444	141800	3210	4417	1	1	79.2	49.8	12
Nashville	34213	59667	21928	272	0	1	62.7	33.5	22
Newark	8870	103822	6710	1547	1	1	74.9	71.7	6
New York	17881	2604992	4406	59123	1	1	78.8	61.3	10
Norwalk	7286	10380	4193	247	0	0	49.1	50.7	0
Paterson-Clifton-Passaic	5849	45710	4502	1015	1	1	74.9	71.7	1
Rochester	6550	161393	2785	5795	1	1	78.8	61.3	29
Sacramento	3223	25190	2006	1255	1	1	73.1	50.6	25
St. Louis	4585	195514	2780	7032	0	1	60.1	51.9	16
San Antonio	19126	39500	3907	1011	0	0	65.5	47.7	48
San Diego	7608	123550	3473	3557	1	0	73.1	50.6	25
San Jose	5835	25513	4650	548	1	1	73.1	50.6	7
Savannah	16114	17535	10901	160	0	0	58.1	33.1	47
Seattle	4081	112200	1885	5952	0	1	56.4	30.9	32
Spokane	2090	61667	620	9946	0	0	56.4	30.9	45
Stamford	18373	29062	13028	223	0	0	49.1	50.7	13
Syracuse	1915	107126	1151	9307	1	0	78.8	61.3	46
Tampa-St. Petersburg	15429	37135	7727	480	0	1	61.4	43.7	36
Toledo	10696	44812	3567	1256	1	1	71.3	51.8	24
Utica-Rome	1545	50387	833	6048	1	1	78.8	61.3	55

Bibliography

Books

Academy of Political Science. "The Urban Problem," *Proceedings*, Vol. XXVIII, No. 1, 1960.

Adams, Robert F. *Determinants of Local Government Expenditures*. Ph.D. Dissertation, University of Michigan, 1963.

Adrian, Charles R. *Governing Our Fifty States and Their Communities*. New York, McGraw-Hill Book Co., 1963.

———. *Governing Urban America*. New York: McGraw-Hill Book Co., 1961.

———. *State and Local Government*. New York: McGraw-Hill Book Co., 1960.

Alderfer, Harold F. *American Local Government and Administration*. New York: The Macmillan Co., 1956.

Anderson, William *Federalism and Intergovernmental Relations*. Chicago: Public Administration Service, 1946.

———. *The Units of Government in the United States*. Chicago: Public Administration Service, 1942.

———. *State and Local Government in the United States*. New York: Holt, Rinehart and Winston, 1951.

———. *The Nation and the States, Rivals or Partners?* Minneapolis: University of Minnesota Press, 1955.

———. *Intergovernmental Relations in Review*. Minneapolis: University of Minnesota Press, 1960.

Anderson, William, and Edward W. Weidener. *American City Government*. New York: Holt, Rinehart and Winston, 1951.

Anderson, William, *et al*. *Government in the Fifty States*. New York: Holt, Rinehart and Winston, 1960.

Baker, Benjamin. *Urban Government*. Princeton: Van Nostrand, 1957.

Baker, Gordon. *Rural vs. Urban Power*. Garden City, N.Y.: Doubleday Book Co., 1956.

Banfield, Edward C. *Urban Government—A Reader in Administration and Politics*. New York: The Free Press, 1963.

———. *Government and Housing in Metropolitan Areas*. New York: McGraw-Hill Book Co., 1958.

Bates, F. G., *et al*. *State Government*, 4th ed. New York: Harper & Row, 1954.

Benson, Charles S. *The Economics of Public Education*. Boston: Houghton Mifflin Co., 1961.

———. *Perspectives on the Economics of Education*. Boston: Houghton Mifflin Co., 1963.

Birkhead, Guthrie S., ed. *Metropolitan Issues: Social, Governmental, Fiscal*. Background Papers for the Third Annual Faculty Seminar on Metropolitan Research, August, 1961. Syracuse University, 1962.

Blair, George S. *American Local Government*. New York: Harper & Row, Publishers, 1964.

Bloomberg, Warner, and Morris Sunshine. *Suburban Power Structures and Public Education: A Study of Values, Influence and Tax Effort*. The Economics and Politics of Public Education Series, No. 10. Syracuse, N.Y.: Syracuse University Press, 1963.

Bollens, John C. *The State and the Metropolitan Problem*. Chicago: Public Administration Service, 1956.

———. *Special District Governments in the United States*. Berkeley: University of California Press, 1957.

Bollens, John C., ed. *Exploring the Metropolitan Community*. Berkeley: University of California Press, 1961.

Bollens, John C., with G. Ross Stephens *et al*. *Metropolitan Challenge*. Dayton, Ohio: Metropolitan Community Studies, November 1959.

Bollens, John C., and Henry J. Schmandt. *The Metropolis: Its*

People, Politics And Economic Life. New York: Harper & Row, 1965.

Bollens, John C., and Stanley Scott. *Local Government in California*. Berkeley: University of California Press, 1951.

Boskoff, Alvin, and Harmon Zeigler. *Voting Patterns in a Local Election*. Philadelphia: J. B. Lippincott, 1964.

Brazer, Harvey E. *City Expenditures in the United States*. Occasional Paper No. 66. New York: National Bureau of Economic Research, 1959.

Bromage, Arthur W. *Introduction to Municipal Government and Administration*. 2d ed. New York: Appleton-Century-Crofts, 1957.

——. *Political Representation in Metropolitan Agencies*. Ann Arbor, Mich.: Institute of Public Administration, University of Michigan, 1962.

Buchanan, James M., and Gordon Tullock. *The Calculus of Consent*. Ann Arbor, Mich.: The University of Michigan Press, 1962.

Buckley, William E. *Connecticut: The State and its Government*. New York: Oxford Books, 1953.

Burkhead, Jesse. *State and Local Taxes for Public Education*. Syracuse, N.Y.: Syracuse University Press, 1963.

Burns, James McGregor. *The Deadlock of Democracy: Four Party Politics in America*. Englewood Cliffs, N.J.: Prentice-Hall, Inc., 1963.

Caldwell, Lynton K. *The Government and Administration in New York*. New York: Crowell-Collier, 1954.

Callahan, Raymond E. *Education and the Cult of Efficiency*. Chicago: University of Chicago Press, 1962.

Chinitz, Benjamin. *City and Suburb*. Englewood Cliffs, N.J.: Prentice Hall, Inc., 1964.

Cohen, Leo. *Comparative Fiscal Capacity and Tax Effort and Units of Government in Madison and St. Clair Counties, Illinois, 1950–1960*. Carbondale, Ill.: Public Administration and Metropolitan Affairs Program, Southern Illinois University, 1963.

Conant, James B. *Slums and Suburbs*. New York: Signet Books, 1964.

Coughlin, Robert E. and Walter Isard. *Municipal Costs and*

Revenues from Community Growth. Wellesley: Chandler-Davis Publishing Co., 1957.

Council of Economic Advisers. *Economic Report of the President.* Washington: U. S. Government Printing Office, 1963.

Council of State Governments. *State-Local Relations.* Chicago, 1946.

——. (John C. Bollens, Director of Study.) *The States and the Metropolitan Problem.* Chicago, 1956.

——. *State Responsibility in Urban Regional Development.* Chicago, 1962.

Crouch, Winston. *Metropolitan Los Angeles: A Study in Integration.* Vol. V, *Intergovernmental Relations.* Los Angeles: Haymes Foundation, 1954.

Crouch, Winston, *et al. State and Local Government in California.* Berkeley: University of California Press, 1952.

Dobriner, William M. *Class in Suburbia.* Englewood Cliffs, N.J.: Prentice-Hall, Inc., 1963.

——. *The Suburban Community.* New York: G. P. Putnam's Sons, 1958.

Downs, Anthony. *An Economic Theory of Democracy.* New York: Harper & Row, 1957.

Duesenberry, James S. *Income, Saving, and the Theory of Consumer Behavior.* Cambridge, Mass.: Harvard University Press, 1949.

Easton, David. *A Framework for Political Analysis.* Englewood Cliffs, N.J.: Prentice-Hall, Inc., 1965.

——. *The Political System.* New York: Alfred A. Knopf, Inc., 1953.

——. *A Systems Analysis of Political Life.* New York: John Wiley & Sons, Inc., 1965.

Eckstein, Otto. *Trends in Public Expenditures in the Next Decade.* New York: Committee for Economic Development, 1959.

Elazar, Daniel J. *American Partnership.* Chicago: University of Chicago Press, 1962.

Erickson, Elmer, Jr. *California Government: State and Local.* New York: American Book Co., 1955.

Ezekiel, Mordecai, and Karl A. Fox. *Methods of Correlation and Regression Analysis.* New York: John Wiley & Sons, Inc., 1959.

Fabricant, Solomon. *The Trend of Government Activity in the*

United States Since 1900. New York: National Bureau of Economic Research, Inc., 1952.

Fairbanks, Robert *Property Tax Behavior in New York State, 1949–1961.* D. S. Sc. Dissertation, Syracuse University, 1963.

Fels Institute of State and Local Government. *Special Education and Fiscal Requirements of Urban School Districts in Pennsylvania, A Research Inquiry: The Impact of Social and Economic Conditions on Urban Education and State Fiscal Policy.* Philadelphia: University of Pennsylvania, 1964.

Ferber, Robert. *Statistical Technique in Market Research.* New York: McGraw-Hill Book Co., 1949.

Ferber, Robert, and P. J. Verdoorn. *Research Methods in Economics and Business.* New York: The Macmillan Co., 1962.

Fesler, James W. *Area and Administration.* Tuscaloosa: University of Alabama Press, 1949.

Frasier, G. W. *The Control of City School Finances.* Milwaukee: The Bruce Publication Co., 1922.

Freeman, Roger A. *School Needs in the Decade Ahead.* Washington: The Institute for Social Science Research, 1958.

Galbraith, John Kenneth. *The Affluent Society.* New York: Mentor Books, 1953.

Gans, Herbert J. *The Urban Villagers.* New York: The Free Press, 1962.

Gibbs, Jack P. *Urban Research Methods.* Princeton: D. Van Nostrand Co., 1961.

Glazer, Nathan, and Daniel P. Moynihan. *Beyond the Melting Pot.* Cambridge, Mass.: M.I.T. Press, 1963.

Goldberger, Arthur S. *Econometric Theory.* New York: John Wiley and Sons, 1964.

Gosnell, C., *Fundamentals in American Government: National, State and Local.* New York: McGraw-Hill Book Co., 1957.

Gosnell, C. and Lynwood Holland. *State and Local Government in the United States.* Englewood Cliffs, N.J.: Prentice-Hall, Inc., 1951.

Government Affairs Foundation, Inc. *Metropolitan Communities: A Bibliography.* Chicago: Public Administration Service, 1956.

———. *Metropolitan Communities: A Bibliography,* Supplement 1955–57. Chicago: Public Administration Service, 1960.

Greer, Scott. *The Emerging City, Myth and Reality*. New York: The Free Press 1962.

——. *Governing the Metropolis*. New York: John Wiley and Sons, Inc., 1962.

Gulick, Luther H. *The Metropolitan Problem and American Ideas*. The Cook Foundation Lectures. New York: Alfred A. Knopf, Inc., 1962.

——. *Growth and Problems of Government in the Metropolitan Areas of the United States of America*. Washington: The Governmental Affairs Institute, 1957.

Haig, Robert M. and Roswell C. McCrae. *Regional Survey of New York and its Environs*. Vol. 1; *Major Economic Factors in Metropolitan Growth and Arrangement: A Study of Trends and Tendencies in the Economic Activities Within the Region of New York and its Environs*. New York: Regional Plan Association, 1927.

Hamilton, Howard D., ed. *Legislative Apportionment*. New York: Harper and Row, 1964.

Hansen, Alvin H. and Harvey S. Perloff. *State and Local Finance in the National Economy*. New York: W. W. Norton and Co., 1944.

Harris, Seymour E. *More Resources for Education*. New York: Harper and Row, 1960.

Harrison, Forrest W., and Eugene P. McLoone. *Profiles in School Support*. Washington: U. S. Office of Education, 1965.

Hatt, Paul K., and Albert J. Reiss, Jr., eds. *Cities and Society*. New York: The Free Press, 1959.

Henry, Nelson B., and Jerome G. Kerwin. *Schools and City Government. A Study of School and Municipal Relationships in Cities of 50,000 or More Population*. Chicago: University of Chicago Press, 1938.

Hirsch, Werner Z. *Paths of Progress for St. Louis*. St. Louis: Metropolitan St. Louis Survey, 1957.

Hoover, Edgar M. *Region in Transition*. Pittsburgh: University of Pittsburgh Press, 1964.

Hoover, Edgar M., and Raymond Vernon. *The Anatomy of a Metropolis*. Garden City, N.Y.: Doubleday Book Co., 1962.

Howard, Lawrence V. *Government in Metropolitan New Orleans*. New Orleans: Tulane University, 1960.

International City Managers' Association. *The Municipal Year Book.* (Individual Series for 1951–1957.) Chicago.

James, H. Thomas. *School Revenue Systems in Five States.* Palo Alto, Calif.: Stanford University Press, 1961.

James, H. Thomas, J. Allen Thomas, and Harold J. Dyck. *Wealth, Expenditures and Decision-Making.* Palo Alto, Calif.: Stanford University Press, 1964.

Janowitz, N., D. Wright, and W. Delaney. *Public Administration and the Public Perspectives Toward Government in a Metropolitan Community.* Government Studies, No. 38. Ann Arbor, Mich.: University of Michigan, 1958.

Johns, R. L., and E. L. Morphet. *Problems and Issues in Public School Finances.* New York: Teachers College, Columbia University, 1952.

Johnson, Byron I. *The Principle of Equalization Applied to the Allocation of Grants-in-Aid.* Federal Security Agency, Social Security Administration. Washington: U. S. Government Printing Office, September, 1947.

Johnson, Claudius O. *American State and Local Government,* 3d ed. New York: Crowell-Collier, 1961.

Jones, Victor. *Metropolitan Government.* Chicago: University of Chicago Press, 1942.

Katona, George. *Psychological Analysis of Economic Behavior.* New York: McGraw-Hill Book Co., 1951.

Kaufman, Herbert. *Politics and Policies in State and Local Governments.* Englewood Cliffs, N.J.: Prentice-Hall, Inc., 1963.

King, Gary W. *Conflict Over Schools: A Sociological Analysis of a School Bond Election.* East Lansing, Mich.: Institute for Community Development and Services, 1963.

Kneier, Charles M., and Gary Fox. *Readings in Municipal Government and Administration.* New York: Holt, Rinehart and Winston, 1953.

Lehman, Maxwell, et al. *"Home Rule" vs. Super Government.* New York: Metropolitan Regional Council, 1961.

Littlefield, Neil., *Metropolitan Area Problems and Home Rule.* Ann Arbor, Mich.: University of Michigan Law School, 1962.

Lutz, Harley L. *Reallocation of Functional Responsibilities and Reorganization of Government Structures as Measures for*

Securing Greater Economy in Local Government. Chicago: Commerce Clearing House, 1933.

Maas, Arthur M. *Area and Power: A Theory of Local Government.* New York: The Free Press, 1959.

McClure, William P. *The Structure of Educational Costs in the Great Cities.* Chicago: Research Council of the Great Cities Program for School Improvement, August 7, 1964.

MacDonald, A. F. *American State Government and Administration,* 5th ed. New York: Crowell-Collier, 1955.

McGaughy, R. J. *The Fiscal Administration of City School Systems.* New York: The Macmillan Co., 1924.

McLaughlin, Frederick C. "Fiscal Administrative Control of City School Systems," in *Fiscal Policy for Public Education in the State of New York.* Albany, 1947.

Mace, Ruth L. *Municipal Cost-Revenue Research in the United States.* Chapel Hill, N.C.: Institute of Government, University of North Carolina, 1961.

Martin, Roscoe C. *Government and the Suburban School.* The Economics and Politics of Public Education Series, No. 2. Syracuse: Syracuse University Press, 1963.

Martin, Roscoe C. *Metropolis in Transition: Local Government Adaptation to Changing Needs.* Washington: Housing and Home Finance Agency, 1963.

Martin, Roscoe C., *et al. Decisions in Syracuse.* Bloomington, Ind.: Indiana University Press, 1962.

Martin, Roscoe C., and H. Douglas Price. *The Metropolis and Its Problems.* Syracuse: Syracuse University, 1959.

Maxwell, James A. *Issues in State-Local Public Finance.* Preliminary Report. Washington: The Brookings Institution, 1964.

May, Samuel C., and Majes M. Fales, Jr. *The State's Interest in the Metropolitan Problem.* Berkeley: University of California Press, 1955.

Mills, Frederic C. *Statistical Method.* New York: Holt, Rinehart & Winston, 1955.

Miner, Jerry. *Social and Economic Factors in Spending for Public Education.* The Economics and Politics of Public Education Series. Syracuse, N.Y.: Syracuse University Press, 1963.

Mort, Paul R., *A New Approach to School Finance: 1961 Review of*

Fiscal Policy for Public Education in New York State, Staff Studies. Albany: New York State Educational Conference Board, September 1, 1961.

Mort, Paul R. and Orlando F. Furno. *Theory and Synthesis of a Sequential Simplex.* New York: Institute of Administrative Research, Teachers College, Columbia University, 1960.

Mort, Paul R., Walter C. Reusser, and John W. Polley. *Public School Finance.* 3d ed. New York: McGraw-Hill Book Co., 1960.

Mumford, Lewis. *The City in History.* New York: Harcourt, Brace, and World, 1961.

Munse, Albert R., and Eugene P. McLoone. *Public School Finance Programs of the United States, 1957–58.* Washington U. S. Government Printing Office, 1960.

Musgrave, Richard A. *The Theory of Public Finance: A Study in Public Economy.* New York: McGraw-Hill Book Co., 1959.

National Bureau of Economic Research. *Public Finances: Needs, Sources and Utilization.* New York, 1961.

National Education Association, Research Division. *Salary Schedules for Classroom Teachers, 1964–65.* Research Report 1964–R12. Washington, 1964.

———. *Selected Statistics of Large School Systems, 1961–62.* Research Report 1963–R8. Washington: National Education Association, August, 1963.

Pate, James E. *Local Government and Administration: Principles and Problems.* New York: American Book Co., 1954.

Philips, Jewell C. *State and Local Government in America.* New York: American Book Co., 1954.

Pierce, T. M. *Controllable Community Characteristics Related to the Quality of Education.* New York: Teachers College, Columbia University, 1947.

Pock, Max A. *Independent Special District: A Solution to Metropolitan Area Problems.* Ann Arbor, Mich.: University of Michigan Law School, 1962.

Raisty, Lloyd B. *Municipal Government and Administration in Georgia.* Athens, Ga.: University of Georgia, 1941.

Ranney, Austin, and Willmore Kendall. *Democracy and The American Party System.* New York: Harcourt, Brace, and World, 1959.

Reeves, Charles E. *School Boards: Their Status, Functions and Activities.* Englewood Cliffs, N.J.: Prentice-Hall, Inc., 1954.

Ridley, Clarence E. *Measuring Municipal Government: Suggested Standards for Measuring the Results of Fire, Health, Police, and Public Works Departments.* New York: Municipal Administration Service, Publication #4, 1927.

Sacks, Seymour. *Municipal Taxation and Regional Development.* East Hartford, Conn.: Capital Regional Planning Agency, March, 1963.

Sacks, Seymour, Robert Harris, and John J. Carroll. *The State and Local Government . . . The Role of State Aid*, Comptroller's Studies in Local Finance, No. 3. Albany: New York State Department of Audit and Control, 1963.

Sacks, Seymour, and William F. Hellmuth, Jr. *Financing Government in a Metropolitan Area.* New York: The Free Press, 1961.

Sayre, Wallace S., and Herbert Kaufman. *Governing New York City: Politics in the Metropolis.* New York: W. W. Norton, Inc. 1965.

Schaller, Howard G., ed. *Public Expenditure Decisions in the Urban Community.* Washington: Resources for the Future, Inc., 1963.

Schreiber, Daniel. *Holding Power/Large City School Systems, Project: School Dropouts.* Washington: National Education Association, 1964.

Schubert, Glendon, ed. *Reapportionment.* New York: Charles Scribner's Sons, 1965.

Scott, Stanley, and Edward L. Feder. *Factors Associated with Variations in Municipal Expenditure Levels.* Berkeley: Bureau of Public Administration, University of California, February, 1957.

Seeley, J. R., R. A. Sems, and E. W. Loosley, *Crestwood Heights.* New York: John Wiley and Sons, 1956.

Sexton, Patricia. *Education and Income: Inequalities in Our Public Schools.* New York: Viking Press, 1961.

Simon, Herbert A. *Fiscal Aspects of Metropolitan Consolidation.* Berkeley: Bureau of Public Administration, University of California, 1943.

Singstock, Frank S. *Extraterritorial Powers in the Metropolitan Area.* Ann Arbor, Mich.: Legislative Research Center, University of Michigan, 1962.

Snider, C. F. *American State and Local Government.* New York: Appleton-Century-Crofts, 1950.
——. *Local Government in Rural America.* New York: Appleton-Century-Crofts, 1957.
Studenski, Paul. *The Government of Metropolitan Areas in the United States.* New York: National Municipal League, Committee on Metropolitan Government, 1930.
Swanson, Bert E. *Current Trends in Comparative Community Studies.* Kansas City: Community Studies, Inc., 1962.
Sweeney, John B., and George S. Blair. *Metropolitan Analysis.* Philadelphia: University of Pennsylvania Press, 1958.
Tableman, Betty. *Governmental Organization in Metropolitan Areas.* Ann Arbor, Mich.: University of Michigan Press, 1951.
Tax Institute, Inc. *Financing Metropolitan Government.* Princeton: The Institute, 1955.
Temporary Commission on City Finances, City of New York. *Toward Fiscal Strength: Overcoming New York City's Financial Dilemma.* New York: Temporary Commission, November, 1965.
Thompson, Wilbur R. *A Preface to Urban Economics: Toward a Conceptual Framework for Study and Research.* Washington: Resources for the Future, Inc., 1963.
Turvey, Ralph. *The Economics of Real Property.* London: George Allen & Unwin, Ltd., 1957.
Vernon, Raymond. *The Changing Economic Function of the Central City.* New York: Committee for Economic Development, 1959.
——. *Metropolis 1985.* Garden City, N.Y.: Doubleday Book Co., 1962.
——. *Myth and Reality of our Urban Problems.* Stratford Little Lectures. Princeton: Princeton University, Spring, 1961.
Vieg, John A., *et al. California Local Finance.* Palo Alto, Calif.: Stanford University Press, 1960.
Wahlke, John C., *et al. The Legislative System: Explorations in Legislative Behavior.* New York: John Wiley & Sons, 1962.
Walker, Mabel L. *Municipal Expenditures.* Baltimore: John Hopkins Press, 1930.
Wardwell, Charles A. R. *Regional Trend in the U. S. Economy.* Washington: U. S. Government Printing Office, 1951.

Whyte, William H., Jr. *The Organization Man*. New York: Doubleday Book Co., 1965.

Wildavsky, Aaron. *The Politics of Budgetary Process*. Boston: Little, Brown & Company, 1964.

Willbern, York. *The Withering Away of the City*. Tuscaloosa, Ala.: University of Alabama Press, 1964.

Williams, Oliver P., and Adrian R. Charles. *Four Cities: A Study in Comparative Policy Making*. Philadelphia: University of Pennsylvania Press, 1963.

Williams, Oliver P., et al. *Suburban Differences and Metropolitan Policies*. Philadelphia: University of Pennsylvania Press, 1965.

Woo Sik Kee. *City Expenditures and Metropolitan Areas: Analysis of Intergovernmental Fiscal Systems*. Ph.D. Dissertation, Syracuse University, 1964.

Wood, Robert C. *1400 Governments*. Cambridge, Mass.: Harvard University Press, 1961.

———. *Metropolis Against Itself*. New York: Committee for Economic Development, 1959.

———. *Suburbia: Its People and Their Politics*. Boston: Houghton, Mifflin, and Company, 1959.

Woodbury, Coleman. *Urban Redevelopment: Problems and Practices*. Chicago: University of Chicago Press, 1953.

———. *The Future of Cities and Urban Redevelopment*. Chicago: University of Chicago Press, 1956.

Woodward, Henry B. *The Effect of Fiscal Control on Current School Expenditures*, Ph.D. Dissertation, Teachers College, Columbia University, 1958.

Wright, Deil S. *Trends and Variations in Local Finance: The Case of Iowa*. Iowa City: Institute of Public Affairs, University of Iowa, 1965.

Wynn, D. Richard. *Organization of Public Schools*. Washington: The Center for Applied Research in Education, Inc., 1964.

Yakel, Ralph. *The Legal Control of the Administration of Public School Expenditures*. New York: Teachers College, Columbia University, 1929.

Yong Hyo Cho. *State-Local Governmental Systems: Their Determinants and Fiscal Implications*. Ph.D. Dissertation, Syracuse University, 1965.

Zimmerman, Joseph F., ed. *Readings in State and Local Government.* New York: Holt, Rinehart, and Winston, 1964.

Articles and Periodicals

American Academy of Political and Social Science. "Metropolis in Ferment," *Annals* (November 1957).

Aronovici, Carol. "Education and Community Planning," *Journal of the American Institute of Planners*, XXI (Fall 1955), 133–137.

Bahl, Roy W., Jr., and Robert J. Saunders. "Determinants of Changes in State and Local Government Expenditures," *National Tax Journal*, XVIII (March 1965), 50–57.

Baumol, William J. "Urban Services: Interactions of Public and Private Decisions," in *Public Expenditure Decisions in the Urban Community*, ed. Howard G. Schaller. (Washington: Resources for the Future, Inc., 1962.

Beck, Morris. "Determinants of the Property Tax Level: A Case Study of Northeastern New Jersey," *National Tax Journal*, XVIII (March 1965), 74–77.

Berolzheimer, Joseph. "Influences Shaping Expenditures for Operation of State and Local Governments," *Bulletin of the National Tax Association*, XXXII (March 1947).

Birdsall, William C. "A Study of the Demand for Public Goods," in *Essays in Fiscal Federalism*, ed. Richard A. Musgrove. Washington: The Brookings Institution, 1965.

Bishop, G. A. "Stimulative versus Substitutive Effects of State School Aid in New England," *National Tax Journal*, XVII (June 1964), 133–143.

Bollens, John C. "Metropolitan and Fringe Area Developments in 1961," in *The Municipal Yearbook, 1962*. Chicago: International City Managers' Association, 1962.

Brazer, Harvey E. "The Role of Major Metropolitan Centers in State and Local Finance," *American Economic Review*, XLVII (No. 2), 305–316.

———. "Some Fiscal Implications of Metropolitanism," in *Metropolitan Issues: Social, Governmental, Fiscal*, ed. Guthrie S. Birkhead. Background Papers for the Third Annual Faculty Seminar on Metropolitan Research, August, 1961.

Bromage, James W. "Political Representation in Metropolitan Areas," *American Political Science Review*, LII (June 1958), 406–418.

Burkhead, Jesse. "Metropolitan Area Budget Structures and Their Significance for Expenditures," *Proceedings of the National Tax Association, 1959*. Harrisburg, 1960.

——. "Uniformity in Governmental Expenditures and Resources in a Metropolitan Area: Cuyahoga County," *National Tax Journal*, XIV (December 1961), 337–348.

Campbell, Alan K. "The Most Dynamic Sector," *National Civic Review*, LIII (February 1964).

——. "National-State-Local Systems of Government and Intergovernmental Aid," *Annals of the American Academy of Political and Social Science*, CCCLIX (May 1965).

——. "Taxes and Industrial Location in the New York Metropolitan Region," *National Tax Journal*, XI (September 1958).

Campbell, Alan K., and Philip J. Meranto. "The Metropolitan Education Dilemma: Matching Resources to Needs," *Urban Affairs Quarterly*, I (September 1966).

Campbell, Alan K., and Seymour Sacks. "Administering the Spread City," *Public Administration Review*, XXIV (September 1964).

Campbell, Ronald. "Process of Policy-Making Within Structures of Educational Government: As Viewed by an Educator," in *Government of Public Education for Adequate Policy Making*, ed. William P. McClure and Van Miller. Urbana, Ill.: Bureau of Educational Research, College of Education, University of Illinois, 1959.

Carroll, John J., and Seymour Sacks. "Local Sources of Local Revenues." *1961 Proceedings of the National Tax Association*, Seattle, 294–311.

Carter, Richard F. "Voters and Their Schools," Cooperative Research Project No. 308 (William R. Odell, Director). Palo Alto, California: Institute for Communication Research, Stanford University, June 20, 1960. Mimeographed.

Carter, Richard F., and John Sutthoff. "Communities and Their Schools," Cooperative Research Project No. 308 (William R. Odell, Director). Palo Alto, California: School of Education, Stanford University, December 1, 1960.

Colm, Gerald. "Public Expenditures and Economic Structure in the United States," *Social Research*, IV (February 1936).

Colm, Gerald, and Manuel Helzner. "Financial Needs and Resources over the Next Decade: At All Levels of Government," in *Public Finances: Needs, Sources and Utilization*, National Bureau of Economic Research (Princeton: Princeton University Press, 1961).

Curran, Donald J. "Intra-Metropolitan Competition," *Land Economics*, XL (February 1964), 93–100.

——. "The Metropolitan Problem: Solution from Within?" *National Tax Journal*, XVI (September 1963), 213–223.

Daver, Manning J., and Robert G. Relsay. "Unrepresentative States," *National Municipal Review* (December 1955), 571–576.

Davies, David. "Financing Urban Functions and Services," *Law and Contemporary Problems*, XXX (Winter 1965).

Davis, Otto A. "Empirical Evidence of Political Influences Upon the Urban Expenditure Policies of Public Schools," *The Public Economy of Urban Communities*, ed. Julius Margolis. Washington: Resources for the Future, Inc., 1965.

Downs, Anthony. "Metropolitan Growth and Future Political Problems," *Land Economics* (November 1961), 311.

Drury, James W. "Townships Lose Ground," *National Municipal Review* (June 1955).

Easterlin, Richard. "State Income Estimates," in *Population Redistribution and Economic Growth. United States, 1870–1950*, Vol. 1 (*Methodological Considerations and Reference Tables*), ed. Simon Kuznets and Dorothy S. Thomas, American Philosophical Society, 1957.

Ecker-Racz, L. Laszlo. "Foreign Scholar Ponders the 1957 Census of Governments," *National Tax Journal*, XII (June 1959), 97–115.

——. "Whither State and Local Finance," *Journal of Finance*. Papers and Proceedings of the Twenty-Second Annual Meeting of American Finance Association (December 1960).

Eckstein, Otto. "A Survey of the Theory of Public Expenditure Criteria," in *Public Finances: Needs, Sources, Utilization*. Princeton: Princeton University Press, 1961.

Educational Policies Commission. "Educational Independence and Human Values," in *Perspectives on the Economics of Public Education, Readings in School Finance and Business Management,* ed. Charles S. Benson. Boston: Houghton, Mifflin Company, 1963.

Elazer, Daniel. "Federal-State Collaboration in the Nineteenth Century United States," *Political Science Quarterly,* LXXIX (June 1964).

Fagin, Henry. "Financing Municipal Services in a Metropolitan Region," *Journal of the American Institute of Planners,* XIX (Fall 1953).

Feinberg, Mordecai S. "The Implications of Core-City Decline for the Fiscal Structure of the Core City," *National Tax Journal,* XVII (September 1964).

Firman, William D. "Fiscal Independence of School Systems," Presented to the Committee on Educational Finance of the *National Education Association,* (April 1965).

Fisher, Glenn W. "Determinants of State and Local Government Expenditures: A Preliminary Analysis," *National Tax Journal,* XIV (December 1961), 349–355.

———. "Interstate Variation in State and Local Government Expenditures," *National Tax Journal,* XVII (March 1964), 71–73.

Friedman, Milton. "The Role of Government in Education," in *Perspectives on the Economics of Public Education, Readings in School Finance and Business Management,* ed. Charles S. Benson. Boston: Houghton Mifflin Company, 1963.

Glazer, Nathan. "The School as an Instrument in Planning," *Journal of the American Institute of Planners,* XXV (November 1959), 191–195.

Greer, Scott. "Social Change and the Metropolitan Problem," in *Metropolitan Issues: Social, Governmental, Fiscal,* ed. Guthrie S. Birkhead. Background Papers for the Third Annual Faculty Seminar on Metropolitan Research, 1961. Syracuse: Syracuse University, 1962.

Groves, Harold M., and C. Harry Kahn. "Stability of State and Local Tax Yields," *American Economic Review,* XLII (March 1952), 87–94.

Groves, Harold M., and John Riew. "Financing Metropolitan Municipalities in Wisconsin," *Land Economics*, XL (February 1964), 29–40.

Gulick, Luther H. "Metropolitan Organization: Problem of Management, Cost and Democracy," *Annals of the American Academy of Political and Social Science* (November 1957).

Hansen, Niles M. "The Structure and Determinants of Local Public Investment Expenditures," *Review of Economics Statistics*, XLVII (May 1965), 150–162.

Havighurst, Robert J. "City-School Cooperation in Developing Educational Policy and Practice," A paper presented at the meeting of *International City Managers Association*, September 21, 1965.

Hawley, Amos H. "The Incorporation Trend in Metropolitan Areas, 1900–1950," *Journal of American Institute of Planners*, XXV (February 1959).

——. "Metropolitan Population and Municipal Government Expenditures in Central Cities," in *Cities and Society*, ed. Paul K. Hatt and Albert J. Reiss, Jr. New York: The Free Press, 1959.

Henderson, Harold L. "State Aids as a Possible Revenue Source for Cities," *Bulletin of the National Tax Association* (November 1946), 43–48.

Herson, Lawrence J. R., Jr. "The Lost World of Municipal Government," *APSR* (June 1957), 330–345.

Hirsch, Werner Z. "The Costs of Public Education," in *Perspectives on the Economics of Public Education, Readings in School Finance and Business Management*, ed. Charles S. Benson. Boston: Houghton Mifflin Company, 1963.

——. "Determinants of Public Education Expenditures," *National Tax Journal*, XIII (March 1960), 29–40.

——. "Expenditure Implications of Metropolitan Growth and Consolidation," *Review of Economics and Statistics*, XLI (August 1959), 232–241.

——. "Fiscal Impact of Industrialization on Schools," *Review of Economics and Statistics*, XLVI (May 1964), 198–208.

——. "Measuring Factors Affecting Expenditure Levels for Local Government Services," St. Louis: Metropolitan St. Louis Survey, 1957. Mimeographed.

———. "Spillover of Public Education Costs and Benefits," Cooperative Research Project No. 1045. Mimeographed.

Holland, Lynwood M. "Atlanta Pioneers in Merger: City Area Tripled and Services are Divided with County in Award-Winning Movement to Solve Metropolitan Problem," *National Municipal Review* (April 1952).

Hoyt, Homer. "Economic Background of Cities," *Journal of Land and Public Utility Economics*, XVII (February 1941), 188–195.

Jones, Victor. "Local Governmental Organization in Metropolitan Area," in *The Future of Cities and Urban Redevelopment*, ed. Coleman Woodbury. Chicago: University of Chicago Press, 1953.

Kessel, John K. "Governmental Structure and Political Environment: A Statistical Note About American Cities," *APSR*, LVI (1962).

Kuh, Edwin, and John R. Meyer. "Correlation and Regression Estimates When the Data are Ratios," *Econometrica*, XXIII (October 1955), 400–416.

Kurnow, Ernest. "Determinants of State and Local Expenditures Reexamined," *National Tax Journal*, XVI (September 1963), 252–253.

Lee, Tong Hun. "Demand for Housing: A Cross-Section Analysis," *Review of Economics and Statistics*, XLV (May 1963), 190–196.

Leonard, Lawrence A. "State and Local Governmental Revenue Structures: A National and Regional Analysis," *National Tax Journal* (March 1958).

Lindblom, Charles E. "Decision Making in Taxation and Expenditures," in *Public Finances: Needs, Sources and Utilization*. National Bureau of Economic Research. Princeton: Princeton University Press, 1961.

Long, Norton E. "The Local Community As An Ecology of Games," *American Journal of Sociology*, LXIV (November 1958), 251–261.

McClure, William P. "Structures of Educational Government: As Viewed by the Educator," in *Government of Public Education for Adequate Policy Making*, ed. William P. McClure and Van

Miller. Urbana, Ill.: Bureau of Educational Research, College of Education, University of Illinois, 1959.

Mansfield, Harvey C. "States in American Systems," *The Forty-Eight States.* New York: Columbia University, 1955.

Margolis, Julius. "Metropolitan Finance Problems: Territories, Functions, and Growth," in *Public Finances: Needs, Sources, and Utilization,* National Bureau of Economic Research. Princeton: Princeton University Press, 1961.

———. "Municipal Fiscal Structure in a Metropolitan Area," *Journal of Political Economy,* LXV (June 1957), 225–236.

———. "On Municipal Land Policy for Fiscal Gains," *National Tax Journal,* IX (September 1956).

Martin, Roscoe C. "Action in Metropolis: Local Government Adaptation to Changing Urban Needs Assumes a Variety of Forms," *National Civic Review* (June and July 1961).

Monypenny, Phillip. "A Political Analysis of Structures for Educational Policy Making," *Government of Public Education for Adequate Policy Making,* ed. William P. McClure and Van Miller. Urbana, Ill.: Bureau of Educational Research, College of Education, University of Illinois, 1959.

Mueller, Eva. "Public Attitudes Toward Fiscal Programs," *Quarterly Journal of Economics,* LXXVII (May 1963), 210–235.

Musgrave, Richard A. "Approaches to Fiscal Theory of Political Federalism," in *Public Finances: Needs, Sources, and Utilization.* Princeton: Princeton University Press, 1961.

———. "The Classification of Public Goods," in *Perspectives on the Economics of Public Education, Readings in School Finance and Business Management,* ed. Charles S. Benson. Boston: Houghton Mifflin Company, 1963.

Mushkin, Selma J. "Intergovernmental Aspects of Local Expenditure Decisions," in *Public Expenditure Decisions in the Urban Community,* ed. Howard G. Schaller. Baltimore: Johns Hopkins Press, 1963.

Netzer, Richard. "Financial Needs and Resources over the Next Decade: State and Local Governments," *Public Finances: Needs, Sources, and Utilization,* The National Bureau of Economic Research. Princeton: Princeton University Press, 1961.

New Jersey Taxpayers Association. *Financial Statistics of New Jersey Local Government* (September 1962).

Ostrom, Vincent, et al. "Organization of Government in Metropolitan Areas," *APSR*, LV (December 1961), 831.

Ostrom, Vincent, Charles M. Tiebout, and Robert Warren. "The Organization of Government in Metropolitan Areas: A Theoretical Inquiry," *American Political Science Review*, LV (December 1961).

Penniman, Clara. "The Politics of Taxation," in *Politics in the American States: A Comparative Analysis*, ed. Herbert Jacob and Kenneth N. Vines. Boston: Little, Brown and Company, 1965.

Polley, John W. "Educational Expenditures in High Expenditure and Low Expenditure School Districts in New York State." New York: Teachers College, Columbia University, 1964. Mimeographed.

Ranney, Austin, and Kendall Willmore. "The American Party System," *APSR* (June 1954).

Ratliff, Charles E., Jr. "Centralization of Government Expenditures for Education and Highways in North Carolina," *National Tax Journal* (September 1956).

———. "Centralization, Ability, and Effort in School Finance," *National Tax Journal*, XIII (March 1960), 41–44.

Reed College. "A Statistical Study of American Cities by Students of Reed College," *Reed College Record*. Social Service Series, No. 4.

Reed, Thomas N. "Changes Needed in Governmental Structure and Metropolitan Areas," *American City* (February 1953).

Renshaw, Edward F. "A Note on the Expenditure Effect of State Aid to Education," *Journal of Political Economy*, LXVIII (April 1960), 170–174.

Rothenberg, Jerome. "A Model of Economic and Political Decision-Making," in *The Public Economy of Urban Communities*, ed. Julius Margolis. Washington: Resources for the Future, Inc., 1965.

Sacks, Seymour. "Central City and Suburban Public Education: Fiscal Needs, Fiscal Resources and Fiscal Realities," *Educational Yearbook, 1966*. Chicago: National Society for the Study of Education, 1966.

Sacks, Seymour, and Alan K. Campbell. "Fiscal Zoning Game," *Municipal Finance*, XXXVI (1964), 140–149.

Sacks, Seymour, and Robert Harris. "The Determinants of State and Local Government Expenditures and Intergovernmental Flow of Funds," *National Tax Journal*, XVII (March 1964).

Sacks, Seymour, and David C. Ranney. "Suburban Education: A Fiscal Analysis," *Urban Affairs Quarterly*. I (September 1966).

Samuelson, Paul A. "Diagramatic Exposition of a Theory of Public Expenditures," *Review of Economics and Statistics*, XXXVII (November 1955), 350–356.

———. "The Pure Theory of Public Expenditures," *Review of Economics and Statistics*, XXXVI (November 1954), 387–389.

Saville, Lloyd. "Regional Contrasts in the Development of Local Public Finance," *National Tax Journal* (June 1962).

Sayre, Wallace S. "Urbanism and Government, 1957–1977: A Rejoinder," *Annals of the American Academy of Political and Social Science*, CCCXIV (November 1957), 82–85.

Sazama, Gerald. "Equalization of Property Taxes for the Nation's Largest Central Cities," *National Tax Journal*, XVIII (June 1965), 51–61.

Schlesinger, Joseph A. "A Two-Dimensional Measure of Inter-Party Competition," *APSR* (December 1955).

Schmandt, Henry J. "The Area Council Approach to Metropolitan Government," *Public Management*, XLII (February 1960).

Schmandt, Henry J., and G. Ross Stephens. "Local Government Expenditures," *Land Economics*, XXXIX (November 1963).

———. "Measuring Municipal Output," *National Tax Journal*, XIII (December 1960), 369–375.

Schnore, Leo F. "The Growth of Metropolitan Suburbs," *American Sociological Review*, XXII (April 1957), 165–173.

Shapiro, Harvey. "Economics of State and Local Government Finance," *Land Economics*, XXXIX (May 1963).

———. "Measuring Local Government Output: A Comment," *National Tax Journal*, XIV (December 1961), 394–397.

Shapiro, Sherman. "Some Socio-Economic Determinants of Expenditures for Education; Southern and Other States Compared," *Comparative Education Review*, VI (October 1962).

Sigafoos, Robert A. "State Financing of U. S. Local Governments: Prospects and Challenges in the Mid- and Later 1960's," *Proceedings of the National Tax Association*. Harrisburg, 1962.

Simon, Herbert A. "The Incidence of A Tax on Urban Real Property," *Readings in the Economics of Taxation*, ed. Richard A. Musgrave and Carl S. Shoup. Homewood, Illinois: Richard D. Irwin, Inc., 1959.

Smith, Luke M. "Territorial Variables in American Local Government," *Social Forces* (May 1949).

Snider, Clyde F. "American County Government: A Mid-Century Review," *APSR* (March 1952).

——. "Twilight of the Townships," *National Municipal Review* (September 1952).

Spangler, Richard. "The Effect of Population Growth Upon State and Local Government Expenditures," *National Tax Journal* (June 1963).

Spencer, Max R. "Town and City Consolidation in Connecticut," *APSR* (June 1942).

Stephens, G. Ross, and Henry J. Schmandt, "Revenue Patterns of Local Governments," *National Tax Journal*, XV (December 1962).

Suits, Daniel B. "Use of Dummy Variables in Regression Equations," *Journal of the American Statistical Association*, LII (December 1957), 548–581.

Tiebout, Charles M. "An Economic Theory of Fiscal Decentralization," in *Public Finances: Needs, Sources, and Utilization*. Princeton: Princeton University Press, 1961.

——. "A Pure Theory of Local Expenditures," *The Journal of Political Economy*, LXIV (October 1956).

——. "Economics of Scale and Metropolitan Governments," *Review of Economics and Statistics*, XLII (November 1960), 442–444.

Tiebout, Charles M., and David B. Houston. "Metropolitan Finance Reconsidered: Budget Functions and Multi-Level Governments," *Review of Economics and Statistics*, XLIV (November 1962), 412–417.

Vernon, Raymond. "Production and Distribution in the Large Metropolis," *Annals of the American Academy of Political and Social Science*, CCCXIV (November 1957).

Webber, Melvin M. "Order in Diversity: Community Without Propinquity," in *Cities and Space: The Future Use of Urban Land*, ed. Lowdon Wingo, Jr. Baltimore: Johns Hopkins Press, 1963.

Weisbrod, Burton. "Geographic Spillover Effects and the Allocation of Resources to Education," in *The Public Economy of Urban Communities*, ed. Julius Margolis. Washington: Resources for the Future, Inc., 1965.

Willbern, York. "Changing Ecology of Urban Local Government," *Metropolitan Issues: Social, Governmental, Fiscal*, ed. Guthrie S. Birkhead. Background Papers for the Third Annual Faculty Seminar on Metropolitan Research, 1961. Syracuse: Syracuse University, 1962.

Wilson, James Q., and Edward C. Banfield. "Public-Regardingness as a Value Premise in Voting Behavior," *American Political Science Review*, LXVII (December 1964), 876–887.

Woo Sik Kee. "Central City Expenditures and Metropolitan Areas," *National Tax Journal*, XVIII (December 1965), 337–353.

Wood, Robert C. "Metropolitan Government 1975: An Extrapolation of Trends," *APSR* (1958), 108–122.

Public Documents

Advisory Commission on Intergovernmental Relations. *Alternative Approaches to Governmental Reorganization in Metropolitan Areas*. Washington: U. S. Government Printing Office, 1962.

——. *Factors Affecting Voter Reactions To Governmental Reorganization in Metropolitan Areas* (1962).

——. *Governmental Structures, Organization, and Planning in Metropolitan Areas* (1962).

——. *Impact of Federal Urban Development Programs on Local Government Organization and Planning*. Prepared in cooperation with the Subcommittee on Intergovernmental Relations of the Committee on Government Operations, United States Senate (1964).

——. *Local Nonproperty Taxes and the Coordinating Role of the State* (1961).

———. *Measures of State and Local Fiscal Capacity and Tax Efforts* (1962).

———. *Metropolitan Social and Economic Disparities: Implications for Intergovernmental Relations in Central Cities and Suburbs* (September 1964).

———. *Performance of Urban Functions: Local and Areawide* (1963).

———. *The Problem of Special Districts in American Government* (1964).

U. S. Bureau of the Budget. *Standard Metropolitan Statistical Areas.* Washington: U. S. Government Printing Office, 1961.

U. S. Bureau of the Census. *Census of Governments: 1957.* Vol. I, No. 2: *Local Government in Standard Metropolitan Areas.* Washington: U. S. Government Printing Office, 1959.

———. *Census of Governments: 1957.* Vol. III, No. 1: *Finances of School Districts* (1958).

———. *Census of Governments: 1957.* Vol. III. No. 5: *Compendium of Government Finances* (1959).

———. *Census of Governments: 1957.* Vol. III, No. 6: *Local Government Finances in Standard Metropolitan Areas* (1959).

———. *Census of Governments: 1957.* Vol. IV, No. 2: *State Payments to Local Governments* (1959).

———. *Census of Governments: 1962.* Vol. I: *Governmental Organization* (1963).

———. *Census of Governments: 1962.* Vol. II: *Taxable Property Values* (1963).

———. *Census of Governments: 1962.* Vol. IV, No. 1: *Finances of School Districts* (1963).

———. *Census of Governments: 1962.* Vol. V.: *Local Government in Metropolitan Areas* (1964).

———. *Census of Governments: 1962.* Vol. VI, No. 2: *State Payments to Local Governments* (1963).

———. *Census of Governments: 1962.* Vol. VI, No. 4: *Historical Statistics on Governmental Finances and Employment* (1964).

———. *Census of Population: 1960.* Vol. I: *Characteristics of the Population, Part A. Number of Inhabitants* (1961).

———. *Census of Population: 1960. General Social and Economic Characteristics, U. S. Summary.* Final Report PC(1)-1C (1961).

———. *Census of Population: 1960. Selected Area Reports, Standard*

Metropolitan Statistical Areas. Final Report PC(3)-1D (1962.)

——. *Census of Population and Housing: 1960. Census Tracts* (1963).

——. *Compendium of City Government Finances in 1961* (G-CP61-No. 2) (1962).

——. *Compendium of City Government Finances: 1962* (G-CF-No. 2) (1963).

——. *County and City Data Book, 1962: A Statistical Abstract Supplement* (1962).

——. *Current Population Reports. Population Characteristics.* Series P-20, No. 131 (September 4, 1964).

——. *Current Population Reports. Technical Studies.* Series P-23, No. 12 (July 31, 1964).

——. *Governmental Finances in 1961* (G-GF61-No. 2) (1962).

——. *Summary of Governmental Finances in 1962* (G-GF62-No. 1) (1963).

——. *Governmental Finances in 1963–4* (G-GF64-No. 1) (1964).

——. *State and Local Government Special Studies No. 45: Local Government Finances and Employment in Relation to Population: 1957* (1961).

U. S. Department of Commerce, Office of Business Economics: *Survey of Current Business*, XLV (August 1965).

U. S. Department of Health, Education, and Welfare. *Current Expenditures Per Pupil in Large Public School Systems, 1959–60* (1962).

——. *Digest of Educational Statistics, 1965* (1965).

U. S. Department of Health, Education, and Welfare. Office of Education, Bureau of Educational Research and Development. *Public School Finance Programs, 1961–1962* (1963).

Index

Index